Single Case Research Designs in Educational and Community Settings

ROBERT E. O'NEILL
University of Utah

JOHN J. MCDONNELL
University of Utah

FELIX F. BILLINGSLEY
University of Washington

WILLIAM R. JENSON
University of Utah

Boston   Columbus   Indianapolis   New York   San Francisco   Upper Saddle River
Amsterdam   Cape Town   Dubai   London   Madrid   Milan   Munich   Paris   Montreal   Toronto
Delhi   Mexico City   Sao Paulo   Sydney   Hong Kong   Seoul   Singapore   Taipei   Tokyo

Vice President and Editor in Chief:
Jeffery W. Johnston
Executive Editor: Ann Castel Davis
Editorial Assistant: Penny Burleson
Vice President, Director of Marketing: Quinn
Perkson
Marketing Manager: Erica DeLuca
Senior Managing Editor: Pamela Bennett
Senior Project Manager: Mary M. Irvin
Senior Operations Supervisor: Matt Ottenweller

Senior Art Director: Diane Lorenzo
Cover Designer: Kristina Holmes
Cover Art: Shutterstock
Permissions Administrator: Rebecca Savage
Full-Service Project Management: S4Carlisle
Publishing Services
Composition: S4Carlisle Publishing Services
Printer/Binder: R. R. Donnelley and Sons Company
Cover Printer: R. R. Donnelley and Sons Company
Text Font: Clearface-Regular

Every effort has been made to provide accurate and current Internet information in this book. However, the Internet and information posted on it are constantly changing, so it is inevitable that some of the Internet addresses listed in this textbook will change.

Library of Congress Cataloging-in-Publication Data
Single case research designs in educational and community settings / Robert E. O'Neill . . . [et al.].
    p. cm.
  Includes bibliographical references and index.
  ISBN 978-0-13-062321-8
 1. Education—Research—Methodology. 2. Single subject research. I. O'Neill, Robert E.,
  LB1028.S5116 2011
  370.7'2—dc22
                                                                    2009050093

www.pearsonhighered.com

ISBN 10:   0-13-062321-0
ISBN 13: 978-0-13-062321-8

Dr. O'Neill would like to dedicate this book: To my lovely daughters Shanna and Daria, who put up with many years of my time and effort spent completing this book, and to all my friends, family, and colleagues who were so patient and who provided so much support in the completion of the project.

PREFACE

WHO THIS BOOK IS FOR AND HOW TO USE IT

We have written this book for practitioners and researchers (or would-be researchers) working in a broad range of applied settings, including schools, residential and vocational programs, and home/family settings. Some of you might be teachers (regular or special education), school counselors or psychologists, administrators, related services personnel (e.g., speech/language therapists, OT/PTs), and/or staff in residential treatment or therapeutic home settings. Others may be students training for a career providing service and/or conducting research in one or more of these types of settings or programs. In all of these, situations will arise in which you will want or need to conduct a controlled evaluation of the impact of some type of strategy, intervention, or program. In recent years there has been greatly increasing emphasis on accountability for services and outcomes in medical, behavioral health, and educational settings. Having the tools to conduct valid evaluations of our treatments and interventions has therefore become even more important. Such evaluations are of great benefit to the applied practice situation. They will also be a potential contribution of broader interest to practitioners and researchers in a given field and other related areas. Such information might be disseminated through informal contacts with other colleagues or via more professional outlets such as presentations at conferences and publications in professional newsletters or journals.

What we have striven for in this book is to provide you with the basic understanding and practical tools you will need to evaluate the impact of your day-to-day practice. The book moves through the research process from the early planning stages, through the actual conduct of a project, to the final evaluation and possible dissemination stages. We have tried to present information in a clear, straightforward, and engaging manner, with a minimum of jargon. Many of the chapters on how to carry out a research effort are structured to provide you with a step-by-step guideline for what, when, and how to do things. The summary tables and checklists throughout the book are meant to be helpful as you follow the process.

Those of us involved in writing the book have participated for many years in practice and research in a variety of applied settings such as classrooms, residential programs, and home/family settings. We strongly believe in the critical importance of sound evaluation and research both to assess the impact of what we do and advance the knowledge base in our respective fields. We sincerely hope that this book is helpful to you as you pursue your own practice and evaluation efforts.

ACKNOWLEDGMENTS

The authors would like to thank profusely the collaborators who contributed in writing all or part of the individual chapters for this book. Their time, expertise, and willingness to work with us are tremendously appreciated; they have collectively helped to make the book a much better product.

We would also like to thank the reviewers: Larry Beard, Jacksonville State University; Margaret Clark, California State University – Los Angeles; E. Paula Crowley, Illinois State University; Georgia Hambrecht, Indiana State University; Thomas Higbee, Utah State University; Tina Sidener, Caldwell College; and R. J. Waller, Piedmont College.

ABOUT THE AUTHORS

Dr. Robert E. O'Neill is the coordinator of the Program in Mild/Moderate Disabilities in the Department of Special Education at the University of Utah, and also teaches courses in the Program in Severe Disabilities and the Department's master's and doctoral programs. He received his M.A. and Ph.D. from the University of California at Santa Barbara, after which he was a member of the faculty at the University of Oregon for nine years prior to coming to the University of Utah. Dr. O'Neill's recent work has focused on strategies for supporting persons exhibiting severe problem behaviors in a variety of community settings, including homes, classrooms, and work sites. His current work is concerned with the areas of functional assessment, teaching communication skills as alternatives to problem behaviors, schoolwide behavioral support, and gender issues in emotional/behavioral disorders. Dr. O'Neill has received over half a million dollars in federal grant support for his research, development, and personnel preparation activities. He has published a number of articles, books, and book chapters, and has done presentations at a variety of state, national, and international conferences. His work has appeared in *Journal of Applied Behavior Analysis, Journal of the Association for Persons with Severe Handicaps, Education and Treatment of Children, Journal of Developmental and Physical Disabilities, Journal of Special Education, Remedial and Special Education,* and *Journal of Positive Behavioral Support.*

Dr. John J. McDonnell received his Ph.D. from the University of Oregon. He joined the faculty in the Department of Special Education at the University of Utah in 1984. His research is focused on curriculum and instruction, transition programs, and inclusive education for students with intellectual and developmental disabilities. He has published a number of journal articles, book chapters, and books in these areas. During his tenure at the University, Dr. McDonnell has obtained a number of federal and state grants and contracts to support his research and personnel training activities. He serves on the editorial boards of several of the top journals in special education, including *Exceptional Children, Intellectual and Developmental Disabilities, Education and Training in Developmental Disabilities,* and *Research for Persons with Severe Disabilities.*

Dr. Felix F. Billingsley received his Ph.D. from the University of Washington in 1974. He is a University of Washington Emeritus Professor. During his years with the College of Education's Area of Special Education, Dr. Billingsley taught courses in instructional methods for students with severe disabilities and single-case research methods. He also published widely on those topics. When he is not playing blues on acoustic or electric guitar, he enjoys sailing and otherwise traveling with his wife, Patti, particularly in Mexico.

Dr. William R. Jenson received his doctorate from Utah State University in 1976, with a specialization in child clinical psychology. His research interests are in the areas of behavioral interventions for tough kids, parent training, generalization of treatment effects, and autism. Dr. Jenson is the author of many journal articles, book chapters, and books, including the widely used *The Tough Kid Book.*

Brief Contents

CONTENTS

HISTORICAL BACKGROUND AND DEVELOPMENT OF SINGLE CASE RESEARCH METHODS

EXPERIMENTAL METHODS AND THE BASICS OF FUNCTIONAL RELATIONSHIPS

The scientific process has been defined in many different ways over the years. Sir Peter Medawar, a Nobel Prize-winning biologist from England, defined science as "all exploratory activities of which the purpose is to come to a better understanding of the natural world" (Medawar, 1979, p. 1). Murray Sidman, a famous behavioral scientist, proposed a variety of reasons for conducting scientific experiments, such as testing hypotheses, investigating new methods and techniques, and even just to indulge the curiosity of the investigator (Sidman, 1960). For our purpose of thinking about educational and community settings, we can think of scientific research as a systematic process for asking and answering questions. That is, we typically start with some type of question or hypothesis to investigate, and then conduct one or more experiments to attempt to find an answer. For example, we may wonder, "Does it make a difference in my students' performance if I add manipulatives along with a whiteboard presentation while teaching a math lesson?" This question could be answered by conducting an experiment.

Single case research (SCR) methods are a category of experimental behavioral research techniques for investigating and demonstrating *causal* or *functional* relationships between *independent* and *dependent* variables. *Independent* variables (IVs) are typically the things that we think of as interventions, or the things that researchers control or manipulate as part of a research study. These might include such things as particular instructional techniques, providing particular types of behavioral consequences (e.g., reinforcement or punishment), or making changes in the context or setting of the participants involved (e.g., changing seating arrangements in a classroom setting). *Dependent* variables (DVs) are the things that we typically observe and measure to determine if the independent variable(s) or intervention(s) had an effect. Dependent variables might include children's social interactive behaviors during recess, the frequency of on-time appointment keeping at a community counseling clinic, or student performance on weekly math or reading assessments. A *functional relationship* means that we have demonstrated that the independent variable(s) or intervention(s) reliably produce changes in the dependent variable(s) (Baer, Wolf, & Risley, 1968). In the example given previously, if we demonstrated that adding manipulatives to the math lesson made a consistent difference, we would have demonstrated a functional relationship between using manipulatives and student performance.

GROUP COMPARISON EXPERIMENTAL DESIGNS

Prior to the development of SCR methods the primary approach for conducting experimental studies was the group comparison (GC; Parsonson & Baer, 1978). This approach involves selecting larger groups of participants, some of whom receive an intervention and some who do not, or different groups who receive different interventions. In a typical scenario a population of interest would be identified (e.g., children in grades 3-5 experiencing significant reading problems). Then, a group of children meeting the desired criteria would be randomly selected from the available population, and subsequently assigned at random to either an *experimental* group or to a *control* group. The experimental group would receive some type of intervention or training aimed at improving their reading skills, while the control group would receive either no intervention or possibly the typical reading intervention provided in their school settings. Following the completion of the intervention the groups would be compared on relevant measures of reading performance (e.g., percent of words read correctly). Most typically the groups' performances would be compared using one or more methods of statistical analysis. These types of experimental approaches, and many variations of them, have been used to investigate questions in a wide range of applied fields (e.g., Gersten et al., 2005; Kendall, Butcher, & Holmbeck, 1999). Use of these types of designs has generally been considered as a *deductive* approach, in which a hypothesis is formulated based on some type of theoretical framework. The experiment is conducted, and the results are analyzed to determine if they do or do not support the hypothesis and its underlying theory (Sidman, 1960).

Concerns and Issues with Group Comparison Designs

As the use of group designs became more prevalent over time, a variety of limitations to their use became more apparent as well. For example, in carrying out research on certain types of questions with various populations, it may be difficult to actually get enough participants to be able to randomly sample and assign the participants for a meaningful study (Shadish, Cook, & Campbell, 2002). This becomes especially important in areas involving lower incidence disabilities such as mental retardation (McDonnell & O'Neill, 2003). A second issue of concern is the use of no-treatment or minimal-treatment control groups. Such approaches raise ethical concerns about withholding treatment from persons who may benefit from it (Griffin & Balandin, 2004). Finally, statistical analyses have traditionally been the primary method for data analysis in GC studies. These typically involve computing mean or average levels of performance and the standard deviation of results and comparing them across the groups through some type of significance test (e.g., a t test; Kazdin, 2003). As pointed out by Sidman (1960) and others, such averaging of data across participants within a group provides little information about the performance of individuals. For example, a group of students receiving a reading intervention may have an average score of 50 on a particular reading measure. However, this could result from half of the students scoring near zero and half of the students scoring 100. While the standard deviation would provide some information about this wide range, individual performance would still be obscured, unless all of the scores were presented. While newer trends in statistical analysis, such as the use of effect size calculations (see Chapter 4), are helping to mitigate this problem, it still remains a significant concern.

DEVELOPMENT OF EXPERIMENTAL SINGLE CASE RESEARCH (SCR) DESIGN METHODOLOGY
Some Historical Background

The intensive study of individual participants has a long history in a variety of disciplines such as physiology, medicine, psychiatry, and clinical psychology. Most readers will be familiar with the ideas of Sigmund Freud. He wrote entire books about some of his individual clients involved in psychoanalysis (e.g., *The Wolf Man*, *The Rat Man*). Along with such analyses there have been ongoing developments in more empirical/experimental approaches to the study of individuals (Dukes, 1965; Gottman, 1973; Kazdin, 1978; Thompson, 1984; Valsiner, 1986). The evolution of current experimental SCR methods has been closely aligned with the development of *behavioral* principles and procedures for studying both human and non-human animal behavior. Such approaches promote a more objective approach to the study of behavior, including direct observation and measurement of overt behavior, and careful operational definitions of experimental (independent) variables. Readers may have heard of, or been familiar with, the work of persons such as Ivan Pavlov, Edward Thorndike, John B. Watson, and Clark Hull (Kazdin, 1978). For example, Pavlov is well known for his work in *respondent* or *classical* conditioning. In this framework, responses that are reliably *elicited* by a particular stimulus can also be brought under the control of other stimuli. Think about being at the eye doctor's office, and undergoing the test where they blast your eye with a puff of air. This will automatically elicit an eye blink response. Suppose each time before the air puff the doctor says "Ready?" With repeated pairings over time simply hearing the word "Ready?" may begin to elicit the eye blink.

Pavlov's work was a stimulus for many other behavioral researchers, such as John B. Watson, who were focused on attempting to make the study of behavior as natural and objective a science as possible (Watson, 1924). Their work in turn was very influential on B.F. Skinner, who has been labeled the most famous psychologist of the 20th century (Bjork, 1993). Building on the work of Pavlov and others, Skinner developed the principles and procedures of *operant* conditioning. In this framework stimuli are said to set the occasion for responses to occur, which are then followed by particular consequences that influence the likelihood that the responses will occur again. To give a simple example, we may present a student with a card with the letter "A" on it and say "What letter?" If the student says "A," we may provide some type of social reinforcement (e.g., praise, pat on the arm, a smile). Over time the experience of many such trials with different letters will typically result in the student being able to name the letters of the alphabet.

Skinner's work primarily took place in the laboratory and involved nonhuman animals such as rats and pigeons. Along with a number of colleagues, Skinner's efforts led to the development of a variety of operant principles and procedures such as reinforcement, punishment, extinction, and stimulus control, which collectively came to be known as the experimental analysis of behavior (EAB).

This work became so widespread that it led to the founding of a journal, the *Journal of the Experimental Analysis of Behavior* (*JEAB*, 1958-present). Around this time Sidman (1960) published a very influential book delineating methodological principles and procedures for carrying out this type of research, which emphasized replication of behavioral effects within and across individual research participants, rather than the typical group comparison approach. For example, a pigeon might initially be exposed to a reinforcement schedule in which it receives a bit of food every third time it pecks a disk in its experimental chamber (an FR3, or fixed ratio 3 schedule). Then the food reinforcement would be discontinued in an extinction condition. Then the reinforcement would be reinstated. In this manner, researchers could examine repeated effects on the animal's behavior during each subsequent condition (Ferster & Skinner, 1957).

Sidman (1960) outlined an important distinction between different types of replication of experimental effects. *Direct* replication involves implementing the same intervention or independent variable(s) with the original participants, or with new participants, to determine if the same results are obtained. So, if having found that using manipulatives improves the math performance of students during a particular year, a teacher may repeat the same procedures with a new group of students the following year to see if the same improvements are evident. *Systematic* replication involves implementing the intervention but with some

---

BOX 1.1

In the course of his research Skinner and his colleagues developed a variety of technical tools, such as experimental chambers (sometimes known as "Skinner boxes"), in which pigeons could peck disks or rats could press levers. Such behaviors were automatically measured and displayed using a device, invented by Skinner, known as a cumulative recorder (which recorded and displayed the accumulated number of responses made by the participant). A recent example of this type of recording and data presentation is shown in Figure 1.1. In a cumulative record each data point is calculated by adding on the number of responses exhibited during a given period. For each group of writers the number of words they wrote and submitted each day was added to the previous day's total to keep a running total of the number of words written. The data indicate that the number of words written by the two groups of writers exceeded the number expected when the intervention was implemented.

Figure 1.1 The graph presents the cumulative number of words written by two small groups of fiction writers ($N = 6$ and 4, respectively) during baseline (no intervention) and Internet intervention periods (during which the authors could obtain feedback on their writing if they met their goals for number of words written). The graph displays trend lines (the solid straight lines) during the intervention phases which indicate the likely number of responses to be expected if no intervention had occurred (see Chapter 4).

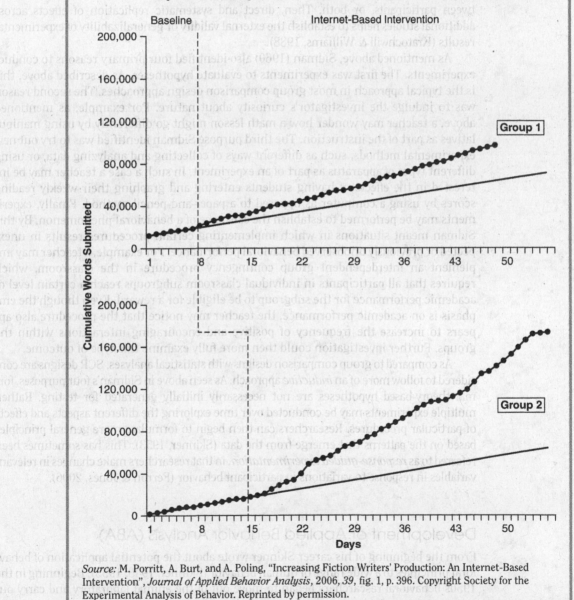

differences. These could involve a different version of the intervention, or implementation with different populations or in different settings. So, our hypothetical teacher might feel that a modification of the manipulatives approach may be more effective, and will implement the modified approach with similar students to assess its effects. Or, our teacher may be in a new job placement with older or younger students, or students with disabilities, and decide to attempt the manipulatives approach with this new population. Most typical individual SCR studies include direct replication of experimental effects either within or between participants, or both. Then, direct and systematic replication of effects across additional studies helps to establish the external validity or generalizability of experimental results (Kratochwill & Williams, 1988).

As mentioned above, Sidman (1960) also identified four primary reasons to conduct experiments. The first was experiments to evaluate hypotheses. As described above, this is the typical approach in most group comparison design approaches. The second reason was to indulge the investigator's curiosity about nature. For example, as mentioned above, a teacher may wonder how a math lesson might go differently by using manipulatives as part of the instruction. The third purpose Sidman identified was to try out new experimental methods, such as different ways of collecting and analyzing data, or using different types of apparatus as part of an experiment. In such a case a teacher may be interested in the effects of having students entering and graphing their weekly reading scores by using a computer as opposed to a paper-and-pencil method. Finally, experiments may be performed to establish the existence of a behavioral phenomenon. By this Sidman meant situations in which implementing certain procedures results in unexpected or previously unobserved behavioral performance. For example, a teacher may implement an interdependent group contingency procedure in the classroom, which requires that all participants in individual classroom subgroups reach a certain level of academic performance for the subgroup to be eligible for a reward. Even though the emphasis is on academic performance, the teacher may notice that the procedure also appears to increase the frequency of positive and encouraging interactions within the groups. Further investigation could then more fully examine this type of outcome.

As compared to group comparison designs with statistical analyses, SCR designs are considered to follow more of an *inductive* approach. As seen above in Sidman's four purposes, formal theory-based hypotheses are not necessarily initially generated for testing. Rather, multiple experiments may be conducted over time exploring the different aspects and effects of particular procedures. Researchers can then begin to formulate more general principles based on the patterns that emerge from the data (Skinner, 1953). This has sometimes been referred to as *response-guided experimentation*, in that researchers make changes in relevant variables in response to variations in participant behavior (Ferron & Jones, 2006).

Development of Applied Behavior Analysis (ABA)

From the beginning of his career Skinner wrote about the potential application of behavioral principles to a wide range of human behavior (Skinner, 1948, 1953). Beginning in the 1950s behavioral researchers began to move out of the animal laboratory and carry out studies in more applied settings, primarily with children and adults with psychiatric and developmental disorders. These settings included psychiatric institutions (Lindsley, 1956). For example, Allyon and Michael (1959) demonstrated how social attention from unit staff, when made contingent on appropriate responding, could improve the behavior of adults with schizophrenia living in an institutional setting. Other research groups demonstrated how behavioral principles and procedures could be used to increase desired behavior (e.g., verbal speech) and decrease undesired behavior (e.g., self-injury) of children with autism (Lovaas, Freitag, Gold, & Kassorla, 1965; Wolf, Risley, & Mees, 1964). Such approaches were also shown to be effective in changing the social play behavior of socially isolated children in preschool classroom settings (Allen, Hart, Buell, Harris, & Wolf, 1964; Hart, Reynolds, Baer, Brawley, & Harris, 1968). Other applications focused on improving student behavior in classroom settings (Becker, Madsen, Arnold, & Thomas, 1967). These and other initial studies demonstrated the power of behavioral principles and procedures to impact real-life social problems outside the more basic laboratory setting. This emphasis on problems of social importance is one of the defining features of ABA (see Table 1.1 below).

Throughout the 1960s and 1970s ABA flourished in a wide variety of areas, including developmental disabilities, education, and organizational behavior management in business (Friman, Allen, Kerwin, & Larzelere, 1993). (A variety of terms were sometimes used to describe this approach, such as behavior modification or behavior management [Kazdin, 1978]). The *Journal of Applied Behavior Analysis* (*JABA*) started publication in 1968, followed by other applied journals in subsequent years (e.g., *Behavior Modification, Analysis and Intervention in Developmental Disabilities, Journal of Organizational Behavior*

Table 1.1   The Critical Characteristics of Applied Behavior Analytic Research Delineated by Baer, Wolf, & Risley (1968).

1) *Applied*—This type of research focuses on problems or challenges of social importance (e.g., education, mental health), as opposed to more basic or abstract laboratory research.

2) *Behavioral*—The focus is on objectively observing and measuring what people say and do (i.e., how they behave), as opposed to less objective measures (e.g., self-reports).

3) *Analytic*—Controlled SCR designs are used to demonstrate functional relationships between interventions and behavior change.

4) *Technological*—The procedures used to bring about behavior change must be operationally defined so that others can replicate and implement them.

5) *Conceptual*—Behavior change procedures must be clearly based on conceptual principles of behavior analysis.

6) *Effective*—Behavioral procedures must produce outcomes that are substantial enough to result in significant benefit to those involved (i.e., social validity—see Chapter 3).

7) *Generalization*—Behavior change procedures must produce results across a range of desired behaviors, settings, and persons.

Management). In the inaugural issue of *JABA*, Baer et al. (1968) delineated the critical characteristics of applied behavior analytic research, which was built on SCR approaches. These characteristics are presented in Table 1.1. Along with these general characteristics, Baer et al. (1968) also described two of the main SCR designs used at the time (the reversal design and the multiple baseline design) and the logic underlying them (see Chapters 6 & 7). Since this early period, effective use of applied behavior analytic approaches has been demonstrated in a wide range of fields, including education, clinical psychology, developmental disabilities, business, pediatrics, and a host of others (Austin & Carr, 2000).

The Link Between SCR and ABA

It is worth noting that, as others have pointed out, SCR designs have not solely been used to evaluate the effects of behavioral intervention approaches (Kazdin, 1982). SCR designs can be used in virtually any situation in which someone might want to study the effect of some type of potential behavior change procedure. In what is referred to as *behavioral pharmacology*, SCR designs have been used in a variety of ways to assess the effects of drugs in both humans and animals (Poling & Byrne, 2000). In addition, SCR designs have been used to evaluate the effects of less strictly behavioral interventions in fields such as clinical psychology, speech-language pathology, and social work (Kendall et al., 1999; McReynolds & Kearns, 1983; Tripodi, 1998). While many examples of SCR investigations described in this book involve behaviorally oriented interventions, it is important for the reader to keep in mind that such design approaches are not limited to the evaluation of behavioral interventions, but have broader potential application.

THE CURRENT ROLE OF SCR DESIGN METHODOLOGY IN DETERMINING EVIDENCE-BASED PRACTICES

Over the last two decades there has been increasing pressure in various fields (e.g., medicine, clinical psychology, education) for clinicians and school personnel to employ interventions or treatments that have been shown to be effective by controlled research studies. This trend has involved a variety of labels including empirically validated treatments, empirically supported treatments, and evidence-based practices. The field of clinical psychology provides an example of this process. In the early 1990s the Division of Clinical Psychology (Division 12) of the American Psychological Association established a task force to identify psychological treatments that were considered to be effective as indicated by the results of empirical research (Chambless et al., 1998; Chambless & Hollon, 1998). Among other activities this process entailed defining a set of criteria for the quality and quantity of research that had to be present in the literature to serve as the basis for identifying a practice as empirically supported or evidence-based.

The criteria that were identified as characteristic of *well-established* or *probably efficacious* treatments are presented in Table 1.2 (Chambless et al., 1998). As can be seen, the Task Force identified criteria for both group comparison and SCR experimental

Table 1.2 A Variety of Criteria for Identifying Intervention or Treatment Practices as Empirically Supported or Evidence-based.

Chambless et al. (1998) Criteria

WELL-ESTABLISHED TREATMENTS

I. At least two good between-group design experiments demonstrating efficacy in one of the following ways:

   A. Superior (statistically significantly so) to pill or psychological placebo or to another treatment.

   B. Equivalent to an already established treatment in experiments with adequate sample sizes.

OR

II. A large series of single case design experiments ($n \geq 9$) demonstrating efficacy. These experiments must have:

   A. Used good experimental designs and

   B. Compared the intervention to another treatment as in IA.

Further Criteria for Both I and II:

III. Experiments must be conducted with treatment manuals.

IV. Characteristics of the client samples must be clearly specified.

V. Effects must have been demonstrated by at least two different investigators or investigating teams.

PROBABLY EFFICACIOUS TREATMENTS

I. Two experiments showing the treatment is superior (statistically significantly so) to a waiting-list control group.

OR

II. One or more experiments meeting the Well-Established Treatment criteria IA or IB, III, and IV, but not V.

OR

III. A small series of single case design experiments ($n \geq 3$) otherwise meeting Well-Established Treatment criteria.

POLSGROVE & FORNESS (2004) CRITERIA EVIDENCE-BASED PRACTICE

I. At least two well-designed randomized group comparison studies demonstrating effectiveness.

OR

II. A meta-analysis of at least 12 group experimental or quasi-experimental studies with a mean effect size of 0.7 or higher.

OR

III. At least 20 well-designed single case studies with a minimum of 60 participants and a mean percent of nonoverlapping data points (PND) of at least 80%.

(Continued)

Table 1.2 A Variety of Criteria for Identifying Intervention or Treatment Practices as Empirically Supported or Evidence-based. (*Continued*)

PARTIALLY EVIDENCE-BASED PRACTICE

I. One randomized group comparison study demonstrating efficacy.

OR

II. Four quasi-experimental studies or a meta-analysis of at least 12 studies with an effect size of 0.4 or higher.

OR

III. A single case synthesis of at least 12 studies with a PND of 70% or higher.

HORNER ET AL. (2005) CRITERIA FOR AN EVIDENCE-BASED PRACTICE

I. A minimum of 5 single case studies that meet minimally acceptable methodological criteria that have been published in peer-reviewed journals.

II. The studies have been conducted by at least 3 different researchers across at least 3 different geographical locations.

III. The 5 or more studies include a total of at least 20 participants.

designs. The criteria for SCR designs specify a minimum number of experiments but not a minimum number of participants. One of the specified characteristics that is only seen in some SCR research designs is Criterion II B (Compared the intervention to another treatment as in IA). Some SCR designs are focused on evaluating only a single intervention (see Chapters 6, 7, & 8), while others focus on comparing the relative effects of multiple treatments (see Chapters 9 & 10). Also, while recent years have seen an increasing emphasis on collecting data to document the consistency or integrity of the implementation of independent variables or interventions (Gresham, Gansle, & Noell, 1993), it is still not common to see SCR that employs treatment manuals (Criterion III).

This emphasis on evidence-based practices was formally brought into the field of education with the passage of the No Child Left Behind Act (NCLB) in 2002. While a widely noted report on scientific research in education emphasized that research involves different types of questions requiring different types of methodologies (Shavelson & Towne, 2002), NCLB defined "scientifically based research" with an emphasis on objective measurement and experimental designs, especially randomized group comparison designs (NCLB, 2002). This last criterion created understandable concern for researchers in areas such as special education. Investigators in this field may face significant challenges in conducting randomized group comparisons, such as difficulties in identifying and involving enough participants, particularly when studying low-incidence disabilities (e.g., severe mental retardation, dual visual/hearing impairments; McDonnell & O'Neill, 2003). As mentioned earlier in this chapter, ethical issues also arise when participants may potentially be assigned to no-treatment control groups. These concerns are important, as they impact very important issues such as the ability of investigators to effectively compete for federal research funding, and thereby develop important interventions for various populations of students with disabilities (Spooner & Browder, 2003).

In response to such concerns various authors and researchers in special education have proposed standards for using SCR studies as the basis for identifying practices as scientifically or evidence-based (Cook & Schirmer, 2006). Polsgrove and Forness (2004) proposed criteria for both group and SCR design studies (see Table 1.2). Their criteria included minimum numbers of studies and participants, as well as (in some cases) specification of average effect sizes obtained from sets of studies, and calculation of the average percentage of nonoverlapping data points between baseline and intervention phases (see Chapter 3). In 2003 the Council for Exceptional Children (CEC) established a task force to address issues in identifying evidence-based practices in special education (Odom et al., 2005). This task force commissioned multiple subcommittees to examine and write about these issues as they relate to a variety of research methodologies, such as group comparisons, correlational and qualitative methods, and SCR design research. With regard to SCR designs, Horner et al., (2005) described a set of quality indicators for evaluating the methodological soundness of such studies, including operational definition and measurement of independent and dependent variables, replication of effects within and across participants, and evaluation of the social validity of intervention procedures and their outcomes. Horner et al. proposed a set of criteria for using SCR design studies to consider a practice to be evidence-based (see Table 1.2). These criteria focus on the methodological soundness of the experiments, a minimum number of studies and participants, and replication of effects across different research groups and locations. Horner et al. identified functional communication training (FCT) as an example of a practice which would meet their proposed criteria. This strategy involves identifying the behavioral function of problem behaviors (e.g., to obtain social attention, to avoid/escape undesired tasks or activities) and then teaching a person to use appropriate alternative communicative responses to indicate their needs/wants (e.g., presenting a card which says "I need a break"). The efficacy of such an approach in reducing problem behavior and increasing appropriate behavior has been demonstrated across a range of participants, settings, research groups, and locales (Chambless et al., 1998; Horner et al., 2005).

There is clearly variability in the criteria proposed by different researchers with regard to the quantity and quality of SCR studies that would be considered sufficient to identify an intervention or practice as being evidence-based. The consistent message, however, is that effects need to be demonstrated across multiple SCR studies involving a variety of participants and research groups. Such an approach fits perfectly with Sidman's (1960) concept of systematic replication (see above) to establish the generality of intervention effects.

SUMMARY AND CONCLUSION

The preceding portions of this chapter have attempted to describe the historical development and current status of SCR design methodology as a scientific research method employed in a variety of basic and applied fields (Dermer & Hoch, 1999). It should be clear that SCR approaches have earned respect and value as an investigative approach

(Morgan & Morgan, 2001). SCR design studies are well suited for demonstrating functional relationships between independent and dependent variables. Replication of effects both within and across studies allows for the establishment of the generality or external validity of interventions (see Chapter 3). Hopefully it is clear at this point that SCR design approaches can be employed to answer experimental questions that may be posed in a broad variety of settings and situations (e.g., schools, community settings, etc.). The remainder of this book will describe the basic features of SCR design approaches, present details of the methodology, and discuss aspects of dissemination of experimental results to relevant audiences.

REFERENCES

Allen, K. E., Hart, B., Buell, J. S., Harris, F. R., & Wolf, M. M. (1964). Effects of social reinforcement on isolate behavior of a nursery school child. *Child Development, 35,* 511–518.

Allyon, T., & Michael, J. (1959). The psychiatric nurse as a behavioral engineer. *Journal of the Experimental Analysis of Behavior, 2,* 323–334.

Austin, J., & Carr, J. E. (Eds.). (2000). *Handbook of applied behavior analysis.* Reno, NV: Context Press.

Baer, D. M., Wolf, M. M., & Risley, T. R. (1968). Some current dimensions of applied behavior analysis. *Journal of Applied Behavior Analysis, 1,* 91–97.

Becker, W. C., Madsen, C. H., Arnold, C. R., & Thomas, D. R. (1967). The contingent use of teacher attention and praise in reducing classroom behavior problems. *Journal of Special Education, 1,* 287–307.

Bjork, D. W. (1993). *B. F. Skinner: A life.* New York: Basic Books.

Chambless, D. L., Baker, M. J., Baucom, D. H., Beutler, L. E., Calhoun, K. S., Crits-Cristoph, P., . . . Woody, S. R. (1998). Update on empirically validated therapies, II. *The Clinical Psychologist, 51,* 3–16.

Chambless, D. L., & Hollon, S. D. (1998). Defining empirically supported therapies. *Journal of Consulting and Clinical Psychology, 66,* 7–18.

Cook, B. G., & Schirmer, B. R. (Eds.). (2006). *What is special about special education: Examining the role of evidence-based practices.* Austin, TX: Pro-Ed.

Dermer, M. L., & Hoch, T. A. (1999). Improving descriptions of single subject experiments in research texts written for undergraduates. *The Psychological Record, 49,* 49–66.

Dukes, W. F. (1965). $N = 1$. *Psychological Bulletin, 64,* 74–79.

Ferron, J., & Jones, P. K. (2006). Tests for the visual analysis of response-guided multiple-baseline data. *Journal of Experimental Education, 75,* 66–81.

Ferster, C. B., & Skinner, B. F. (1957). *Schedules of reinforcement.* New York: Appleton-Century-Crofts.

Friman, P. C., Allen, K. D., Kerwin, M. L., & Larzelere, R. (1993). Changes in modern psychology: A citation analysis of the Kuhnian displacement thesis. *American Psychologist, 48,* 658–664.

Gersten, R., Fuchs, L. S., Compton, D., Coyne, M., Greenwood, C., & Innocenti, M. S. (2005). Quality indicators for group experimental and quasi-experimental research in special education. *Exceptional Children, 71,* 149–164.

Gottman, J. M. (1973). N-of-one and N-of-two research in psychotherapy. *Psychological Bulletin, 80,* 93–105.

Gresham, F. M., Gansle, K. A., & Noell, G. H. (1993). Treatment integrity in applied behavior analysis with children. *Journal of Applied Behavior Analysis, 26,* 257–263.

Griffin, T., & Balandin, S. (2004). Ethical research involving people with intellectual disabilities. In E. Emerson, C. Hatton, T. Thompson, & T. R. Parmenter (Eds.), *The international handbook of applied research in intellectual disabilities* (pp. 61–82). West Sussex, England: John Wiley & Sons.

Hart, B. M., Reynolds, N. J., Baer, D. M., Brawley, E. R., & Harris, F. R. (1968). Effect of contingent and non-contingent social reinforcement on the cooperative play of a preschool child. *Journal of Applied Behavior Analysis, 1*, 73–76.

Horner, R. H., Carr, E. G., Halle, J., McGee, G., Odom, S. L., & Wolery, M. (2005). The use of single-subject research to identify evidence-based practice in special education. *Exceptional Children, 71*, 165–179.

Kazdin, A. E. (1978). *History of behavior modification*. Baltimore, MD: University Park Press.

Kazdin, A. E. (1982). *Single case research designs*. New York, NY: Oxford University Press.

Kazdin, A. E. (2003). *Research design in clinical psychology* (4th ed.). Boston, MA: Allyn & Bacon.

Kendall, P. C., Butcher, J. N., & Holmbeck, G. N. (1999). *Handbook of research methods in clinical psychology* (2nd ed.). New York, NY: John Wiley & Sons.

Kratochwill, T. R., & Williams, B. L. (1988). Perspectives on pitfalls and hassles in single-subject research. *Journal of the Association for Persons with Severe Handicaps, 13*, 147–154.

Lindsley, O. R. (1956). Operant conditioning methods applied to research in chronic schizophrenia. *Psychiatric Research Reports, 5*, 118–139.

Lovaas, O. I., Freitag, G., Gold, V. J., & Kassorla, I. C. (1965). Experimental studies in childhood schizophrenia: Analysis of self-destructive behavior. *Journal of Experimental Child Psychology, 2*, 67–84.

McDonnell, J. J., & O'Neill, R. E. (2003). A perspective on single/within subject research methods and "scientifically based research." *Research and Practice for Persons with Severe Disabilities, 28*, 138–142.

McReynolds, L. V., & Kearns, K. (1983). *Single-subject experimental designs in communicative disorders*. Austin, TX: Pro-Ed.

Medawar, P. B. (1979). *Advice to a young scientist*. New York, NY: Basic Books.

Morgan, D. L., & Morgan, R. K. (2001). Single-participant research design: Bringing science to managed care. *American Psychologist, 56*, 119–127.

No Child Left Behind Act of 2001. Public Law 107-110, 115 Stat. 1425. (2002, January 8).

Odom, S. L., Brantlinger, E., Gersten, R., Horner, R. H., Thompson, B., & Harris, K. R. (2005). Research in special education: Scientific methods and evidence-based practices. *Exceptional Children, 71*, 137–148.

Parsonson, B. S., & Baer, D. M. (1978). The analysis and presentation of graphic data. In T. R. Kratochwill (Ed.), *Single subject research: Strategies for evaluating change* (pp. 101–165). New York, NY: Academic Press.

Poling, A., & Byrne, T. (Eds.). (2000). *Behavioral pharmacology*. Reno, NV: Context Press.

Polsgrove, L., & Forness, S. R. (2004). *Evidence-based practice in special education*. Presented at the Annual Teacher Educators of Children with Behavioral Disorders Conference, Tempe, AZ.

Shadish, W. R., Cook, T. D., & Campbell, D. T. (2002). *Experimental and quasi-experimental designs for generalized causal inference*. Boston, MA: Houghton-Mifflin.

Shavelson, R. J., & Towne, L. (Eds.). (2002). *Scientific research in education*. Washington, DC: National Academy Press.

Sidman, M. (1960). *Tactics of scientific research: Evaluating data in experimental psychology*. New York, NY: Basic Books.

Skinner, B. F. (1948). *Walden Two*. New York: MacMillan.

Skinner, B. F. (1953). *Science and human behavior*. New York: Free Press.

Spooner, F., & Browder, D. M. (2003). Scientifically based research in education and students with low incidence disabilities. *Research and Practice for Persons with Severe Disabilities, 28*, 117–125.

Thompson, T. (1984). The examining magistrate for nature: A retrospective review of Claude Bernard's *An Introduction to the Study of Experimental Medicine*. *Journal of the Experimental Analysis of Behavior, 41*, 211–216.

Tripodi, T. (1998). *A primer on single-subject design for clinical social workers*. Washington, DC: NASW Press.

Valsiner, J. (Ed.). (1986). *The individual subject and scientific psychology*. New York, NY: Plenum Press.

Watson, J. B. (1924). *Behaviorism*. New York: Norton.

Wolf, M. M., Risley, T. R., & Mees, H. (1964). Application of operant conditioning procedures to the behavior problems of an autistic child. *Behaviour Research and Therapy, 1*, 305–312.

Defining What to Measure and How to Measure It

John J. McDonnell and
Lora Tuesday Heathfield

2

As discussed in Chapter 1, establishing a functional relationship between the dependent and independent variables in single case research designs requires repeated measurement of the study participant's behavior prior to and following the implementation of the intervention (Barlow & Hersen, 1984; Tawney & Gast, 1984). The researcher's confidence in the observed relationship between these variables hinges on the development and implementation of effective measurement systems (Horner et al., 2005). As such, two of the most important decisions that researchers make in designing a study are related to how the target behavior is defined and how changes in the behavior will be measured. Once the measures have been selected, the researcher must take steps to ensure that the procedures used to record changes in the target behavior are reliable. In addition, the researcher must ensure that the implementation of the independent variable is consistent across study participants, behaviors, and settings. Finally, the researcher must assess the social validity of the intervention. The combination of these factors enhances the ability of the researcher to document experimental control and to effectively communicate the results of the study. This chapter will discuss recommended procedures for ensuring these outcomes.

PARAMETERS OF MEASUREMENT

It is important to remember that the general parameters of a measurement system for any study are dictated by the proposed research questions. Consider a research question such as: "Does constant-time delay promote the acquisition of dressing skills by students with developmental disabilities?" Obviously, the target behaviors for the study will include one or more dressing skills for each student participating in the study, and the measures would logically focus on assessing variables such as the accuracy of the students' responses, their level of independence in completing the

DEFINING WHAT TO MEASURE
AND HOW TO MEASURE IT

skills, and/or the amount of time they required to complete the skill. In contrast, addressing a question such as "Is constant time-delay or the system of most to least prompts more effective in promoting the acquisition of dressing skills by students with developmental disabilities?" would require additional measures that focused on variables such as the number of trials to criterion or the amount of time in instruction. The research question provides direction to the researcher in defining the target behavior and dimensions of the target behavior that should be measured.

Defining the Target Behavior

The first step in developing an effective measurement system is to operationally define the behavior that will be used as the dependent variable in the study. Hawkins and Dotson (1975) identified three criteria that are necessary for behavior to be considered operationally defined: (1) it is objective, (2) it is clear, and (3) it is complete. Objectivity implies that the behavior is observable and can be recorded reliably by others. Clarity indicates that the definition is unambiguous and does not require extensive explanation in order to distinguish the targeted behavior from other behaviors. Completeness is demonstrated when there are clear guidelines denoting what the inclusion and exclusion criteria are so that minimal judgment is required as to whether a behavior occurred or did not occur. When judgment is required, a complete operational definition will ensure the same judgment on multiple occasions or by more than one observer. An example of a good operational definition for putting on a shirt might be "the shirt is right-side out, the student's arms are in the correct sleeves, buttons are inserted into the correct holes, and the shirt tail is straight." In contrast, the statement "the student puts on his shirt" would be a poor example of an operational definition because it requires the observer to make a number of judgments about whether the student has done it correctly. Similarly, an example of a good operational definition of a student's aggressive behavior might be: "any striking out with arms, hands, legs, feet, or teeth that is in the direction of another individual and accompanied by an audible verbal threat, whether or not contact is made with the other individual." A poor example of an operational definition of this behavior would be the student is "aggressive toward others" because it leaves the observer in the position of having to decide, for example, whether the student hitting a desk or yelling at someone is an aggressive behavior.

Specifying an operational definition is important in the measurement of behavior for several reasons. The first is to ensure that the resulting measure of behavior is accurate. On the same occasion, two different individuals should agree on whether the behavior occurred or not. If the operational definition lacks objectivity, clarity, or completeness, it is possible that two individuals could be measuring different behaviors and accuracy is compromised. Increased precision serves to enhance the accuracy of the data collected. Secondly, a comprehensive operational definition is critical in order to accurately evaluate the effectiveness of a specific intervention on the targeted behavior. Otherwise, a clear determination cannot be made as to whether the behavior change was due to the intervention strategy, a change in the behavior measured, or both. As the data collection process begins, it is possible that ambiguous situations will arise that the operational definition does not address adequately and it will be unclear whether a specific instance is considered an occurrence of the behavior or not. For example, in the example of aggressive behavior described above, the student may pick up a rock and throw it at a classmate on the playground. This scenario was not anticipated in the initial operational definition because it had never occurred before. In these cases slight alterations of the operational definition may be necessary to increase precision, but ideally they should be determined prior to beginning data collection. Once the target behavior is specified adequately, formal data collection can commence.

Identifying the Dimension of the Behavior to Be Measured

Any response made by a study participant can be assessed on multiple dimensions. For example, in assessing a student's performance in putting on a shirt, the researcher could look at the consistency of the student's response with the operational definition of the behavior (accuracy), the amount of assistance the instructor had to provide the student to put on the shirt, the amount of time it took the student to put on the shirt, or all three. Similarly, in assessing aggressive behavior by a student the researcher could count the frequency of aggressive behaviors, the duration of a particular behavior, and/or the intensity of a behavior. Choosing which of these dimensions, or perhaps multiple dimensions, to use to assess changes in the target behavior depends on the research question proposed for the study. The goal is to select one or more dimensions that will allow the researcher to clearly answer the research question and document the functional relationship between the dependent and independent variables. Common dimensions of behavior that are used in single case research studies include frequency (rate), accuracy, duration, latency, and intensity (Table 2.1).

Frequency (Rate)

Frequency refers to how often a behavior occurs in a specified time period. Data regarding a behavior's frequency such as the number of occurrences per minute or hour are often described as the rate of behavior. The frequency or rate of a behavior may be the most appropriate dimension to measure when the focus of the research question is on the increase or decrease in the rate of a particular behavior, such as the number of math problems that a student completes correctly in one minute on a worksheet or the number of circuit boards assembled in an hour by a worker in an electronics plant. Frequency or rate is not an appropriate dimension to measure when the behavior can only occur under specific conditions or when the behavior occurs continuously over an extended period of time.

For example, frequency or rate would not be a particularly usefully dimension to measure when a student is reading sight words from flashcards being presented by a teacher. In this case, the number of words read by the student is impacted by how quickly the teacher shows the flashcards to the student.

Frequency or rate would also not be a good dimension to measure for a behavior such as a student's engagement in a science lesson or walking to and from the grocery store. In these cases, the researcher is likely more interested in the proportion of time

Table 2.1   Summary of Dimensions of Behavior.

Dimensions	Definition	Potential Uses	Typical Measures
Frequency/ Rate	Number of occurrences or nonoccurrences of the target behavior within a specified period of time.	Track the acceleration or deceleration of the target behavior across observational sessions.	Number of times the target behavior occurs or does not occur within a constant time period. The number of times the target behavior occurs divided by the total number of time units (seconds, minutes, or hours).
Accuracy	Completion of the target behavior in relation to the operational definition of the target behavior or a preestablished performance criterion.	Track improvements in the ability of the participant to complete the target behavior.	Number of correct responses completed. Percent of correct responses (number of correct responses divided by the total number of opportunities).
Duration	The amount of time a target behavior occurs.	Track increases or decreases in the amount of time a behavior occurs during each occurrence or during an observation period.	Number of seconds, minutes, or hours a behavior occurs. Mean, median, and range of occurrence.
Latency	The amount of time between the presentation of a specific stimulus and the initiation of the target behavior.	Track increases or decreases in the amount of time the participant requires to start the target behavior.	Number of seconds, minutes, or hours. Mean, median, and range of occurrence.
Intensity/ magnitude	Severity or strength of the target behavior.	Determine whether the target behavior meets a specified performance criterion.	Number or percentage of responses that met or did not meet the performance criterion.

that the study participant took to complete the behavior within the observation period or the total amount of time it took the participant to complete the behavior.

Accuracy

This dimension refers to the number or percentage of correct responses made by the study participant. Typically, this dimension is designed to assess the student performance in relation to the definition of the target behavior or a preestablished performance criterion within a discrete and controlled opportunity to complete the target behavior. Accuracy is an appropriate dimension to measure when the research question is focused on the acquisition of new behaviors. For example, the number of trials that a student puts a shirt on correctly or the percent of math problems completed correctly during an intervention session.

Duration

Duration indicates how long a behavior occurs from its starting point to stopping point. Duration can be assessed based on the amount of time that elapses during each occurrence of the target behavior (e.g., 85 seconds to put on a shirt) or the amount of time in which the target behavior occurs during an observation period (e.g., 3.5 minutes during math). Measuring how long a behavior occurs from start to end may be most appropriate when the goal is to increase or decrease the duration of a behavior, such as the amount of time attending in class or the amount of time required to put on a shirt.

Latency

Latency is defined as the length of time between the presentation of a specified stimulus and the start of the specified behavior. For example, the length of time between the presence of a snake and a fear response such as a scream, or the amount of time it takes a person to begin to cross a street after the signal changes from "Don't Walk" to "Walk." In these cases measurement of latency might be the most appropriate dimension to measure when attempting to increase or decrease the length of time between one event and a specific response.

Intensity/Magnitude

Intensity generally refers to the severity of a behavior, but could also refer to a behavior's "magnitude, strength, amplitude, force, or effort" (Kazdin, 2001, p. 87). The intensity of a behavior is difficult to measure accurately due to the level of judgment required. Physiological measures, such as pulse or heart rate, might provide a more precise measure of intensity; but more commonly, intensity is simply estimated by measuring outcomes (e.g., "Did a student hit the object with enough intensity to damage it?"). Another more objective measure of intensity is to specify and define discrete categories, such as mild, moderate, and severe, in order to increase accuracy of measurement, although some degree of judgment is still involved. Measuring a behavior's intensity would be most appropriate when attempting to either increase or decrease the force of a behavior, such as swinging a baseball bat, or self-hitting.

MEASUREMENT PROCEDURES

The selection of the most appropriate data collection procedure relies on several considerations including the characteristics of the research setting, the target behavior and the dimension to be assessed, the nature of the intervention, and the resources available. Two types of measurement procedures frequently used in single case research studies include the measurement of permanent products and direct observation of the participant's behavior.

Measurement of Permanent Products

Permanent product measurement is used when there are tangible items resulting directly from a particular behavior. For example, if a student is having difficulty completing independent seatwork in math their work completion can be gauged by determining the percentage of math problems completed on math worksheets by the end of the seatwork time period. The advantages of permanent product measurement is that it is both convenient and minimally disruptive to ongoing activities since it does not require direct observation, which can sometimes be impractical, and can be recorded long after the event occurs.

The primary disadvantage to permanent product measurement is that it does not provide information regarding how the product was actually produced. For example, if a student only completes 30% of the math problems on a worksheet the researcher would not be able to determine if it was because the student was distracted and off-task during math seatwork or because the student had not mastered the required basic math facts. The other disadvantage is that permanent product measurement is limited to those behaviors that result in tangible items that are considered permanent products.

Observational Recording

Observational recording refers to the recording of data in real time or as it is actually occurring. An alternative involves using audiotape or videotape recordings to obtain a sample of behaviors to listen/view and document later. In either case, one or more onlookers (or the actual target individual) participate in data recording. Direct observation of an individual's behavior can provide accurate information regarding the actual occurrence or nonoccurrence of a target behavior versus the perceived occurrence (or nonoccurrence) that is obtained through report. Prior to the beginning of the study, four decisions regarding the observation procedures must be made: the number of observation sessions, how long observation sessions last, when observation sessions are conducted, and how the target behavior will be coded (Kazdin, 2001).

The first determination is the number of observation sessions in which to collect data. This depends on how variable the target behavior is over time and more practical considerations such as the availability of observers and potential restrictions such as scheduling difficulties. Ultimately the goal is to conduct observations on as many occasions as possible in order to accurately measure the target behavior prior to and during the implementation of the intervention (Horner et al., 2005). The general recommendation is that a minimum of five data collection sessions occur within baseline and again after an intervention is initiated.

A second determination is how long each observation period will last. The goal is to conduct long enough observations to obtain an accurate sample of the target behavior. Some behaviors may occur at specified times so observation sessions should be planned accordingly. For example, if a student's disruptive behavior occurs primarily after working for 20 minutes, observation periods should probably be 30 minutes long or longer. In this case, a 15-minute observation period might not accurately measure the targeted behavior. The length of an observation period may also be dictated by the number of opportunities to respond (or) the number of instructional trials provided to the student during an intervention session. In this case, the length of the observation might vary from one intervention session to the next based on how long it takes the participant to complete the scheduled number of trials.

The third decision is when the observation periods should be conducted. This will depend largely on the nature of the target behavior and the context in which it is typically performed. For example, to observe a student's use of a fork and knife, mealtimes are the most appropriate context in which to be certain to observe and collect data. Ideally, observation sessions should be planned across multiple time periods and multiple settings (being sure to include the settings in which behavior change is desired). The ultimate goal of any data collection method is to obtain a representative sample of the individual's behavior of concern.

The final decision relates to how the participant's performance of the target behavior will be coded during observations (Bijou, Peterson, & Ault, 1968). Observational coding procedures can be designed to focus on a single behavior or multiple behaviors. For example, the researcher can record the frequency that a behavior occurs by simply placing a check mark on a data sheet or indicate whether a response was correct or incorrect by recording a "+" or "−." Recording procedures can also be designed to track multiple behaviors simultaneously, usually by using a coding scheme to represent different behaviors (e.g., "T" for talking-out and "O" for out-of-seat). Some research questions may require that the researcher not only record a code describing the participant's behavior but the stimuli that set the occasion for the behavior or that follow the behavior. In designing the observational coding system the researcher should strive to make it as simple as possible while ensuring that a sufficient amount of data are collected to allow the research question to be answered.

Direct observation permits the recording of behavior in real time as it occurs in the natural environment. Approaches to measuring behavior can be classified as being either continuous or discontinuous. Continuous measures are designed to allow the researcher to detect all instances of a response during the observation period (Johnson & Pennypacker, 1993). Discontinuous measures are designed to record some but not all occurrences of a response and are used to develop estimates of the occurrence or nonoccurrence of a behavior during the observation period.

Continuous Measures

Continuous measures include event, duration, and latency recording. Event recording is structured to document the exact number of occurrences (or nonoccurrences) of a particular behavior that are observed. A code (i.e., notation or mark) is recorded on the data sheet each time the behavior occurs. In some cases, the code may simply focus on a frequency count of the occurrence of the target behavior during an observation period (e.g., the student shouted out inappropriate words 12 times during morning circle time; Figure 2.1). In other cases, the code may describe the nature of the student response (e.g., whether a student read cooking sight words correctly or incorrectly; Figure 2.2). Event recording is best suited for target behaviors that have a clearly definable beginning and ending in order to yield an accurate count. The advantages of event recording are

Figure 2.1 Illustrative data recording for behavior frequency

Participant: John		Observer: Rob	
Target Behaviors: Out-of-seat			
Date	Time	Frequency Count	Total Behaviors
1/15	10:00 – 10:20	✓✓✓✓✓✓✓✓✓✓✓✓✓✓✓✓✓✓✓✓	20

Figure 2.2 Illustrative data recording form for accuracy

Student: Don						Teacher: Mrs. Smith			
Example/Item + = correct 0 = incorrect	Date								
	1/9	1/11	1/16	1/18	1/22				
Casserole	0	0	0	+	+				
Tongs	0	0	+	+	+				
Spatula	0	+	+	+	+				
T	+	+	+	+	+				
Whisk	0	+	+	+	+				
Percent Correct	20	60	80	100	100				

Source: McDonnell, J., Johnson, J. W., & McQuivey, C. *Embedded instruction for students with developmental disabilities in general education classes.* CEC, vol. 6, Figure 4-9, p. 51. Copyright 2008 by The Council for Exceptional Children. Reprinted with permission.

that it is simple to use and summarize, and provides for a direct assessment of the participant's performance during each observation period. The primary disadvantage of event recording is that it is not well suited for behaviors that occur at extremely high rates or occur over extremely long periods of time. For example, it might be difficult for an observer to accurately count the number of strokes a participant made in brushing his or her teeth or the number of times a participant flapped his or her hands up and down during self-stimulation. Event recording is also less useful for measuring behaviors such as playing a video game or throwing temper tantrums where the amount of time that the participant engages in a behavior is of more concern than how often it occurs.

Duration recording is used to record the length of time of each occurrence of the target behavior (e.g., the amount of time it takes a student to get ready for school; Figure 2.3). For accurate data collection, behaviors must have a discrete onset and conclusion, which necessitates a clear operational definition of when the behavior starts (description of the behavior at onset) and when the behavior terminates (description of the behavior at conclusion). Data collected using duration recording can be converted to an average duration if the behavior occurs regularly (e.g., "The student's tantrums lasted an average of 6.3 minutes in the mornings and 10.1 minutes in the afternoon") or a total duration if appropriate (e.g., "It took the student 68 seconds to put on his shirt"). If the time periods in which observations occur remain stable, a percentage can be computed (e.g., "The student was out of his seat during seatwork activities 35% of the time").

Latency recording is very similar to duration recording; however, the measurement focuses instead on the duration of the interval between two events. Typically, latency recording is used to determine the length of time between a stimulus, such as a request, and a behavior, such as the response. For example, recording the length of time between the teacher's request, such as "Get out your pencils," and a student having a pencil in hand. Latency recording also differs from duration recording in that the observer must attend to two different behavioral events (e.g., initial stimulus and behavioral response) at two different points in time. Again, for precise recording of the length of a latency period, clear operational definitions of the termination of the stimulus (e.g., when a request ends) and the onset of the behavior (e.g., when a response begins) are critical.

Discontinuous Measurement

This group of measures includes interval recording and time sampling procedures. Interval recording can be used to record the frequency of a behavior occurrence (or nonoccurrence); however, as pointed out above, interval recording results in an *estimate* of the duration or frequency of the target behavior rather than the exact amount of time the behavior occurs or number of occurrences of the target behavior as measured by event recording. For interval recording, the observation period is divided into equal intervals of time, usually denoted by a box on a data recording sheet (Figure 2.4). Each box then represents one interval of a predetermined length of time. Interval length is decided upon based on the perceived frequency and duration of the target behavior in question. Intervals usually are no longer than 30 seconds in length

Figure 2.3 Illustrative data recording form for duration

Participant: John			Observer: Rob
Target Behavior: Get dressed for school.			
Date	Start	Stop	Total Duration
1/15	7:10	7:23	13 min
1/16	7:04	7:14	10 min

(Cooper, 1981) and most commonly are 10 to 15 seconds in length (Kazdin, 2001), particularly for high frequency behaviors. Intervals smaller than 10 seconds in length are rarely used since the rate at which observers must record data increases the likelihood of errors. Typically, the observation period is divided into equal periods (e.g., a ten-minute observation would be divided into 60 ten-second intervals). Interval recording

Figure 2.4 Illustrative interval data recording form

Student: John												Observer: Rob	
Target Behavior: Hits during free time/min												**Observation Period: 10 min**	
Date	Time	Intervals											Percent of Intervals
		1	2	3	4	5	6	7	8	9	10	
1/15	10:15 – 10:25	✔		✔ ✔				✔				30

results in the proportion of time in which the target behavior occurred, which is typically reported as the number or percentage of intervals in which the target behavior occurred (e.g., "The student was observed to be off-task during 75% of the intervals"). By considering interval recording as a proportion of time, in addition to estimating the frequency of behavior, it can also be used to estimate the duration of a behavior. There are two types of interval recording: whole interval and partial interval.

In whole interval recording, the behavior is only marked as occurring if it is exhibited during the entire interval. Using whole interval recording, the student would be considered "off-task" during an interval only if the student was engaged in off-task behavior for the entire 10-second interval. In partial interval recording, the behavior is marked as occurring if it is observed at any time or multiple times during the interval. Using partial interval recording, a student would be considered "off-task" during an interval if the student was engaged in off-task behavior during the first second of the 10-second interval, the last second of the 10-second interval, or multiple times during the 10-second interval. On a cautionary note, whole interval recording can result in an underestimate of a behavior's frequency since a behavior must occur across an entire interval for it to be counted, while partial interval recording can result in either an overestimate of a behavior's frequency, since a behavior can occur as briefly as 1 second to be counted as occurring, or an underestimate, since a behavior can occur multiple times during the interval but be counted only once. Interval recording is appropriate to use when measuring high frequency behaviors that do not have a long duration or for low frequency behaviors that occur across an extended time. Interval recording also can be appropriate for behaviors that do not have a discrete beginning or ending, such as being "off-task." Both whole interval and partial interval recording require continuous observation and data recording and attention to precise time intervals, all of which make it difficult to carry out while performing another task at the same time, such as teaching. As a result, most interval recording is conducted by an independent observer with the aid of a pre-written data sheet and a time-signaling device, such as a beep tape. The data sheet typically has the intervals marked across the page, which are continued in the next row, with each row representing equal time lengths. For example, for 10-second intervals, each row may have six intervals across the page, with each row then representing one minute of time.

Momentary time sampling is a variation of interval recording that does not require continuous observation. Similar to interval recording, the observation time period is divided into equal intervals, with the interval length dependent upon the target behavior's frequency and duration. Also like interval recording, time sampling is used to estimate a behavior's frequency or duration of occurrence (or nonoccurrence) and results are typically summarized in terms of the percentage of intervals in which the target behavior occurred. Momentary time sampling is best used to record high-frequency behaviors, such as stereotypy, or behaviors that occur for a longer duration, such as work refusal. Although interval recording requires continuous observation, time sampling only requires observation at specified times. With momentary time sampling, a target behavior is marked as occurring only if it is exhibited at the end of the interval. As with interval recording, a beep tape can be used to provide an auditory signal at the pre determined interval length, but with momentary time sampling the auditory signal cues the observer to observe whether the target behavior is occurring at that moment. The advantages to using time sampling are that it is easier to use than interval recording and that it can be used while simultaneously engaged in another task since it only requires attending to the target behavior at specified moments. Another advantage is that time sampling can be used to track a target behavior across multiple individuals. This can be accomplished in a round-robin format (Cooper,

1981), by observing one individual at the end of each interval. For example, at the end of the first interval the observer notes whether one student is on-task; at the end of the second interval, the observer notes whether another student is on-task; and so on. Group scanning can also be used with time sampling by scanning a group of individuals and counting the number of individuals engaged in a particular target behavior at the cued end of the interval. For example, it may be helpful to determine the proportion of students in a classroom who are on-task in comparison with the target student. At the end of one interval, the observer notes whether the target student is on-task. At the end of the next interval, the observer quickly counts the number of students in the class who are on-task and the procedure continues using alternate intervals to focus on the target student on-task behavior or the on-task behavior of the classroom as a whole. Momentary time sampling can result in a fairly accurate estimate of a target behavior's frequency, but can also underestimate frequency (a) if the target behavior occurs multiple times during an interval since recording only occurs at the end of the interval, and or (b) if the behavior occurs frequently but often not at the end of the interval (when observing and recording the behavior's occurrence). Similarly to interval recording, time sampling typically involves a pre-written data sheet, with intervals marked across the rows, and a time signaling device, such as a beep tape.

As pointed out, all discontinuous measurement procedures can result in an under- or overestimate of the frequency or duration of a behavior. This is referred to as a measurement artifact. Figure 2.5 illustrates how the use of whole-interval recording, partial-interval recording, and momentary time sampling procedures can lead to substantially different results. The shaded bars indicate the actual duration of time the participant engaged in the target behavior during the observation period using continuous duration recording procedures. The whole-interval recording procedure indicates that the participant engaged in the target behavior during 30% of the intervals. The partial-interval procedure indicates that the participant engaged in the behavior during 70% of the intervals. Finally, the momentary time sampling procedure indicates that the participant engaged in the behavior during 50% of the intervals. However, it should not be concluded that the momentary time sampling procedure provides a more accurate estimate of the behavior in this example. It simply illustrates how the different recording procedures can lead to widely different results depending on the distribution of the target behavior during the observation period.

This example highlights two important points in developing a measurement system. First, continuous measures are the preferred methods for recording target behavior. Second, when resource limitations prevent the use of continuous measures the researcher must carefully consider which sampling procedure will provide the most accurate estimate of the occurrence or nonoccurrence of the target behavior. This will require the researcher to determine how many observation sessions are needed, how long the observation must be, the length of the observation intervals, and when the observation sessions should occur in order to obtain the most valid sample of the target behavior.

Advanced Observation Tools

Recent advances in computer technology have led to the development of extremely powerful data recording systems that can be used in applied research settings (Thompson, Felce, & Symons, 2000). The availability of these systems has prompted researchers to

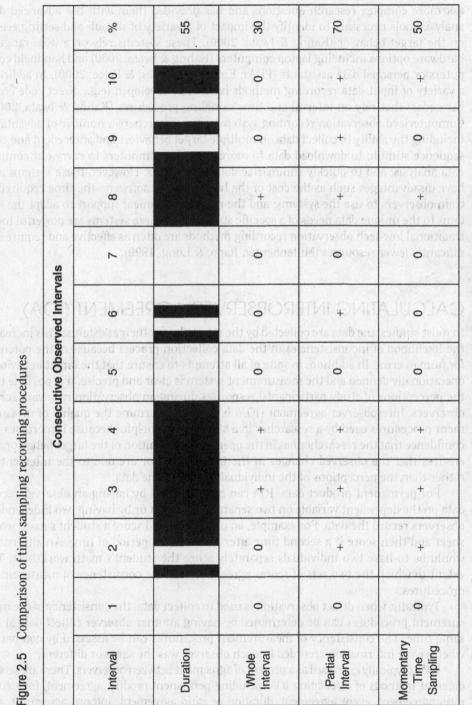

Figure 2.5 Comparison of time sampling recording procedures

	Consecutive Observed Intervals									
	1	2	3	4	5	6	7	8	9	%
Interval										
Duration	0				0	+	0			55
Whole Interval	0			+	0	+	0		0	30
Partial Interval	0			+	0	+	0		0	70
Momentary Time Sampling	0			+	0	0	0		0	50

Note: Adapted from Cooper, J. O., Heron, T. E., & Heward, W. L. (2007). *Applied Behavior Analysis* (2nd Edition). Upper Saddle River, NJ: Pearson.

■ = Actual occurrence of behavior measured by continuous duration recording.

+ = Behavior recorded as occurring in the interval.

0 = Behavior recorded as not occurring in the interval.

ask more complex research questions and has provided them with the advanced data analysis tools necessary to identify the impact of a variety of stimuli and setting events on the target behavior (Kahng & Iwata, 2000). These systems rely on a wide range of hardware options including laptop computers (Kahng & Iwata, 2000) and handheld computers or personal data assistants (PDAs; Emerson, Reeves, & Felce, 2000). In addition, a variety of input data recording methods have been developed (e.g., direct code entry, bar codes) that rely on interval and time sampling procedures (Kahng & Iwata, 2000). Computerized observation recording systems offer researchers a number of advantages including the ability to collect data on multiple target behaviors and antecedent and consequence stimuli; to download data to more powerful computers to carry out complex data analysis; and to quickly summarize data for analysis. However, these systems also have disadvantages such as the cost of the hardware and software; the time required to train observers to use the systems; and the need for technical support to adapt the systems to the unique data needs of a specific study. While these systems are powerful tools, traditional low-tech observation recording methods are often as effective and require significantly fewer resources (Miltenberger, Rapp, & Long, 1999).

CALCULATING INTEROBSERVER AGREEMENT (IOA)

In most studies, the data are collected by the researcher or their assistants. This increases the likelihood of inconsistencies in the data collection process because of the potential for human error. In addition, in spite of all attempts to ensure that the target behavior is operationally defined and the measurement system is clear and precise, it is possible that the perceptions of study participants' responses during an observation may vary across observers. Interobserver agreement (IOA) is used to determine the quality of measurement procedures used by a researcher in a study. IOA is helpful because it increases the confidence that the researcher has in the operational definition of the target behavior and ensures that the observed changes in the target behavior are due to the intervention rather than the perceptions of the individual recording the data.

For permanent product data, IOA can be conducted by having an observer record data on the dependent variable on two separate occasions or by having two independent observers record the data. For example, an observer could score a student's math worksheet and then score it a second time after a prescribed period of time. An alternative would be to have two individuals separately score the student's math worksheet. The extent to which the two sets of scores agree indicates the consistency of measurement procedures.

Typically, when direct observation is used to collect data, the consistency of the measurement procedures can be determined by having another observer collect data at the same time. The consistency of measurement procedures can be assessed by comparing whether the information recorded by each observer was the same or different.

IOA is typically expressed as a percent of agreement between observers. There are several different methods of calculating IOA including permanent product agreement, frequency-ratio agreement, event agreement, duration or ratio agreement, interval agreement, and occurrence/nonoccurrence agreement. The specific method selected by the researcher should match the dimension of the target behavior being measured and data recording system being used.

Permanent Product Agreement

IOA for permanent products can be calculated by dividing the number of agreements on each observation and multiplying by 100. In the example described above, if the observer scored 15 math problems as correct on the first scoring and 18 problems as correct on the second scoring, the IOA would be 83.3% ($15/18 = 0.833 \times 100 = 83.3\%$). A similar approach would be used if two observers scored the student's math worksheet separately. If Observer 1 scored 14 problems as correct and Observer 2 scored 15 problems as correct the IOA would be 93.3% ($14/15 = 0.933 \times 100 = 93.3\%$).

Frequency-Ratio Agreement

When frequency or ratio of responses is the primary dependent variable, IOA can be calculated by dividing the lower frequency count of first observer by the higher frequency count of the second observer and multiplying by 100. For example, if Observer 1 recorded 70 instances of the behavior and Observer 2 recorded 75 instances of the behavior, the IOA would 93.3% ($70/75 = 0.933 \times 100 = 93.3\%$).

Duration or Latency Agreement

For duration recording and latency recording, the shorter length of time recorded by one observer is divided by the longer length of time recorded by the second observer and multiplied by 100. For example, if Observer 1 recorded 98 seconds and Observer 2 recorded 100 seconds, the IOA would 98% ($98/100 = 0.98 \times 100 = 98\%$).

Event Agreement

This procedure (sometimes referred to as point-by-point agreement) is used when calculating IOA for discrete behaviors in which the observer is coding the nature of the participant's response (Kazdin, 1982). For example, recording whether a participant read sight words correctly or completed the steps of a task analysis correctly when putting on a shirt. In this case IOA is calculated by dividing the number of agreements in the codes recorded by observers for each event by the total number of agreements plus disagreements in the codes recorded, multiplied by 100. For example, if two observers were coding whether a participant read sight words correctly during an observation, IOA would be calculated based on whether the observers agreed or disagreed on whether the participant read each sight word correctly or incorrectly. If the observers agreed that the student read nine words correctly and disagreed on one word the IOA would be 90% (9 agreements/10 [9 agreements + 1 disagreement] = 0.90 × 100 = 90%).

Interval Agreement

The calculation of IOA for interval or time sampling data often is based on a point-by-point IOA procedure. In which the number of intervals in which both observers agreed that the target behavior occurred is divided by the total number of intervals (agreements plus disagreements) and that amount is multiplied by 100. For example, out of 100 possible intervals 90 were recorded the same by both Observers 1 and 2, and 10 were recorded differently; consequently, the IOA would be 90% (90/100 = 0.90 × 100 = 90%). It is important to note, however, that even though an interval may have been coded the same by two observers, it does not imply that the two observers saw exactly the same behavior within that interval (Tawney & Gast, 1984). For example, it is possible that the two observers noted different frequencies of the target behavior within a specified interval.

Occurrence/Nonoccurrence Agreement

The potential limitations of using simple agreements and disagreements for calculating IOA for interval and time sampling data has prompted some researchers to use a more rigorous method called occurrence/nonoccurrence agreement (Alberto & Troutman, 1999). For example, if a low frequency behavior occurs in only three times out of 100 possible intervals and two observers each record three instances of the target behavior but not as occurring in the same intervals, the calculation method described previously would still result in a very high level of agreement despite the fact that the two observers did not agree on when the target behavior occurred. The number of "agreements" due to the large number of intervals in which the target behavior did not occur artificially inflates the estimation of IOA. The method of calculation of occurrence/nonoccurrence is similar to that outlined above except that the researcher calculates two IOA coefficients, one for occurrence of the behavior and another of nonoccurrence of the behavior.

Standards of IOA

At this point, there are no empirically validated standards for determining the number of IOA observations that should be conducted with a study or the level of IOA that should be achieved. Professional conventions suggest that researchers should collect IOA data during 20%–33% of the observations or intervention sessions. It is also important that IOA data be collected during each phase of the study (i.e., baseline, intervention). Further, the IOA data collection sessions should be randomly selected whenever possible. The conventional minimum standard for acceptable IOA is a mean of 80%–85% across all observations (Kazdin, 1982), although it is recommended that researchers strive to achieve a mean of 90%–100% IOA across observations.

Researchers should be concerned if the IOA falls below 80% during any observation. There are a number of possible reasons for not achieving acceptable levels of IOA (Kazdin, 1977). First is a lack of clarity in the operational definition of the target behavior. This can be addressed by providing training to the observers on examples of behaviors that are included or excluded from the definition through naturalistic observations or via videotaped segments. A second possibility is observer drift. In this circumstance, the operational definition of the target behavior is modified over time in the mind of one or both of the observers. Observer drift can be controlled by having the observers periodically review the operational definition and engage in practice data recording sessions similar to the practice opportunities provided during the initial training. Third, the complexity of the data coding system may be a potential source of agreement error. Coding systems become more complex if multiple behaviors or multiple target individuals are being observed simultaneously. To minimize this source of agreement error, it is important to simplify the data recording process as much as possible by minimizing the number of behaviors or individuals to be observed at the same time to those that are most critical, or by using observation forms with a simplified coding scheme. Finally, agreement error may be attributed to the presence of the second observer when IOA data are collected. For example, due to the second observer's presence, the primary observer may alter behavior by attending more closely to the target individual or target behavior, or engaging in more self-questioning of whether an observed behavior meets the operational definition, thereby potentially altering data collection accuracy during agreement checks. This source of agreement error can be minimized by attempting to keep IOA checks as covert as possible, or by physically separating the two observers during agreement checks.

TRAINING OBSERVERS

The quality of data taken on the dependent variable and the ability of the researcher to establish the reliability of the data is based on the skills of the observers to accurately identify the target behavior and record the correct information. This can only be accomplished if the observers are rigorously trained on data collection methods prior to the implementation of the study. Although there is no widely accepted convention on the best methods for training observers, it is generally recommended that the researcher and observer complete several steps (Cooper, Heron, & Heward, 2007; Tawney & Gast, 1984):

1. Develop an observer training manual that provides a clear operational definition of each target behavior, the codes that will be used to record data on the behavior, and observation procedures and etiquette.
2. Observers should memorize the operational definitions and coding scheme and be required to demonstrate mastery of the information through verbal or written tests.
3. Observers should be required to practice data recording using role-plays and/or videotapes of individuals in natural environments. This phase of training should continue until the observers meet a prespecified accuracy criterion.

4. Observers should simultaneously carry out data collection with an experienced observer in natural environments until they meet a prespecified accuracy criterion.
5. The consistency of observers' data recoding should be regularly assessed using IOA procedures.

MEASURING THE FIDELITY OF THE INTERVENTION

A clear demonstration of experimental control by the independent variable requires that the researcher document that the intervention was consistently implemented during the study (Gresham, Gansle, & Noell, 1993; Horner et al., 2005). This is of particular concern in single case research studies because of the length of time that the independent variable may be implemented with study participants. The possibility of procedural drift increases with the amount of time that the intervention is implemented. This creates a significant threat to the internal validity of the study and reduces the ability of the researcher to draw firm conclusions about the impact of the intervention on the target behavior. The way to avoid this problem is to regularly assess the fidelity of the intervention throughout the study (Peterson, Homer, & Wonderlitch, 1982).

Gresham et al. (1993) suggest that researchers can document the fidelity of the intervention through several simple steps. First, the researcher should develop a comprehensive operational definition of the independent variable. The definition should describe the exact procedural steps that will be implemented with the study participant across sessions. In essence the researcher develops a "task analysis" of the intervention that lays out procedural steps that are both observable and measurable. It is often helpful to develop a written description (or script) of the steps of the intervention for the individuals implementing it.

Second, the individuals implementing the intervention should be evaluated on the extent to which their implementation of the intervention matches the operational definition developed by the researcher. For example, Figure 2.6 presents a treatment fidelity evaluation form used by McDonnell and his colleagues to assess treatment fidelity in a series of studies examining the effects of embedded instruction on students with developmental disabilities in general education classes (McDonnell, Johnson, Polychronis, & Riesen, 2002; Johnson & McDonnell, 2004; Johnson, McDonnell, Holzwarth, & Hunter, 2004). In this example, one of the researchers would observe the individual implementing embedded instruction procedures. If the teacher implemented the intervention step as described in the operational definition it was scored as a "+." If the teacher's implementation of the step was inconsistent with the definition it was scored as "−." The percentage of treatment fidelity during the sessions was calculated by dividing the correct steps by the total steps and multiplying by 100.

Finally, the researcher needs to collect a sufficient amount of treatment fidelity data to obtain a representative sample of all intervention sessions. Although there are no empirically validated rules governing the number of observations that should be done, it is generally recommended that they mirror the standards suggested for calculating

Figure 2.6   Illustrative treatment fidelity checklist

Student: Don Instructor: Karen		EI Program Step: II/2 Date: 1/17				
Program Step	Trial	1	2	3	4	5
1. Initiates an instructional trial at planned times or when a natural opportunity occurs.		+	+	+	+	+
2. Varies instructional materials.		+	0	+	+	+
3. Obtains student's attention.		+	+	+	+	+
4. Delivers instructional cue.		+	+	+	+	+
5. Implements designated delay.		+	0	+	0	+
6. Delivers controlling prompt.		+	+	+	+	+
7. Provides correct level of reinforcement (unprompted or prompted). OR Implements error correction procedure.		+	+	+	+	+
8. Records trial on tracking form.		+	+	+	+	+
Percent Correct (Total Correct Steps/Total Steps × 100)		37/40 × 100 = 92.5%				

Source: McDonnell, J., Johnson, J. W., & McQuivey, C. *Embedded instruction for students with developmental disabilities in general education classes.* CEC, vol. 6, p. 56. Copyright 2008 by The Council for Exceptional Children. Reprinted with permission.

IOA on the dependent variable (Peterson et al., 1982). In general we recommend that treatment fidelity be obtained for a minimum of 25% of all intervention sessions. Given the importance of ensuring the consistency of the intervention to demonstrating experimental control, the level of treatment fidelity should be extremely high. Researchers should strive for a 90% or higher level of treatment fidelity during each observation. Failure to achieve this level should prompt the researcher to take additional steps to operationally define the intervention and to train the individuals how to properly implement it.

MEASURING SOCIAL VALIDITY

The concept of social validity was initially introduced for use in intervention research to determine whether the intervention outcomes were considered socially important and whether they made a difference in the lives of the individuals receiving the intervention (Kazdin, 1977, 1980; Wolf, 1978). Two approaches have been advocated for assessing the social validity of an intervention. The first approach relies on the subjective reports by study participants and others who were directly impacted by the implementation of the intervention. The focus is on obtaining the perceptions of the respondents on the importance, acceptability, and sustainability of the intervention. The second approach is to compare the performance of study participants to other individuals who represent typical performance in a particular setting (Van Houten, 1979); for example, comparing the rates of "academic engagement" or "academic performance" of students with disabilities participating in general education classes with peers without disabilities (e.g., Carter, Cushing, Clark, & Kennedy, 2005; McDonnell, Thorson, Allen, & Mathot-Buckner, 2000). The social validity of the intervention is established if the study participant's behavior approximates the individuals in the comparison group. Although the assessment of social validity is widely accepted as a key indicator of the quality of a single case research study (Horner et al., 2005), reviews of the research literature suggest it is often not addressed in published studies (Carr, Austin, Britton, Kellum, & Bailey, 1999).

The most widely used approach to assessing social validity is through subjective evaluation. Although standardized scales of social validity are available (e.g., The Behavior Intervention Rating Scale, Elliott & Treuting, 1991), in most cases the researcher will develop an assessment approach that best matches the intervention, study participants, and research setting. The steps of carrying out subject evaluations of social validity are relatively straightforward:

1. Identify the respondent groups. Obviously the most important group to gather data from are the study participants. They are in the best position to evaluate the outcomes and acceptability of the intervention. In many cases, it is also important to gather social validity data from the individuals who implement the intervention in order to assess the feasibility and sustainability of the intervention in the natural environment. It may also be necessary to gather data from individuals who may not be the direct recipients of the intervention or its implementation such as parents, peers, and other community members.

2. Select the data collection method. A number of strategies have been used to gather the perceptions of study participants about the social validity of interventions including questionnaires, forced-choice procedures, structured interviews, and open-ended interviews (Kennedy, 1992). Each approach has its own advantages and disadvantages; the key is to select the approach that allows the researcher to obtain a comprehensive understanding of the impact of the intervention in the most efficient way.

3. Analyze and report the data. The key to effectively using social validity data is to integrate it with the empirical findings of the study. All too often, social validity is reported as an afterthought without being directly linked to the study's research questions and findings. At a minimum, the researcher should discuss how the social validity data impact the interpretation of the primary findings; the effect on the generalization of the findings to other individuals, behaviors, and settings; and the implications for practice.

SUMMARY AND CONCLUSION

High quality single case research studies must employ procedures that ensure that data collection is reliable and valid (Horner et al., 2005). This includes a clear operational definition of the target behavior; the selection of measures that allow the researcher to comprehensively describe the changes in the target behavior; the implementation of IOA procedures that allow the researcher to document the consistency of data collection on the dependent variable; the implementation of procedures that ensure that the independent variable was implemented consistently across all study participants, behaviors, or settings; and gathering information on whether the intervention resulted in socially important outcomes and whether it can be sustained within the typical resources of the intervention settings. The decisions that the researcher makes for each of these issues can have a significant effect on the internal and external validity of the study, as well as the contribution the study will make to research and practice.

REFERENCES

Alberto, P. A., & Troutman, A. C. (1999). *Applied behavior analysis for teachers* (5th ed.). Upper Saddle River, NJ: Prentice-Hall.

Barlow, D. H., & Hersen, M. (1984). *Single case experimental designs: Strategies for studying behavior change* (2nd ed.). New York: Pergamon Press.

Bijou, S. W., Peterson, R. F., & Ault, M. H. (1968). A method to integrate descriptive and experimental studies at the level of data and empirical concepts. *Journal of Applied Behavior Analysis, 1,* 175–191.

Carr, J. E., Austin, J. L., Britton, L. N., Kellum, K. K., & Bailey, J. S. (1999). An assessment of social validity trends in applied behavior analysis. *Behavioral Interventions, 14,* 223–231.

Carter, E. W., Cushing, L. S., Clark, N. M., & Kennedy, C. H. (2005). Effects of peer support interventions on students' access to the general curriculum and social interactions. *Research and Practice for Persons with Severe Disabilities, 30,* 15–25.

Cooper, J. (1981). *Measurement and analysis of behavioral techniques.* Columbus, OH: Merrill.

Cooper, J. O., Heron, T. E., & Heward, W. L. (2007). *Applied behavior analysis* (2nd ed.). Upper Saddle River, NJ: Pearson.

Elliot, S. N., & Treuting, M. V. B. (1991). The behavior intervention rating scale: Development and validation of a pretreatment acceptability and effectiveness measure. *Journal of School Psychology, 29,* 43–51.

Emerson, E., Reeves, D. J., & Felce, D. (2000). Palmtop computer technologies for behavioral observation research. Computer systems for collecting real-time observational data. In T. Thompson, D. Felce, and F. J. Symons (Eds.), *Behavioral observation: Technology and applications in developmental disabilities* (pp. 47–60). Baltimore: Paul H. Brookes.

Gresham, F. M., Gansle, K. A., & Noell, G. H. (1993). Treatment integrity in applied behavior analysis with children. *Journal of Applied Behavior Analysis, 26,* 257–263.

Hawkins, R. P., & Dotson, V. S. (1975). Reliability scores that delude: An Alice in Wonderland trip through the misleading characteristics of inter-observer agreement scores in interval recording. In E. Ramp & G. Semp (Eds.), *Behavior analysis: Areas of research and application* (pp. 359–376). Englewood Cliffs, NJ: Prentice-Hall.

Horner, R. H., Carr, E. D., Halle, J., McGee, G., Odom, S., & Wolery, M. (2005). The use of single-subject research to identify evidence-based practice in special education. *Exceptional Children, 71,* 165–179.

Johnson, J. W., & McDonnell, J. (2004). An exploratory study of the implementation of embedded instruction by general educators with students with developmental disabilities. *Education and Treatment of Children, 27,* 46–63.

Johnson, J. W., McDonnell, J., Holzwarth, V., & Hunter, K. (2004). The efficacy of embedded instruction for students with developmental disabilities enrolled in general education classes. *Journal of Positive Behavioral Interventions, 6,* 214–227.

Johnson, J. M., & Pennypacker, H. S. (1993). *Strategies and tactics for human behavioral research* (2nd ed.). Hillsdale, NJ: Erlbaum.

Kahng, S. W., & Iwata, B. A. (2000). Computer systems for collecting real-time observational data. In T. Thompson, D. Felce, and F. J. Symons (Eds.), *Behavioral observation: Technology and applications in developmental disabilities* (pp. 35–46). Baltimore: Paul H. Brookes.

Kazdin, A. E. (1977). Assessing the clinical or applied significance of behavior change through social validation. *Behavior Modification, 1,* 427–452.

Kazdin, A. E. (1980). Acceptability of alternative treatments for deviant child behaviors. *Journal of Applied Behavior Analysis, 13,* 259–273.

Kazdin, A. E. (1982). *Single-case research designs: Methods for clinical and applied settings.* New York: Oxford University Press.

Kazdin, A. E. (2001). *Behavior modification in applied settings* (6th ed.). Belmont, CA: Wadsworth/Thompson Learning.

Kennedy, C. H. (1992). Trends in the measurement of social validity. *The Behavior Analyst, 15,* 147–156.

McDonnell, J., Johnson, J. W., Polychronis, S., & Riesen, T. (2002). The effects of embedded instruction on students with moderate disabilities enrolled in general education classes. *Education and Training in Mental Retardation and Developmental Disabilities, 37,* 363–377.

McDonnell, J., Thorson, N., Allen, C., & Mathot-Buckner, C. (2000). The effects of partner learning during spelling for students with severe disabilities and their peers. *Journal of Behavioral Education, 10,* 107–121.

Miltenberger, R. G., Rapp, J. T., & Long, E. S. (1999). A low-tech method for conducting real-time recording. *Journal of Applied Behavior Analysis, 32,* 119–120.

Peterson, L., Homer, A. L., & Wonderlitch, S. A. (1982). The integrity of independent variables in behavior analysis. *Journal of Applied Behavior Analysis, 15,* 477–492.

Tawney, J. W., & Gast, D. L. (1984). *Single subject research in special education.* New York: Merrill Publishing.

Thompson, T., Felce, D., & Symons, F. J. (Eds.). (2000). *Behavioral observation: Technology and applications in developmental disabilities.* Baltimore: Paul H. Brookes.

Van Houten, R. (1979). Social validation: The evolution of standards of competency for target behaviors. *Journal of Applied Behavior Analysis, 12,* 581–591.

Wolf, M. M. (1978). Social validity: The case for subjective measurement, or how applied behavior analysis is finding its heart. *Journal of Applied Behavior Analysis, 11,* 203–214.

INTERNAL AND EXTERNAL VALIDITY AND BASIC PRINCIPLES AND PROCEDURES OF SINGLE CASE RESEARCH (SCR) DESIGNS

Previous chapters have covered the foundational steps that need to be completed prior to formally beginning a research study. These include identifying dependent measure(s), developing a data collection system, training observers or data collectors as needed, and carefully defining and setting up intervention strategies. Other aspects, such as obtaining appropriate reviews and approvals, recruiting participants, and obtaining informed consent, will be covered later (Chapter 5). Part of this process also involves selecting an appropriate experimental design that will allow the research question(s) under consideration to be answered. Subsequent chapters will present and discuss the basic design options available for single case research. Some of these designs rely on comparisons of conditions implemented *within* an individual over time to demonstrate a functional relationship, while others rely on comparisons made *across* individuals (Kazdin, 1982).

As discussed in Chapter 1, the main purpose of conducting a study within the context of an experimental design is to allow the researcher to make conclusions about the relationship between an independent variable or variables and changes in a dependent variable or variables (Hayes, 1981). That is, the experimental design allows for the demonstration of a *functional relationship* by helping to rule out threats to *internal validity* and *external validity* for the study in question. This chapter will describe issues related to internal and external validity, as well as the basic principles underlying single case designs and their general procedural features.

INTERNAL VALIDITY

The *internal validity* of a study refers to the likelihood that we can be sure that the intervention or independent variable was responsible for any observed changes in the dependent variable(s) or behavioral performance being measured (Drew, Hardman, & Hart, 1996; Kennedy, 2005). That is, any observed changes in behavioral performance are not due to uncontrolled or extraneous factors or variables encountered by the participants. For example, suppose a school psychologist was attempting to evaluate the impact of a self-monitoring strategy on the task completion of a 3rd grade student labeled as having Attention Deficit Hyperactivity Disorder (ADHD). Such a strategy might involve having the student self-evaluate behavior every two minutes, and record whether she was on- or off-task on a self-monitoring recording sheet. Such interventions have been demonstrated to have positive effects on on-task behavior and task completion in classroom settings (Wehmeyer, Agran, & Hughes, 1998). However, if unbeknownst to the school psychologist the student's parents had recently visited their family pediatrician and had begun administering a medication aimed at improving the student's behavior, the effects of the medication would be an alternative explanation for any observed change in the student's performance, and therefore would pose a threat to the internal validity of the study.

The scenario described above is an example of a threat to internal validity known as *history effects* (Campbell & Stanley, 1966).

These are events that occur outside of the context or situation under study that may influence the participant's behavior. Other examples include changes in a family situation (e.g., divorce); unanticipated changes in the classroom or school (e.g., a substitute teacher); larger environmental events (e.g., a hurricane); or changes in a participant's physical functioning (e.g., sleep problems, medication changes).

Maturation effects refer to changes in a participant's behavior that may occur due to typical developmental processes, such as changes in height, weight, or intellectual development. For example, in a study focused on accelerating the language development of young children with disabilities, it may become difficult to determine whether observed progress is due to the intervention or independent variable, or to the effects of basic developmental processes.

Testing or practice effects may be an issue when participants are repeatedly exposed to particular evaluation experiences, which may lead to changes in their performance. For example, elementary students repeatedly given the same set of spelling words may begin to learn the words independently of any intervention aimed at increasing their spelling ability.

Measurement or instrumentation effects occur when apparent changes in behavioral performance are actually due to problems with the measurement process or system. In measuring the noisiness of students in a school cafeteria or on a school bus, the decibel meter may malfunction. This could lead evaluators to conclude that a behavioral intervention was having an impact, when in fact the changing measurements were due to problems with the measurement instrument. Similarly, over time the manner in which human observers perceive and categorize the occurrence of behavioral events may change, leading to changes in the resulting data (see Chapter 2).

Regression to the mean may come into play as a threat to internal validity, particularly when participants are selected due to their extreme performances on a particular behavioral dimension. For example, participants may be included in a study based on very low initial levels of on-task behavior or task completion, or very high rates of aggressive or disruptive behavior. If such performances were not representative of the participants' "usual" behavior, subsequent regressions to their more typical levels of behavior may be mistakenly interpreted as being due to the intervention under study. However, this type of regression is less likely to be an issue in a research process involving frequently repeated measurement (see below).

Selection bias relates primarily to a group comparison design approach (see Chapter 1). In this case, differences between groups may be observed due to the fact that the initial selection and assignment of participants to groups resulted in groups with different characteristics and levels of performance. Observed differences may then be due to the selection and assignment process, rather than the effects of an intervention. Again, this kind of issue is not necessarily applicable in a single case design paradigm, which typically does not involve group comparisons.

Participant attrition effects refer to situations in which an experiment may be affected by the fact that particular participants were not able to complete the study. This could be due to a variety of factors such as families moving to another city or parental decisions to opt out due to time constraints. Such changes in the participant group could influence the study results. Attrition could affect both group and single case type experiments, although it is more likely to be a concern in group comparison studies. In the single case context, attrition could be a problem in a variety of ways. For example, suppose there were five initial participants in a study, but two of them did not complete the study due to various logistical factors. If those two participants were not responding positively to the study intervention, but the remaining three participants were, this would produce a biased outcome with regard to interpreting the results of the study.

Diffusion of treatment threatens the validity of a study when participants are exposed to some or all aspects of an intervention when they are not supposed to be. Consider a situation in which a prompting and reinforcement intervention is being implemented in a playground setting to increase social interactions of students exhibiting social withdrawal. Students who are not supposed to be receiving the intervention (i.e., who are in a baseline condition—see below) may observe other students receiving prompts and positive feedback for engaging in social interactions. The non-intervention students may begin to change their social behavior as a result of this exposure, thus compromising their baseline condition and resulting data.

Finally, *multiple-treatment interference* refers to a situation in which participants may be exposed to more than one intervention in some kind of sequence. If this is not done in a systematic and controlled manner (see Chapters 10 & 11), it may be impossible to draw conclusions about which treatment was responsible for any observed changes in performance.

The range of single case designs to be described includes a variety of features (e.g., replication within and across participants) that control for these types of threats to internal validity and allow for conclusions to be drawn about functional relationships.

EXTERNAL VALIDITY AND REPLICATION

The threats previously discussed potentially influence the confidence that may be placed in an observed functional relationship; that is, whether or not there appears to be a causal relationship between an intervention and changes in behavioral performance. *External validity* concerns how the results of an experiment may be generalized beyond the conditions of that particular study. What are the implications of the results with regard to their application to other types of persons, situations, and behaviors? Factors that limit this generalizability or generality are considered to be threats to external validity.

External validity concepts have their roots in group comparison and statistical inference approaches (Kennedy, 2005). The larger a group of study participants and the more representative it is of the population of interest (e.g., middle school students in inner-city schools), the greater the external validity. However, many writers and researchers have raised concerns about how effective many group comparison studies are in adequately sampling from a population of interest, and then randomly assigning the sample participants to groups (e.g., Barlow & Hersen, 1984). In contrast, single case designs have traditionally approached establishing external validity through the *replication* of experimental effects, both within and across experiments. Sidman (1960) defined two types of replication approaches to establish external validity or generality: *direct* and *systematic*. A direct replication involves the same types of participants, settings, and procedures as in the original experiment. A systematic replication involves changes in one or more characteristics of the participants, settings, and/or procedures.

As discussed in Chapter 1, the term "single case design" is misleading in that studies employing such methodology typically involve small groups of participants (e.g, 3–5). This allows for direct replication of experimental effects multiple times within a given experiment (Horner et al., 2005). Subsequent experiments involving variations in the types of participants, settings, change agents, and procedures can provide further evidence for the generality of effects of the intervention procedure(s) under investigation. For example, beginning in the early 1960s, empirical research began to demonstrate that structured behavioral intervention procedures were effective in increasing the academic, social, and communicative behavior of children with autism, and decreasing their problem behavior (Lovaas, Koegel, Simmons, & Long, 1973). Much of this work was conducted in clinic-based settings in hospitals or universities. Subsequent studies demonstrated that such procedures could be taught to, and effectively used by, classroom teachers and parents in school, home, and other settings (Koegel, Glahn, & Nieminen, 1978; Koegel, Schreibman, Britten, Burke, & O'Neill, 1982), thus demonstrating their generality or external validity.

This type of approach has been central to recent efforts to ensure that single case design approaches are given due consideration in federal efforts to identify evidence-based practices in education and special education. As mentioned in Chapter 1, Horner et al. (2005) delineated a set of quality indicators to be used to evaluate individual investigations (e.g., operational definition of independent and dependent variables, controls for threats to internal validity). They also proposed certain parameters for designating a practice or intervention as "evidence-based" (and therefore worthy for relevant persons to consider adopting). These were: (1) a minimum of five single case studies published in peer-reviewed journals that meet methodological criteria and demonstrate experimental control; (2) the five studies must have come from at least three different researchers or research groups in at least three different geographical locations; and (3) the five or more studies must have involved a minimum of at least 20 participants. While it remains to be seen how these standards will be evaluated and used by researchers and policy makers, it is heartening to see that single case design methodology is viewed as a potentially important approach to identifying effective practices in this era of accountability (Odom et al., 2005).

COMMON BASIC PRINCIPLES AND PROCEDURES OF SINGLE CASE DESIGNS

Some of these principles and procedures have been mentioned in previous chapters. However, it is worthwhile to summarize them more completely at this point before moving into specific design approaches.

A Small Number of Participants

Complete single case design experiments can be conducted with only one participant. However, typical studies involve a small group of participants (e.g., 3–5). As previously discussed, this allows for the critical replication of effects to be demonstrated. Most often individuals are the primary unit of analysis; that is, each participant serves as his/her own control so that the participant's behavioral performance is compared between at least one baseline (nonintervention) condition and one intervention condition (Baer, Wolf, & Risley, 1968; Horner et al., 2005). In some cases groups may serve as the unit of analysis when behavioral performance measures are generated from a larger set of participants. For example, Kartub, Taylor-Greene, March, and Horner (2000) evaluated the effects of a package of strategies to reduce noise generated by middle school students moving through their building's hallways. The main dependent variable was the noise level in decibels as measured by a decibel meter placed in the hallway. Even though a single case experimental design format was followed (a multiple baseline across groups of students), in this case the unit of analysis were three larger groups of participants.

Repeated Measures Over Time

Chapter 2 covered the key process of defining and reliably measuring the dependent variable(s) of interest. In single case designs such measurement occurs repeatedly over time as participants proceed through the different phases of the study. This allows for ongoing evaluation of the participants' behavioral performance as well as decision making about such issues as considering when to change phases, and so on. (see Chapter 4). As a general rule, data would be collected on a participant approximately 3–5 times per week. In some cases, depending on the situation and dependent variable, "probe" measures might be taken on a less frequent basis (e.g., once a week; see Chapter 7).

Graphing and Visual Analysis of Data

As described in detail in Chapter 4, the primary data analysis strategy for single case designs has been the visual analysis of data in a graphic format. As mentioned previously, graphing data as they are generated over time allows the researcher to continually evaluate the participants' performance and make decisions as needed during a study. Being able to assess the data in "real time" as a study is conducted may also be an important reinforcer to the researchers involved!

Integrity of the Independent Variable(s)

It is important to ensure that a data collection system produces reliable and valid information on the *dependent variable* measure(s) of interest. However, as described in Chapter 2, in recent years the expectation has also developed that researchers document the fidelity with which their independent variables or interventions are being implemented (Gresham, Gansle, & Noell, 1993). It is important to be able to document that an intervention was implemented consistently during the course of a study in order to be able to draw clear conclusions about functional relationships between variables.

Initial Baseline Evaluation

Most (but not all) single case designs will begin with an initial phase or condition during which the planned intervention or independent variable is not being implemented. The basic idea is to be able to get a sense of the participants' performance under typical current conditions. Baselines serve both *descriptive* and *predictive* functions (Kazdin, 1982). *Descriptively* they provide such information as how often behaviors of interest are occurring, and/or how long they last. A baseline condition also provides a pattern that allows us to *predict* how the behavioral performance would continue if an intervention was not implemented. Once the data are relatively stable (see Chapter 4), the intervention can be implemented and the resulting data pattern can be compared to the pattern predicted from the baseline (Bailey & Burch, 2002). Figure 3.1 provides a hypothetical example in presenting the frequency per day of obscene verbalizations by an adolescent in a residential treatment program. In this case one can see that the verbalizations are relatively consistent across multiple days, allowing for a prediction of their likely frequency in subsequent days, which differs from the pattern once the intervention is implemented.

It is important to note that baselines come in "all shapes and sizes." In most cases participants in a home, classroom, or other community setting of interest will be experiencing various types of interactions and activities during the baseline period (i.e., they will not be just sitting around doing nothing). It is important to be able to fully describe the people, settings, interactions, and activities that are present during baseline assessment. This will ultimately allow readers and other researchers to clearly understand the initial baseline situation and how it was changed when the intervention was implemented (Kennedy, 2005).

Figure 3.1   A hypothetical demonstration comparing the predicted data path (dashed line) to the actual path (solid line with diamonds) that is observed once intervention is implemented

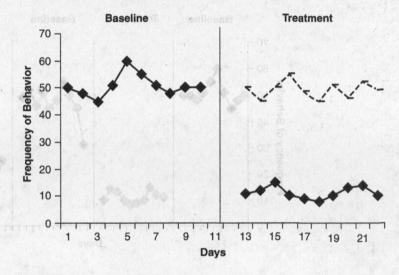

Demonstration of Experimental Control by Replication of Effects

Single case designs control for threats to internal and external validity (see the previous discussion) by demonstrating the replication of experimental effects at repeated points in time (Sidman, 1960). Depending on the design involved this may occur within and/or across participants. A general consensus has evolved in the field that in order to be convincing, clear experimental effects must be demonstrated at a minimum of three points in time (Horner et al., 2005; Kennedy, 2005). From a within-participant perspective, this means that there must be a change from an initial baseline phase to an initial intervention phase, then a change from the intervention phase back to a second baseline phase, and then a change from the second baseline phase to a second intervention phase (A-B-A-B design; see Figure 3.2 and Chapter 6). In other designs, such as a multiple baseline across participants or behaviors (see Chapter 7), the change is demonstrated across three different participants or behaviors. In some cases there will be a combination of within- and across-participant effects.

Social Validity of Behaviors, Procedures, and Outcomes

As described more fully in Chapter 2, social validity addresses the social importance of the goals or behaviors targeted in an experiment, the acceptability of the procedures employed, and the significance of the outcomes (Bailey & Burch, 2002; Kazdin, 1977;

Figure 3.2 A hypothetical example of an A-B-A-B design with changes in behavioral performance at three points in time (baseline to intervention; intervention back to baseline; and baseline back to intervention)

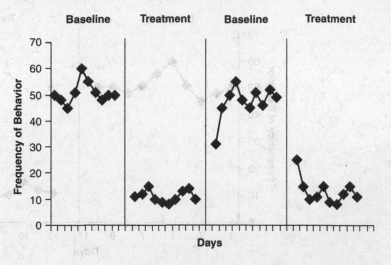

Wolf, 1978). As described earlier, social validation assessments are too often lacking in applied research studies (Kennedy, 2005). Assuming investigators have at least identified target behaviors to change that are of importance to participants and relevant other persons (e.g., parents, teachers), at a minimum researchers should attempt to assess the acceptability of the procedures involved and outcomes achieved (Schwartz & Baer, 1991).

A Flexible and Dynamic Approach to Research?

In 1956 B. F. Skinner published a paper entitled "A Case History in Scientific Method" (Skinner, 1956). In this paper he attempted to illustrate how scientific investigation can, in some cases, be a disorderly and "accidental" process. He described his informal principles of scientific method, such as "When you run onto something interesting, drop everything else and study it!" (p. 223). Obviously such principles may not always be feasible in applied settings such as classrooms and other community settings, where human and other costs are involved in research activities that are attempting to improve individuals' lives. However, one frequently cited advantage is that single case design approaches may sometimes allow an investigator to more easily accommodate changes in the people and situations under study (Kazdin, 1982). That is, it may be possible to change aspects of an ongoing study and experimental design without compromising internal and external validity. Hayes (1981) characterized this as an "attitude of investigative play" (p. 424). Data from repeated measurements should be graphed and assessed on a frequent basis to make decisions about potentially needed changes (see Chapter 4). Examples provided in the next several chapters will illustrate this flexible and dynamic aspect of single case designs.

A Note on Terminology in Referring to Design Components

In most basic descriptions and discussions of single case designs conventions have developed for referring to different phases of such designs. For example, the letter "A" typically refers to a baseline condition, and the letter "B" refers to an intervention of some type, such as the A-B-A-B designs described in the next chapter (Bailey & Burch, 2002). In designs involving more than one intervention, they would be referred to by subsequent letters such as "C", "D", etc. (e.g., A-B-C-B-C; Hayes, Barlow, & Nelson-Gray, 1999).

REFERENCES

Baer, D. M., Wolf, M. M., & Risley, T. R. (1968). Some current dimensions of applied behavior analysis. *Journal of Applied Behavior Analysis, 1,* 91–97.

Bailey, J. S., & Burch, M. R. (2002). *Research methods in applied behavior analysis.* Thousand Oaks, CA: Sage.

Barlow, D. H., & Hersen, M. (1984). *Single case experimental designs: Strategies for studying behavior change* (2nd ed.). Boston, MA: Allyn & Bacon.

Campbell, D. T., & Stanley, J. C. (1966). *Experimental and quasi-experimental designs for research.* Chicago, IL: Rand McNally.

Drew, C. J., Hardman, M. L., & Hart, A. W. (1996). *Designing and conducting research: Inquiry in education and social science.* Boston, MA: Allyn & Bacon.

Gresham, F. M., Gansle, K. A., & Noell, G. H. (1993). Treatment integrity in applied behavior analysis with children. *Journal of Applied Behavior Analysis, 26,* 257–263.

Hayes, S. C. (1981). Single case experimental design and empirical clinical practice. *Journal of Consulting and Clinical Psychology, 49,* 192–211.

Hayes, S. C., Barlow, D. H., & Nelson-Gray, R. O. (1999). *The scientist practitioner: Research and accountability in the age of managed care* (2nd ed.). Boston, MA: Allyn & Bacon.

Horner, R. H., Carr, E. G., Halle, J., McGee, G., Odom, S., & Wolery, M. (2005). The use of single-subject research to identify evidence-based practice in special education. *Exceptional Children, 71,* 165–179.

Kartub, D. T., Taylor-Greene, S., March, R. E., & Horner, R. H. (2000). Reducing hallway noise: A systems approach. *Journal of Positive Behavior Interventions, 3,* 179–182.

Kazdin, A. E. (1977). Assessing the clinical or applied significance of behavior change through social validation. *Behavior Modification, 1,* 427–452.

Kazdin, A. E. (1982). *Single-case research designs: Methods for clinical and applied settings.* New York: Oxford University Press.

Kennedy, C. H. (2005). *Single-case designs for educational research.* Boston, MA: Allyn & Bacon.

Koegel, R. L., Glahn, T. J., & Nieminen, G. S. (1978). Generalization of parent-training results. *Journal of Applied Behavior Analysis, 11,* 95–109.

Koegel, R. L., Schreibman, L., Britten, K., Burke, J. C., & O'Neill, R. E. (1982). A comparison of parent training with direct child treatment. In R. L. Koegel, A. Rincover, and A. L. Egel (Eds.), *Educating and understanding autistic children* (pp. 260–279). San Diego, CA: College-Hill Press.

Lovaas, O. I., Koegel, R., Simmons, J. Q., & Long, J. S. (1973). Some generalization and follow-up measures on autistic children in behavior therapy. *Journal of Applied Behavior Analysis, 6,* 131–165.

Odom, S. L., Brantlinger, E., Gersten, R., Horner, R. H., Thompson, B., & Harris, K. R. (2005). Research in special education: Scientific methods and evidence-based practices. *Exceptional Children, 71,* 137–148.

Schwartz, I. S., & Baer, D. M. (1991). Social validity assessments: Is current practice state of the art? *Journal of Applied Behavior Analysis, 24,* 189–204.

Sidman, M. (1960). *Tactics of scientific research: Evaluating experimental data in psychology.* New York, NY: Basic Books.

Skinner, B. F. (1956). A case history in scientific method. *American Psychologist, 11,* 221–223.

Wehmeyer, M. L., Agran, M., & Hughes, C. (1998). *Teaching self-determination to students with disabilities: Basic skills for successful transition.* Baltimore, MD: Paul H. Brookes.

Wolf, M. M. (1978). Social validity: The case for subjective measurement, or how applied behavior analysis is finding its heart. *Journal of Applied Behavior Analysis, 11,* 203–214.

MAKING SENSE OF YOUR DATA: USING GRAPHIC DISPLAYS TO ANALYZE AND INTERPRET IT

4

Most readers of this book have seen or heard the phrase "a picture is worth a thousand words." This maxim is especially true when it comes to analyzing data produced by various experimental procedures. There is a very long history in the behavioral and social sciences of analyzing data that are presented via visual or graphic displays (Smith, Best, Cylke, & Stubbs, 2000; Tufte, 1983, 1990). Recent analyses by Smith and colleagues have demonstrated that the use of graphic displays of data is directly correlated with the "hardness" or empirical and objective nature of the scientific enterprise in fields such as biology and various specialty areas of psychology (Best, Smith, & Stubbs, 2001; Smith, Best, Stubbs, Archibald, & Roberson-Nay, 2002; Smith, Best, Stubbs, Johnston, & Archibald, 2000). Smith et al. (2002) noted that "graphs provide a compact, rhetorically powerful way of presenting research findings" (p. 749).

As mentioned in Chapter 3, analysis of graphic or visual displays of data has long been a hallmark of SCR design strategies (Baer, Wolf, & Risley, 1968). One of the basic rationales for emphasizing this approach is that behavioral research should be identifying powerful interventions that can produce socially important changes in targeted behavior. Such changes should be detectable by visually examining changes in data across different study conditions or phases (Parsonson & Baer, 1978). A second rationale for a focus on visual/graphic displays is that once they are presented and/or published (see Chapter 11), other persons can examine the data and draw their own conclusions about the results. This differs from an approach focused on group comparison and statistical analyses (see Chapter 1).

This chapter will provide an overview of the purposes and characteristics of graphic displays of data, a process for their analysis, and information on developments in statistical analysis to supplement the visual analysis process. (For readers desiring more detailed information, Parsonson and Baer [1978, 1986, 1992], Parsonson [2003], and Tawney and Gast [1984] have provided more in-depth rationales for and descriptions of this type of data analysis.)

Table 4.1   A List of the Functions of Graphic Displays of Data.

1) Communicates overall experimental design
2) Communicates sequence of experimental conditions
3) Communicates amounts of time in different conditions
4) Identifies independent and dependent variables
5) Organizes information during data collection to facilitate decision making
6) Provides a compact and detailed picture of relationship(s) between independent and dependent variable(s)
7) Allows for independent evaluation of data by individuals not involved in the study (via presentation or publication)

PURPOSES AND CHARACTERISTICS OF GRAPHIC DISPLAYS OF DATA

Graphic displays of data serve a variety of functions both for investigators involved in a study and for others who may be examining the resulting data (Poling, Methot, & LeSage, 1995). These functions are presented in Table 4.1. Plotting data in a visual display allows researchers to make decisions during the course of a study and to evaluate the overall outcomes once a study is completed. Once the resulting data are presented and/or published, such a display allows others to conduct their own analyses and draw their own conclusions about the outcome(s) of a study.

Typical Characteristics of Graphic Displays

Figure 4.1 presents an example of a typical SCR design graph (Lee & Odom, 1996).

This basic line graph presents data on the frequency of both stereotypic (hand flipping, mouthing objects) and social interactive behavior with peers displayed by two elementary age children with autism spectrum disorders (ASD). The design employed was a basic A-B-A-B or withdrawal design (see Chapter 6) in which data were initially collected during a baseline or pre-intervention phase. Following this an intervention was implemented in which typically developing peers were trained to initiate social interactions with the children with ASD. This intervention was then withdrawn during a second baseline or A phase, and then re-implemented during the final intervention or B phase.

The figure includes the basic components of typical SCR design graphs. These include the *vertical* and *horizontal axes* (also sometimes referred to as the ordinate and the abscissa), which present the dependent variables (vertical axis–percentage of intervals with stereotypic or social interactive behavior) and the time sequence of the study (horizontal axis–daily sessions over time). The different conditions or *phases* of the study (i.e., baseline and intervention) are separated by solid vertical *phase lines*. The *phase labels* indicate what was going on during the different parts of the study

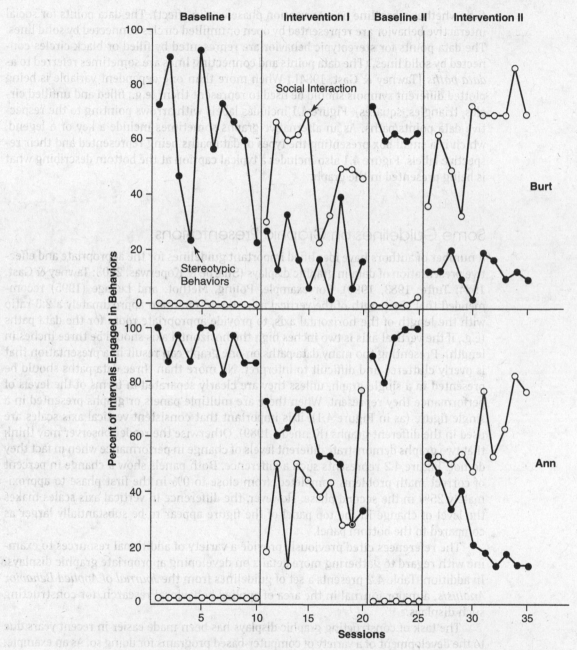

Figure 4.1 The graph presents data on the frequency of occurrence (as indicated by the percentage of intervals–see Chapter 3) of both stereotypic and social interactive behavior of two children with autism spectrum disorders

Source: Lee S. & Odom S. L., "The Relationship Between Stereotypic Behavior and Peer Social Interaction for Children with Severe Disabilities", *Journal of The Association for Persons with Severe Handicaps*, 1996, vol. 21, p. 93. Copyright 1996 by the Association for Persons with Severe Handicaps. Reprinted with permission.

(i.e., whether a baseline or intervention phase was in effect). The data points for social interactive behavior are represented by open or unfilled circles connected by solid lines. The data points for stereotypic behavior are represented by filled or black circles connected by solid lines. (The data points and connecting lines are sometimes referred to as *data paths* [Tawney & Gast, 1984].) When more than one dependent variable is being plotted different symbols should be used to represent them (e.g., filled and unfilled circles, triangles, squares). Figure 4.1 includes labels with arrows pointing to the respective data points/paths. As an alternative graphs sometimes include a key or a legend, which is a small box presenting the types of data paths being represented and their respective labels. Figure 4.1 also includes a typical caption at the bottom describing what is being presented in the graph.

Some Guidelines on Graphic Presentations

A number of authors have identified important guidelines for the appropriate and effective presentation of data in graphic displays (Sharpe & Koperwas, 2003; Tawney & Gast, 1984; Tufte, 1983, 1990). For example, Poling, Methot, and LeSage (1995) recommended that the length of the vertical axis should maintain approximately a 2:3 ratio with the length of the horizontal axis, to provide appropriate room for the data paths (e.g., if the vertical axis is two inches high the horizontal axis should be three inches in length). Presenting too many data paths on one graph can result in a presentation that is overly cluttered and difficult to interpret. No more than three data paths should be presented in a single graph, unless they are clearly separated in terms of the levels of performance they represent. When there are multiple panels or graphs presented in a single figure (as in Figure 4.1), it is important that consistent vertical axis scales are used in the different graphs (Kennedy, 1989). Otherwise the reader/observer may think that two graphs demonstrate different levels of change in performance when in fact they do not. Figure 4.2 represents such a difference. Both panels show a change in percent of correct math problems completed, from close to 0% in the first phase to approximately 25% in the second phase. However, the difference in vertical axis scales makes the level of change in the top panel of the figure appear to be substantially larger as compared to the bottom panel.

The references cited previously provide a variety of additional resources to examine with regard to gathering more details on developing appropriate graphic displays. In addition, Table 4.2 presents a set of guidelines from the *Journal of Applied Behavior Analysis*, a major journal in the area of applied behavioral research, for constructing such displays.

The task of constructing graphic displays has been made easier in recent years due to the development of a variety of computer-based programs for doing so. As an example, Appendix A presents an article by Lo and Konrad (2007) that describes the basic steps for constructing graphs using Microsoft Excel. Although such programs do not necessarily make it a simple task(!), they do make graph construction easier and more readily available to a wide range of researchers and practitioners.

Figure 4.2 An illustration of how data paths in sequential phases may appear very different when different vertical axis scales are used

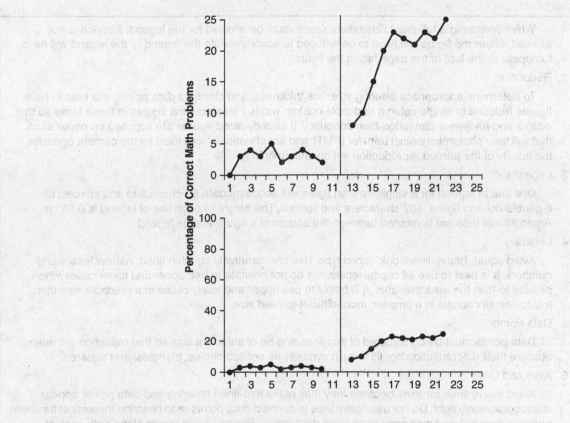

Table 4.2 A List of Guidelines for Preparing Graphic Displays from the *Journal of Applied Behavior Analysis.*

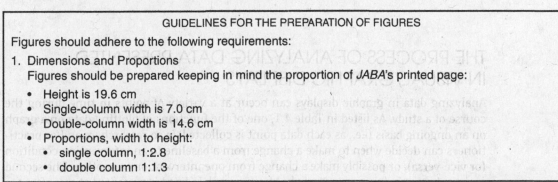

GUIDELINES FOR THE PREPARATION OF FIGURES

Figures should adhere to the following requirements:

1. Dimensions and Proportions
   Figures should be prepared keeping in mind the proportion of *JABA's* printed page:

   - Height is 19.6 cm
   - Single-column width is 7.0 cm
   - Double-column width is 14.6 cm
   - Proportions, width to height:
     - single column, 1:2.8
     - double column 1:1.3

(Continued)

Table 4.2   A List of Guidelines for Preparing Graphic Displays from the *Journal of Applied Behavior Analysis.* (*Continued*)

When preparing a full-page illustration, space must be allowed for the legend. If space is not allowed, either the figure will have to be reduced to accommodate the legend or the legend will have to appear at the foot of the page facing the figure.

2. Reduction

   To determine appropriate lettering size, line thickness, and clarity of data points, it is best to have figures reduced to single-column or double-column width. Please submit figures in these sizes so that editors and reviewers can judge their adequacy. If already sized figures are supplied on paper stock that will take photomechanical transfer (PMT) and are chemically well fixed by the camera operator, the quality of the printed reproduction will be uniformly high.

3. Legends

   One line of legend for a single-column figure will accommodate 52 characters and spaces; for a double-column figure, 107 characters and spaces. The height of each line of legend is 0.35 cm. An additional 0.35 cm is needed between the bottom of a figure and its legend.

4. Lettering

   Avoid squat, heavy-lined, bold-faced type. Use comparatively tall, thin-lined, narrow letters and numbers. It is best to use all capital letters, but do not hesitate to use upper and lower cases when needed to fit in the area available. It is better to use upper and lower cases in a readable size than it is to use all capitals in a smaller, more-difficult-to-read size.

5. Data Points

   Data points must be constructed of thin lines and be of sufficient size so that reduction will neither obscure their differentiation nor fill in such symbols as unfilled circles, triangles, and squares.

6. Axes and Lines

   Avoid heavy lines for axes because they may make thin-lined lettering and data points appear disproportionately light. Do not use heavy lines to connect data points or to describe theoretical functions because they will de-emphasize or obscure data points. Provide scale marks along both axes at sufficiently frequent intervals to permit x and y values of data points to be read accurately. Be sure that axes meet at a right angle and that labels parallel their axes.

THE PROCESS OF ANALYZING DATA PRESENTED IN VISUAL/GRAPHIC DISPLAYS

Analyzing data in graphic displays can occur at a variety of points in time during the course of a study. As listed in Table 4.1, one of the functions of plotting data on a graph on an ongoing basis (i.e., as each data point is collected) is so researchers and/or practitioners can decide when to make a change from a baseline to an intervention condition (or vice-versa), or possibly make a change from one intervention to another. The second main point in time is once a study has been completed and is presented at a conference or published in a professional journal. At that point a graphic display allows others to

Table 4.3 The Steps/Questions Involved in a Comprehensive Analysis of a Visual/Graphic Display of Data.

1) The first question—What are the basic independent and dependent variables involved in the study?

2) The second question—Does the research design presented allow for a demonstration of experimental control by the independent variable(s)?

3) The third question—Do the data presented provide a convincing demonstration of control by the independent variable(s) with regard to changes in level, trend, variability, immediacy of effect, etc.?

4) The fourth question—If there is a demonstrated functional relationship between the independent and dependent variable(s), does it represent a socially valid impact on the target behavior(s) of interest?

(1) examine and analyze the data and draw their own conclusions as to whether or not a functional relationship has been demonstrated, and (2) evaluate the social or clinical importance of any apparent behavior change. Horner et al. (2005) and Horner, Sugai, Swaminathan, & Smolkowski (2008) have recently described a set of questions and processes required for a comprehensive analysis of graphic displays of data. These steps/questions are summarized in Table 4.3.

The First Question: Understanding the Basic Variables Involved in a Study

The first step in analyzing a visual display of data is to examine the figure(s) to determine the basic variables involved in the study being presented. As described in Table 4.1, a graphic figure should identify the dependent variable(s) or measure(s) being presented (on the ordinate or vertical axis), the time frame involved in the study (e.g., sessions per day or per week on the abscissa or horizontal axis), and the independent variable(s) or interventions implemented in the study, as indicated by the phase labels on the figure (e.g., Baseline, Self-Management). Ideally, after examining a figure a reader should be able to phrase the general research question(s) that were addressed in the study (e.g., "What is the effect of peer initiations on the frequency of stereotypic behaviors by children with autism spectrum disorders?").

The Second Question: Does The Study Design Presented Allow for an Assessment of Experimental Control?

This step entails an evaluation of the research design and data presented to decide whether or not it is possible to demonstrate experimental control by the independent variable(s) under investigation. Subsequent chapters in this book present details on a wide variety of design approaches to demonstrate such rigorous experimental control. While there is a role for studies which do not include such clear experimental control (e.g., see Chapter 6), the demonstration of such control has become increasingly important for convincing relevant audiences that particular interventions are supported by scientific research (see Chapter 1).

The Third Question: Do the Data Presented Demonstrate a Functional Relationship Between the Independent and Dependent Variable(s)?

Once it is determined that a research design has been employed that allows for the demonstration of experimental control, the first question to be asked of a set of data has sometimes been referred to as the *experimental* criterion (Kazdin, 1982). That is, do the data demonstrate a clear functional relationship between the independent and dependent variables of interest? Answering this question requires a systematic process for evaluating data patterns within and across phases of a study.

Within-phase Characteristics

One primary characteristic is the overall *level*, or the *average* or *mean* performance within a phase. For example, consider the data on stereotypic behavior during the initial baseline phase for Burt and Ann (see Figure 4.1). Burt's data average approximately 50–60% of the intervals per session, while Ann's data average approximately 90% of the intervals per session. (The level or average corresponds to the mean [X] as used in a statistical sense.)

Burt's data exemplify a second important characteristic, which is the *variability* of the data within a phase, or how much the data vary in relation to the overall mean or level. As can be seen in Figure 4.1 Burt's initial baseline data vary between approximately 20% and 90%, while Ann's data vary in a much smaller range between approximately 80% and 100%. (In a sense variability corresponds to the statistical *standard deviation* [SD] of a set of data as typically presented for a set of group scores.)

A third important characteristic is the *trend* or *slope* of the data, with regard to whether the level is increasing, decreasing, or remaining flat or neutral across the phase. The evaluation of potential trends in data is affected by the characteristics of level and variability, as changes in those aspects of the data will produce increasing or decreasing trends. As can be seen in Burt's initial baseline data, the large amount of variability makes it difficult to discern whether or not any clear trends are present; however, in general Burt's rate of behavior does not appear to be consistently increasing or declining. Ann's data in the Baseline I phase indicate a relatively flat or *neutral* trend, in that her behavior appears to be staying relatively consistent within a small range (i.e., it is neither increasing nor decreasing).

Due to the fact that it is sometimes difficult to discern clear trends in data due to issues such as substantial variability, some authors (e.g., Parsonson & Baer, 1978, 1992) have discussed fitting what are known as *regression* or *trend* lines to data within a phase, which may allow for a clearer determination of the presence of trends (Bailey, 1984; Rojahn & Schulze, 1985). Examples of this are presented in Figure 4.3. The data in both

Figure 4.3 An illustration of a graphic display of data from two phases with superimposed lines to evaluate possible trends in the data

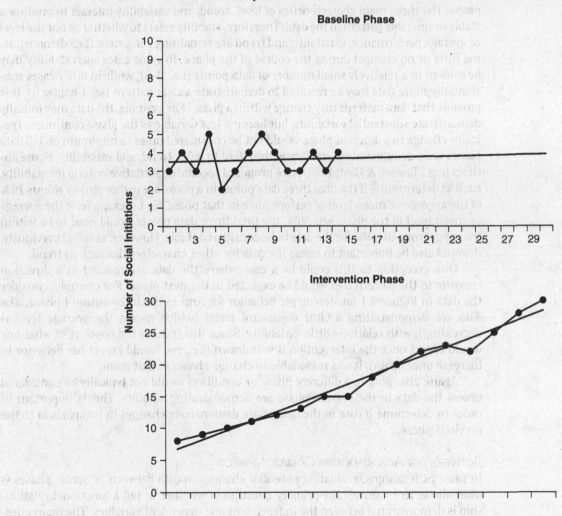

the baseline and intervention phases exhibit different levels of variability. Fitting the regression or trend lines onto the data allow an observer to more clearly determine the direction in which the data are heading. Fitting such trend lines is made relatively easy by programs such as Microsoft Excel, which will automatically calculate and superimpose trend lines on a data chart, as was done in Figure 4.3.

Another within-phase issue is whether or not a phase contains enough data points to allow for a reasonable evaluation. There is no specific minimum number of data points that are required, although some authors have recommended "rules of thumb" such as a minimum of three data points, as this might be considered the smallest number which could demonstrate a trend (Horner et al., 2008). The question is whether or not enough data are presented to allow a clear conclusion about the *stability* of the data within a phase. The three main characteristics of level, trend, and variability interact to produce a stable or unstable pattern in the data. Therefore, stability refers to whether or not the level or average performance, variability, and trend are remaining consistent (i.e., demonstrating little or no change) during the course of the phase. In some cases such stability may be evident in a relatively small number of data points (i.e., 3–5), while in other cases substantially more data may be required to demonstrate a clear pattern (see Chapter 6). It is possible that data patterns may change within a phase. For example, the data may initially demonstrate substantial variability, but become less variable as the phase continues. Typically, change to a different phase would not be considered unless a minimum of 3–5 data points were demonstrating stability with regard to level, trend, and variability. Some authors (e.g., Tawney & Gast, 1984) have proposed specific quantitative criteria for stability, such as determining if the final three data points in a phase are within plus or minus 10% of the average or mean level of performance in that phase. So for example, if the average or mean level of the phase was 50%, the final three data points would need to be within the range from 40–60% for the data to be considered stable. However, as noted previously, it would also be important to assess the data for other characteristics such as trend.

One exception to this could be a case where the data are moving in a direction *opposite* to the pattern that would be expected in the next phase. For example, consider the data in Figure 4.1 on stereotypic behavior for Ann in the Intervention I phase. The data are demonstrating a clear downward trend (which means the average level is decreasing), with relatively little variability. Since this trend is the opposite of what one would expect once the intervention is withdrawn (i.e., you would expect her behavior to increase once again), it was reasonable to change phases at that point.

Again, changing to a different phase or condition would not typically be considered unless the data in the current phase are demonstrating stability. This is important in order to determine if data in the new phase demonstrate changes in comparison to the previous phase.

Between or Across-phase Characteristics

In most SCR designs, evaluating potential changes in data between or across phases is what allows us to answer the primary question of whether or not a functional relationship is demonstrated between the independent and dependent variables. The main question here is what, if any, changes between phases are seen in the main characteristics of level, trend, and variability. Data in a new phase may demonstrate changes in one or more of these characteristics. If we examine the data in Figure 4.1 for Ann in the Baseline I and Intervention I phases, we can see a variety of changes in the data between the phases. In the Baseline I phase the data for both stereotypic and social interactive behavior are quite stable, demonstrating a consistent level, minimal or no variability, and flat or neutral trend. Once the peer social intervention is implemented (Intervention I) Ann's stereotypic behavior begins to consistently decline and her social interactive behavior increases with regard to level and variability. Therefore, it makes sense to conclude that the intervention has had an impact on both types of behaviors.

Changes in the basic characteristics of level, trend, and variability may result in a variety of other apparent changes in data patterns across phases (Parsonson & Baer, 1978). For example, *immediacy of effect* refers to how quickly changes are apparent from the end of one phase and the beginning of another. Ann's data in Figure 4.1 indicate relatively rapid changes in level and other characteristics when shifts were made from baseline to intervention phases and vice-versa. Such rapidity of change provides more convincing evidence of the impact of the intervention. The overall *overlap* of the data between phases is also viewed as an indication of the strength or magnitude of intervention effects. Overlap refers to the extent to which data points in different phases fall within the same range of values, and is the result of changes (or lack thereof) in the basic characteristics of level, trend, and variability across phases. Burt's data in Figure 4.1 demonstrate more data points with similar values across phases, while Ann's data demonstrate essentially no overlap in values across phases, indicating a stronger effect. There have been a variety of proposals for calculating various measures of the numerical overlap of data points between phases, such as the *percentage of nonoverlapping data points*, or PND (Parker, Hagan-Burke, & Vannest, 2007; Scruggs, Mastropieri, & Casto, 1987; Scruggs & Mastropieri, 2001; White, 1987). PND involves calculating the percentage of data points in an intervention phase that are either higher or lower than the highest or lowest data points in a baseline phase. Such measures have been used to aggregate data across larger numbers of studies (Didden, Duker, & Korzilius, 1997). However, a number of concerns have been raised with such measures, such as the fact that they can be strongly affected by a single extreme outlier data point in the baseline phase(s). Other alternative measures have been proposed (e.g., Parker et al., 2007). At this point, it is reasonable to say that there are no universally accepted measures of data overlap that are being used to examine differences between and across phases in SCR studies.

Finally, some authors (Horner et al., 2008; Parsonson & Baer, 1978) have posited that similarity of data patterns across similar phases in an experimental design provides a stronger demonstration of experimental control. For example, in Figure 4.1 the data patterns for Burt and Ann in both baseline phases, and in both intervention phases, are relatively similar with regard to characteristics such as level, trend, and variability. Such similarity can be taken to indicate that successful assessment and control of the relevant variables has been established.

The Critical Importance of Considering *All* Variables Simultaneously

A very important point to reiterate is that when evaluating single case research data presented in a graphic format it is critical to simultaneously consider *all* of the variables previously described. It is very important to consider all of the factors of level, trend, variability, overlap, immediacy of effect, and similarity of data across phases in evaluating the results of an experimental study (Horner et al., 2008). Not all studies will necessarily demonstrate effects across all of these aspects, but they still may demonstrate important effects.

The Fourth Question: If There Is a Functional Relationship Demonstrated by the Data, Does It Represent a Socially Valid Impact on the Target Behavior(s) of Concern?

Chapter 2 described a variety of strategies for assessing the social or clinical validity or importance of the set of data from a particular study. This assessment addresses the clinical or therapeutic impact of a particular intervention. It would be possible that there may be a clear functional relationship between an intervention and the dependent variables being measured, but the effects or impact are not substantial enough to make a socially valid difference in the lives of the participants. For example, someone may learn to complete a work activity in a successful manner (e.g., clearing and resetting tables in a restaurant), but not be able to complete the activity quickly enough to be employable in a real life situation. As described in Chapter 2, it is *critical* that studies begin to more routinely include social validity evaluations as part of the research process. Authors and journal editors should begin to routinely include and require such assessments in the publication process (Carr et al., 1999).

Fluency Building: One More Example

Over the years there has been substantial concern expressed about the purportedly "subjective" nature of the visual analysis process, as compared to other more strictly quantitative methods such as various statistical analyses. Such concerns have been addressed in studies examining variables such as inter-rater agreement when assessing single case data displays (Furlong & Wampold, 1982; Jones, Weinrott, & Vaught, 1978; Knapp, 1983; Wampold & Furlong, 1981). In such studies agreement among observers has not always been demonstrated at what would be considered desired levels. However, such studies have often involved a number of problematic components. Persons asked to judge data displays have often been presented with non-characteristic stimuli, such as graphs that (1) don't describe the dependent variables of interest and their actual range of values, (2) don't provide typical phase labels, and (3) don't provide a complete sequence of phases typical of a complete experimental design (Horner et al., 2008). More recent research has demonstrated that systematic training in the process of visual analysis can produce more consistent agreement between persons evaluating single case design results (e.g., Fisher, Kelley, & Lomas, 2003; Hagopian et al., 1997; Horner et al., 2008). In the interest of such fluency building, we will consider another example of data presentation and analysis, following the major question format previously described (Table 4.3).

Figure 4.4 presents data from a study by Rasmussen & O'Neill (2006; see also Chapter 6). With regard to the first main question, it is apparent from the figure presented that the study involved assessing the effects of fixed-time reinforcement schedules on the frequency of disruptive talk-outs by students in a classroom setting. All three participants were attending a day treatment program for students with significant emotional/behavioral disorders (two of the students had been diagnosed as having a bipolar disorder; the third was diagnosed as having an anxiety disorder). Fixed-time

Figure 4.4 The graph presents data on the frequency of occurrence of disruptive talk-outs in a classroom setting by three children with emotional/behavioral disorders

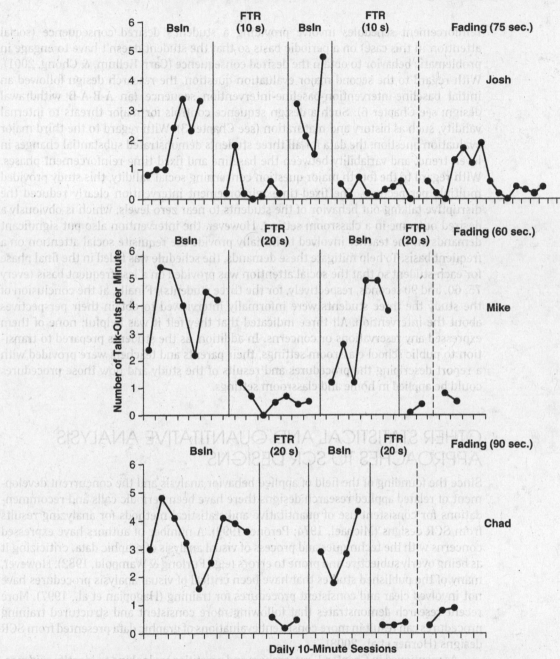

Source: Figure 1 from Rasmussen & O'Neill, The Effects of Fixed-time reinforcement schedules on problem behavior of children with emotional and behavioral disorders in a day-treatment setting—JABA, 2006, v. 39, p. 455. Reprinted with permission.

reinforcement schedules involve providing a student's desired consequence (social attention in this case) on a periodic basis so that the student doesn't have to engage in problematic behavior to obtain the desired consequence (Carr, Kellum, & Chong, 2001). With regard to the second major evaluation question, the research design followed an initial baseline-intervention-baseline-intervention sequence (an A-B-A-B withdrawal design; see Chapter 6). Such a design sequence controls for major threats to internal validity, such as history and maturation (see Chapter 3). With regard to the third major evaluation question, the data for all three students demonstrated substantial changes in level, trend, and variability between the baseline and fixed-time reinforcement phases. With regard to the fourth major question concerning social validity, this study provided multiple perspectives. The fixed-time reinforcement intervention clearly reduced the disruptive talking-out behavior of the students to near zero levels, which is obviously a desired outcome in a classroom setting. However, the intervention also put significant demands on the teacher involved to initially provide the requisite social attention on a frequent basis. To help mitigate these demands, the schedule was faded in the final phase for each student so that the social attention was provided on a less frequent basis (every 75, 60, and 90 seconds, respectively, for the three students). Finally, at the conclusion of the study the three students were informally interviewed to obtain their perspectives about the intervention. All three indicated that they felt it was helpful; none of them expressed any reservations or concerns. In addition, as the students prepared to transition to public school classroom settings, their parents and teachers were provided with a report describing the procedures and results of the study and how those procedures could be applied in home and classroom settings.

OTHER STATISTICAL AND QUANTITATIVE ANALYSIS APPROACHES TO SCR DESIGNS

Since the founding of the field of applied behavior analysis and the concurrent development of related applied research designs there have been periodic calls and recommendations for consistent use of quantitative and statistical methods for analyzing results from SCR designs (Michael, 1974; Perone, 1999). A number of authors have expressed concerns with the techniques and process of visual analysis of graphic data, criticizing it as being overly subjective and prone to errors (e.g., Furlong & Wampold, 1982). However, many of the published studies that have been critical of visual analysis procedures have not involved clear and consistent procedures for training (Hagopian et al., 1997). More recent research demonstrates that following more consistent and structured training procedures can result in more consistent evaluations of graphic data presented from SCR designs (Horner et al., 2008).

As mentioned in Chapter 1, researchers and practitioners looking to identify *evidence-based practices* in education and related fields (e.g., school psychology) have begun to increasingly use measures such as the *effect size* resulting from a study as part of the process of aggregating and evaluating results from various interventions (Olive & Smith, 2005). An effect size measure goes beyond a basic evaluation of statistical significance by providing an assessment of the *magnitude* of the impact of the intervention implemented either within or across studies. As an example, one approach involves dividing the difference between the baseline and intervention phase means by the standard deviation of the baseline phase (Busk & Serlin, 1992). Cohen (1988) presented general guidelines for assessing the magnitude of such effect size measures (i.e., 0.0–0.20 as a small effect size, 0.20–0.50 as a medium effect size, and 0.80 and above as a large effect size). For example, consider the data presented for Chad in Figure 4.4. As has often been done in aggregating results from the single case research literature, one can combine the data from the two baseline phases and the two intervention phases to calculate an effect size. In this case the mean for the combined baseline phases is 2.37 talk-outs per minute; the mean for the combined intervention phases is 0.38 talk-outs per minute. The difference between these means is 1.99. The standard deviation of the initial baseline phase is 1.02. Dividing the mean difference of 1.99 by 1.02 results in an effect size measure of 1.95. Given the previously described guidelines, this would obviously be considered a large effect size. (However, it should be noted that effect sizes from SCR studies are typically larger than those obtained from group comparison studies [Jenson, Clark, Kircher, & Kristiansson, 2007].)

There have been a large number of proposals with regard to what might be appropriate effect size measures for data from SCR designs (Campbell, 2004; Jenson et al., 2007; Nagler, 2008; Olive & Smith, 2005; Parker et al., 2005). It is safe to say at this point that there is no clear consensus on what the most appropriate measure(s) might be. However, it will be critically important for researchers employing SCR designs to keep abreast of developments in this field, and to work with other researchers and statisticians to employ measures that will be viewed as most acceptable and effective by the larger research community (Horner et al., 2008). This will be particularly important as SCR plays an increasingly important role in identifying evidence-based practices in various fields.

Other researchers have increasingly begun to employ other statistical analysis approaches in addition to effect size measures, particularly to aggregate results across studies. For example, *hierarchical linear modeling* (HLM) is being increasingly developed and used to evaluate results within and across SCR studies (Fisher, Kelley, & Lomas, 2003; Jenson et al., 2007). Again, it is safe to say that such approaches are under development and there is no clear consensus on how and when to use them. However, as noted previously, it behooves researchers using SCR approaches to keep abreast of the use and application of new developments in these areas (Horner et al., 2008; Nagler, 2008).

REFERENCES

Baer, D. M., Wolf, M. M., & Risley, T. R. (1968). Some current dimensions of applied behavior analysis. *Journal of Applied Behavior Analysis, 1,* 91–97.

Bailey, D. B. (1984). Effects of lines of progress and semilogarithmic charts on ratings of charted data. *Journal of Applied Behavior Analysis, 17,* 359–365.

Best, L. A., Smith, L. D., & Stubbs, D. A. (2001). Graph use in psychology and other sciences. *Behavioural Processes, 54,* 155–165.

Busk, P. L., & Serlin, R. C. (1992). Meta-analysis for single case research. In T. R. Kratochwill & J. R. Levin (Eds.), *Single case research design in psychology and analysis: New directions for psychology and education* (pp. 187–212). Hillsdale, NJ: Lawrence Erlbaum Associates.

Campbell, J. M. (2004). Statistical comparison of four effect sizes for single-subject designs. *Behavior Modification, 28,* 234–246.

Carr, J. E., Austin, J. L., Britton, L. N., Kellum, K. K., & Bailey, J. S. (1999). An assessment of social validity trends in applied behavior analysis. *Behavioral Interventions, 14,* 223–231.

Carr, J. E., & Burkholder, E. O. (1998). Creating single-subject design graphs with Microsoft Excel™. *Journal of Applied Behavior Analysis, 31,* 245–251.

Carr, J. E., Kellum, K. K., & Chong, I. M. (2001). The reductive effects of noncontingent reinforcement: Fixed-time versus variable-time schedules. *Journal of Applied Behavior Analysis, 34,* 505–509.

Cohen, J. (1988). *Statistical power analysis for the behavioral sciences* (2nd ed.). Hillsdale, NJ: Lawrence Erlbaum Associates.

Didden, R., Duker, P. C., & Korzilius, H. (1997). Meta-analytic study on treatment effectiveness for problem behaviors of individuals with mental retardation. *American Journal on Mental Retardation, 101,* 387–399.

Fisher, W. W., Kelley, M. E., & Lomas, J. E. (2003). Visual aids and structured criteria for improving visual inspection and interpretation of single-case designs. *Journal of Applied Behavior Analysis, 36,* 387–406.

Furlong, M. J., & Wampold, B. E. (1982). Intervention effects and relative variation as dimensions in experts' use of visual inference. *Journal of Applied Behavior Analysis, 15,* 415–421.

Hagopian, L. P., Fisher, W. W., Thompson, R. H., Owen-DeSchryver, J., Iwata, B. A., & Wacker, D. P. (1997). Toward the development of structured criteria for interpretation of functional analysis data. *Journal of Applied Behavior Analysis, 30,* 313–326.

Horner, R. H., Carr, E. G., Halle, J., McGee, G., Odom, S., & Wolery, M. (2005). The use of single-subject research to identify evidence-based practice in special education. *Exceptional Children, 71,* 165–179.

Horner, R. H., Sugai, G., Swaminathan, H., & Smolkowski, K. (2008). Toward a comprehensive analysis of single-case designs. Presented at the IES Training Institute on Single-Case Designs, Washington, D.C.

Jenson, W. R., Clark, E., Kircher, J. C., & Kristiansson, S. D. (2007). Statistical reform: Evidence-based practice, meta-analysis, and single subject designs. *Psychology in the Schools, 44,* 483–493.

Jones, R. R., Weinrott, M., & Vaught, R. S. (1978). Effects of serial dependency on the agreement between visual and statistical inference. *Journal of Applied Behavior Analysis, 11,* 277–283.

Kazdin, A. E. (1982). *Single case research designs.* New York: Oxford University Press.

Kennedy, C. H. (1989). Selecting consistent vertical axis scales. *Journal of Applied Behavior Analysis, 22,* 338–339.

Knapp, T. J. (1983). Behavior analysts' visual appraisal of behavior change in graphic display. *Behavioral Assessment, 5,* 155–164.

Lee, S., & Odom, S. L. (1996). The relationship between stereotypic behavior and peer social interaction for children with severe disabilities, *Journal of the Association for Persons with Severe Handicaps, 21,* 88–95.

Michael, J. (1974). Statistical inference for individual organism research: Some reactions to a suggestion by Gentile, Roden, and Klein. *Journal of Applied Behavior Analysis, 7,* 627–628.

Nagler, E. (2008). *Analyzing data from single subject designs.* Presented at the IES Training Institute on Single-Case Designs, Washington, D.C.

Olive, M. L., & Smith, B. W. (2005). Effect size calculations and single subject designs. *Educational Psychology, 25,* 313–324.

Parker, R. I., Brossart, D. F., Vannest, K. J., Long, J. R., de Alba, R. G., Baugh, F. G., & Sullivan, J. R. (2005). Effect sizes in single case research: How large is large? *School Psychology Review, 34,* 116–132.

Parker, R. I., Hagan-Burke, S., & Vannest, K. (2007). Percentage of all non-overlapping data (PAND): An alternative to PND. *Journal of Special Education, 40,* 194–204.

Parsonson, B. S. (2003). Visual analysis of graphs: Seeing *is* believing. In K. S. Budd & T. Stokes (Eds.), *A small matter of proof: The legacy of Donald M. Baer* (pp. 35–51). Reno, NV: Context Press.

Parsonson, B. S., & Baer, D. M. (1978). The analysis and presentation of graphic data. In T. R. Kratochwill (Ed.), *Single subject research: Strategies for evaluating change* (pp. 101–165). New York: Academic Press.

Parsonson, B. S., & Baer, D. M. (1986). The graphic analysis of data. In A. Poling & R. W. Fuqua (Eds.), *Research methods in applied behavior analysis: Issues and advances* (pp. 157–186). New York: Plenum Press.

Parsonson, B. S., & Baer, D. M. (1992). The visual analysis of data, and current research into the stimuli controlling it. In T. R. Kratochwill & J. R. Levin (Eds.), *Single-case research design and analysis: New directions for psychology and education* (pp. 15–40). Hillsdale, NJ: Lawrence Erlbaum Associates.

Perone, M. (1999). Statistical inference in behavior analysis: Experimental control is better. *The Behavior Analyst, 22*, 109–116.

Poling, A., Methot, L. L., & LeSage, M. G. (1995). *Fundamentals of behavior analytic research.* New York: Plenum.

Rasmussen, K., & O'Neill, R. E. (2006). The effects of fixed-time reinforcement schedules on problem behavior of children with emotional and behavioral disorders in a day-treatment classroom setting, *Journal of Applied Behavior Analysis, 39*, 453–457.

Rojahn, J., & Schulze, H. (1985). The linear regression line as a judgemental aid in visual analyis of serially dependent A-B time-series data. *Journal of Psychopathology and Behavioral Assessment, 7*, 191–206.

Scruggs, T. E., & Mastropieri, M. A. (2001). How to summarize single-participant research: Issues and applications. *Behavior Modification, 22*, 221–242.

Scruggs, T. E., Mastropieri, M. A., & Casto, G. (1987). The quantitative synthesis of single subject research: Methodology and validation. *Remedial and Special Education, 8*, 24–33.

Sharpe, T., & Koperwas, J. (2003). *Behavior and sequential analyses: Principles and practice.* Thousand Oaks, CA: Sage.

Smith, L. D., Best, L. A. Cylke, V. A., & Stubbs, D. A. (2000). Psychology without *p* values: Data analysis at the turn of the 19th century. *American Psychologist, 55*, 260–263.

Smith, L. D., Best, L. A., Stubbs, D. A., Archibald, A. B., & Roberson-Nay, R. (2002). Constructing knowledge: The role of graphs and tables in hard and soft psychology. *American Psychologist, 57*, 749–761.

Smith, L. D., Best, L. A., Stubbs, D. A., Johnston, J., & Archibald, A. B. (2000). Scientific graphs and the hierarchy of the sciences: A Latourian survey of inscription practices. *Social Studies of Science, 30*, 73–94.

Tawney, J. W., & Gast, D. L. (1984). *Single subject research in special education.* Columbus, OH: Merrill.

Tufte, E. (1983). *The visual display of quantitative information.* Cheshire, CT: Graphic Press.

Tufte, E. (1990). *Envisioning information.* Cheshire, CT: Graphics Press.

Wampold, B. E., & Furlong, M. J. (1981). The heuristics of visual inference. *Behavioral Assessment, 3*, 79–92.

White, O. R. (1987). Some comments concerning "The quantitative synthesis of single-subject research." *Remedial and Special Education, 8*, 34–39.

COMMON STEPS AND BARRIERS YOU MAY HAVE TO DEAL WITH IN CONDUCTING A RESEARCH STUDY

Leanne Hawken, PhD, *University of Utah*

5

The research process can be broadly divided into the following phases: planning, implementation, evaluation, and dissemination (Elmes, Kantowitz, & Roediger, 2003; Graziano & Raulin, 2003). The purpose of this chapter is to provide an in-depth look at the planning and implementation phases of the research process for single case research designs, including potential obstacles that may occur in this process. The steps involved in evaluating and disseminating research are detailed in subsequent chapters. In this chapter, information will be provided on gaining access to school or community settings for research, obtaining institutional review board approval, obtaining consent from study participants, and gathering resources to carry out a research study.

Many of the steps detailed in this chapter are based on the University of Kentucky Checklist for Collaborative Field-Based Research, which was developed by Hemmeter, Doyle, Collins, and Ault (1996) for researchers interested in implementing single case research in applied settings. (See Table 5.1 for a copy of this checklist.) In addition, Maruyama and Deno (1992) have provided clear and concise guidelines for conducting research in applied settings.

GETTING ACCESS TO APPLIED RESEARCH SETTINGS FOR RESEARCH AND EVALUATION

One of the most difficult steps in conducting research is finding and gaining access to a site that meets your needs and desires as a researcher (Maruyama & Deno, 1992). The first step to gaining access to research sites is to ask people in your department or work setting who are currently conducting research in school or community settings. These people can help you to connect with key individuals in the settings you are interested in and can provide you with tips for how to best solicit the site for research. Tapping into the relationships that have already been developed between a university

Table 5.1   University of Kentucky Checklist for Collaborative Field-Based
Research (Hemmeter et al., 1996).

Getting Started
  1) Identify potential research questions
  2) Select setting and field-based personnel
  3) Discuss benefits of research with field-based personnel
  4) Assess personnel skill and knowledge of research process
  5) Conceptualize research question with field-based personnel and select research design
  6) Select the number of personnel
  7) Define roles of all personnel
  8) Define field-based personnel role in final product
  9) Obtain field-based personnel permission
  10) Obtain university permission
  11) Obtain educational system permission
  12) Determine schedule of contact with personnel
  13) Select participants with assistance of field-based personnel
  14) Obtain parent/legal guardian permission
  15) Identify methods for obtaining participant records
  16) Develop written materials
  17) Implement training of field-based personnel
  18) Obtain miscellaneous materials
  19) Set due date for any data collection

Implementation
  1) Schedule and conduct procedural and dependent variable reliability observations
  2) Retrain field-based personnel as necessary
  3) Update written materials
  4) Schedule meetings with field-based personnel
  5) Review field-based personnel needs
  6) Schedule data summary for field-based personnel
  7) Provide positive feedback to field-based personnel

Completion
  1) Deliver reinforcers to field-based personnel as agreed on in Getting Started
  2) Provide final data summary
  3) Follow-up with parents and administrators
  4) Include field-based personnel in final products
  5) Interview field-based personnel regarding their participation in the project

and the school or community setting is another excellent way to gain access to a research site (Maruyama & Deno, 1992). Note that if you are working in a college of education, psychology, or communication, students in these departments are often required to complete practicum experiences. For example, your department may consistently place student teachers with a certain school district in your area. Or, there may be a community agency that focuses on mental health issues at which students from your department are placed for practicum hours. Assuming that the relationship between your institution and the site has been positive, this may be an excellent route to access school and community settings.

Building positive relationships with schools and community settings takes time. These sites may be more willing to allow you to conduct your research if they feel they are receiving something in return. One way to build relationships with potential research sites is to offer free consultation or in-service workshops. What are the needs in the school or community setting? Can you offer your expertise? For example, a school may be interested in improving transition services for students with disabilities from high school to college or work settings. You may be able to provide a workshop, help the school staff link with community or college staff, or provide input during transition team meetings. Or if you are interested in conducting research in a community mental health setting, perhaps you can create a practicum so students receive hands-on experience while the site receives extra support for its staff. By creating a situation that is mutually beneficial for both the research site and researcher, you likely improve your odds of obtaining a research site.

Another way to gain access to a research site is to determine if the site is in need of support in implementing a new initiative, program or obtaining outside funding. For example, a state department of education may have money allocated to fund programs to increase reading achievement of students in grades K-3. As a researcher interested in reading interventions and their outcomes, you could help the school write a proposal for funding and build your research agenda around the activities involved in the proposal. In a community setting the same issue applies. The question to ask is, "how can I build and support current service agendas of interest?" Many agencies are underfunded or could use additional resources to improve facilities, hire more staff, or provide more opportunities for the clients or consumers they support. If your research project involves providing a needed service or comes with supplementary funding, this will typically help you get your foot in the door.

Contacting and building relationships with superintendents of school districts is another way to gain access to a school site for research. If you are interested in working in a school setting, particularly with students who are at-risk or who have disabilities, the school district's director of special education or the district curriculum specialist may also be appropriate people to contact to help get your foot in the door (Maruyama & Deno, 1992). These individuals will typically have a wealth of knowledge in terms of what schools need in their district and which schools would be good candidates for your research project.

In each community and school setting, you typically find a few people who are sincerely interested in the "cutting edge" technology in their field (i.e., education, psychology, social work, etc.). These people are the ones who love to continuously learn new skills and readily integrate new information/research into their daily work lives. Finding one of these people who works in a school or community setting can help you gain access to that site. The main issue when going this route is that you need to be certain that you are respectful of the school or community setting approval process. More information on this issue will be provided in the next section.

Being Respectful During the Research Process

When you are making contacts with a research site, it is important to recognize and follow the chain of command that exists in the school or community setting (more information on securing *formal* site approval is provided later in this chapter). For example, even if an individual teacher is interested and willing to be involved in your proposed study, you still need to secure the necessary approvals from the principal and the school district.

Getting to Know the Culture of the School or Community Setting

Often when you are attempting to secure research sites you will not have the luxury of choosing between multiple sites. However, if you do have choices among multiple sites, Maruyama and Deno (1992) stress the importance of getting to know the culture of the school or community setting prior to making the formal decision to conduct research at that site. There are several ways that this can be done. Perhaps you can offer a short workshop or in-service to staff and get a feel for the people you will likely be working with. In such situations you may be able to determine how well staff get along and whether the administrator is supportive.

Maruyama and Deno (1992) also recommend conducting a pilot study in the site you are interested in to confirm whether it would be a good site for your research project. Pilot studies are typically scaled-down versions of the actual study you are interested in implementing (Graziano & Raulin, 2003); so, if staff are having difficulty following through with expectations for the pilot study or are clearly not supporting your research, you may want to choose a different site. A pilot study could also allow you a chance to try out some of your research materials and get the school or community setting staff excited to be involved in your research project.

Increasing Your Odds of Finding and Keeping a Research Site

In both schools and community settings where we are interested in doing research, staff are extremely busy completing the tasks that must be accomplished each day. The idea of adding one more thing, such as a research project, to their busy schedules may seem overwhelming. You may be asking staff to engage in activities that involve additional time on their part. For these reasons, it is typically important to provide some type of incentive for participating in research. There are many different types of incentives that researchers can provide that may aid in securing a research site. It may be possible to offer participants continuing education or some other type of university credit for engaging in a study. For some single case research studies, staff may need to receive a significant amount of training before an intervention is implemented.

Another incentive for participation in research is to provide the school or community setting with money to release staff while they are receiving training related to the study. For example, in a care home setting for adults with disabilities, money could be provided for substitute staff to fill in while full-time staff attend a training session or engage in other activities related to implementing the research. The same concept could be applied to a school setting. Wherever you conduct your research, if staff are being asked to do more and engage in activities above and beyond the scope of their job descriptions, it is helpful to provide resources so that the setting is not spending its own resources to help implement your study.

One of the biggest incentives tends to be providing some type of monetary compensation for participation in research. For example, each member of a school team who agrees to meet after school once a month could receive a $300 honorarium for the school year for engaging in activities outside the scope of his or her job description. The amount of money that is offered as an incentive should correspond to the amount of effort and time that is involved in implementing your research project (Sieber, 1992).

Other incentives that could be provided include purchasing new materials for a classroom or school or purchasing needed equipment for community settings. As mentioned previously in relation to securing a research site, it would also be possible to offer training in particular areas of expertise. It is important to realize that it is a privilege to be allowed to do research in a school or community setting. The job of school and community setting staff is to support the students or clients with whom they work, and research is likely an extra task added to their job responsibilities. Providing some type of incentive for participating in research acknowledges that staff are going above and beyond their job responsibilities.

Making the Final Decision: What to Look for in Potential Research Sites

Getting access to a research site is a critical step in the research process. However, when looking at potential research sites there could be some signs that the school or community setting may be in a state of flux or transition which could make implementing your research difficult (Crone, Horner, & Hawken, 2004). Table 5.2 provides a summary of the questions you may want to ask the site administrator prior to making a final decision on your research site.

One of the things to look for in a site is relatively low administrative and staff turnover. Also, many school and community staff members may be part of a union. Research may be interrupted due to a staff strike or walkout. Such issues need to be taken into account in choosing a potential setting for your research project.

A related issue in choosing a research site is the rate of student or client mobility. Students or clients may be likely to move within a short time frame, which may potentially impact research activities.

Table 5.2 Questions for Potential Research Sites.

1) Is there a high rate of staff turnover?
2) Is there a high rate of administrator turnover?
3) What is the mobility rate of your student/client population?
4) What new initiatives/programs are currently being implemented?
5) Is the school/agency involved in other research projects?
6) Does your school/agency have experience participating in research?
7) What are your district/agency timelines for approval of research projects?
8) Are there any other issues that you feel may affect implementing a research study?

It is also important to assess whether the school or community setting is currently implementing new initiatives, curricula, or programs. In schools, for example, it is not unheard of for the staff to be implementing a new reading curriculum, focusing on school-wide character development, and/or improving the technology in the school. If there are many new programs or initiatives being implemented, your research study may take a back seat to what is currently being implemented because teachers or staff will be so overwhelmed with implementing the new initiatives that they are unable to focus any energy on your research study.

Finally, an essential question to ask potential research sites involves district or community setting timelines for approval of research projects. It will be important to determine if a project can be approved within the necessary timelines for carrying it out.

OBTAINING APPROVAL FROM RELEVANT REVIEW AND APPROVAL COMMITTEES

Once you have a site in mind that is interested in your research project, the next step is to obtain approval from the relevant committees that oversee research approvals. If you are working or studying in a university and are interested in doing research in school or community settings, there are typically two levels of approval that you will need to go through: the university Institutional Review Board (IRB), and whatever review board the school or community setting has in place to screen research proposals (Hemmeter et al., 1996).

Definition and Purpose of the IRB

An Institutional Review Board (IRB) is a committee that reviews research proposals prior to studies being conducted to ascertain whether researchers are following ethical guidelines set forth by the relevant agencies (e.g., the United States Department of Health and Human Services). Each university or community setting that receives funding from the federal government and conducts research is required to establish a formal IRB process (Sieber, 1992).

The purpose of the IRB is to weigh the benefits of conducting research with the risks that are involved. IRB proposals are typically approved if they have sound research designs and the benefits (e.g., knowledge gained, students helped) outweigh the possible risks (e.g., loss of confidentiality) of conducting the research. IRBs may have different timelines for the conduct of research. For example, a common approach is that approval is given for one year to complete research before an application is required to renew the approval for a project.

Timelines for Getting Your IRB Proposal Approved

Of greatest importance when working through IRB approval is to understand the timelines that surround the process. The frequency with which the IRB meets will vary by university or agency. Realize that the IRB will likely require revisions prior to giving final approval to conduct research. Sources for information regarding the IRB process can be colleagues or fellow students who have recently gone through the process and had a study approved.

School or Agency Approval

If you are a student or faculty researcher in a university, once the university IRB approval process is complete, you may need to go through the process again with the community or school setting in which you are interested in doing research. University IRBs may require a letter from the community setting or school district stating that they have agreed to allow you to do research in their setting.

If you are interested in doing research in a school setting, the approval process for research varies widely depending on the district and settings of interest. Large school districts may have a centralized research approval process and a full-time person to review and approve research proposals. Other districts have a more decentralized decision-making structure and allow research approval at the individual school level (Maruyama & Deno, 1992).

It is in everyone's best interests to develop a research agreement form that lists the expectations for both the staff at the research site and research staff. Hemmeter et al. (1996) recommend that a research agreement contain the following components: (a) the anticipated beginning and ending dates of the research project, (b) names and contact information of the people from the school or community setting who will be involved in the research project, (c) names and contact information of personnel from the university who will be involved in the research, and (d) the expectations for all individuals involved in a study.

OBTAINING CONSENT AND ASSENT FOR PARTICIPATION

Once a research project has received the stamp of approval from relevant IRBs, the next hurdle will be to obtain consent and assent from the participants who will be involved in the research study. This sequence usually involves 1) getting consent from school or community setting personnel, 2) obtaining parental permission, as needed for children to participate, and 3) obtaining the children's assent to participate. (See Table 5.3)

Table 5.3 Federal Regulations of Information that Must Be Provided to Each Participant.

> 1) A statement that the study involves research, an explanation of the purposes of the research and the expected duration of the participant's participation, a description of the procedures to be followed and identification of any procedures which are experimental;
>
> 2) A description of any reasonably foreseeable risks or discomforts to the participant;
>
> 3) A description of any benefits to the participant or to others which may reasonably be expected from the research;
>
> 4) A disclosure of appropriate alternative procedures or courses of treatment, if any, that might be advantageous to the participant;
>
> 5) A statement describing the extent, if any, to which confidentiality of records will be maintained;
>
> 6) An explanation of whom to contact for answers to pertinent questions about the research and research participants' rights, and whom to contact in the event of a research-related injury to the participant; and
>
> 7) A statement that participation is voluntary, refusal to participate will involve no penalty or loss of benefits to which the participant is otherwise entitled and the participant may discontinue participation at any time without penalty or loss of benefits to which the participant is otherwise entitled.

Source: From: Penslar, R. L. (n.d.). *Institutional Review Board Guidebook.* Retrieved August 31, 2003, from http://ohrp.osophs.dhhs.gov/irb/irb_guidebook.htm.

PLANNING RESOURCES FOR A STUDY

Jumping through the hoops of the IRB process, securing approval from a school or community setting, and obtaining consents for participation are significant hurdles in the research process. During the planning step of the research process it is also important to think about the other logistical resources that will be required to carry out a research study.

Resources Needed and Steps for Acquiring Resources

Project Personnel

Most studies will require the services of data collectors, who will either be paid or will be involved for course credit. Ideally, individuals working on a project should have some knowledge of the research process. Hemmeter et al. (1996) recommend interviewing potential project personnel to assess their knowledge of the research process. This would include determining any previous research experience, research courses they have taken, knowledge of research terminology (e.g., interobserver reliability, treatment integrity), and data collection processes. Project personnel should also already have knowledge of, or receiving training in, appropriate ethical standards about research (Sieber, 1992).

Equipment and Materials

The vast majority of single case studies will involve some type of direct observation data collection system (see Chapter 2 on "Defining What to Measure and How to Measure It"). Some direct observation may include a computer-based data collection system while others will involve hard copy data sheets and a timing device that signals when to record behavior. Research costs for the relevant equipment and materials need to be included in the budget as part of the research process.

During the planning phase of the research process you will also need to select a method for measuring the extent to which the experimental intervention or treatment is being implemented as planned (i.e., with fidelity). There are several different ways to assess the extent to which the independent variable is being implemented with fidelity. These include reviewing permanent products (e.g., audio and/or video recordings of training lessons), having community setting personnel complete checklists upon implementing an intervention, or directly observing the school or community setting staff during intervention implementation (McIntyre, Gresham, DiGennaro, & Reed, 2007).

CREATIVE METHODS TO ACQUIRE THE RESOURCES NEEDED FOR SINGLE CASE RESEARCH

Teachers and Staff as Data Collectors

There may be times in which the help of school or program staff can be solicited for data collection. For example, in a school setting a teacher could help gather archival and demographic data needed for a study. In a community setting, a staff member may be willing to rate the client's behavior at the end of each hour. Such participation from staff may facilitate the data collection processes needed to implement a study.

Offering Research Experience

Some colleges or departments in universities require students to participate in research as part of their program requirements. Students may sign up for an internship or independent study; in this case, they could receive credit for participating in a research project rather than some form of hourly payment.

There are several ways students can obtain funds for research. Many institutions of higher education have undergraduate or graduate research awards. These research awards or grants help cover some or all of the costs related to implementing research. Additionally, students should look for research funding from the professional organizations they belong to. Organizations such as the Council for Exceptional Children, the National Association of School Psychologists, the American Psychological Association, and the Association for Behavior Analysis all have some type of research award or grant competition to fund student research.

SETTING YOUR START DATE FOR DATA COLLECTION: TIMELINE ISSUES

Maruyama and Deno (1992) state that if you are doing research in schools, the best time to collect data is between January and spring break. During this period there are typically some interruptions to the school schedule such as two presidential holidays, but in the fall there are parent-teacher conferences, Halloween, the Thanksgiving break, and the Christmas/holiday break. In many schools, instruction stops or is put on hold right before breaks to allow time for parties, plays, and other school events surrounding holidays. Whether conducting research in a school or community setting, it is important to obtain a calendar of events that will likely occur during the course of a study.

The main message in relation to finalizing timelines and setting data collection start dates is that it is important to be flexible with expectations of how quickly you will be able to finish.

IMPLEMENTING YOUR RESEARCH PROJECT

Once all of the planning steps of the research process have been completed, the project can get underway.

Conducting Interobserver Reliability and Treatment Fidelity Checks

During implementation, it will be important to schedule and conduct interobserver reliability checks across baseline and intervention. It will also be important to schedule times to check the fidelity of implementation of the intervention.

Meeting Regularly with Staff and Maintaining Commitment to the Project

One way to maintain commitment to a study is to set up a communication system so that personnel involved in the project can provide feedback on a regular basis (Maruyama & Deno, 1992). This gives the project staff and research site personnel a feeling that they are being supported and will hopefully lead to them staying on board. Being available on site to answer questions and provide feedback is an essential way to let people know you are involved and interested in how the research is going (Maruyama & Deno, 1992).

Earlier in this chapter information was shared on the importance of providing incentives for individuals who participate in research. Typically, research participants (e.g., school or community setting staff) receive these incentives at the end of the research project. Depending on the design, some single case studies may involve daily data collection and go on for several months. It is often helpful to provide encouragement and acknowledgement along the way so that the school or community setting staff realize that their efforts are truly appreciated. This may involve a "Thank You" note to relevant personnel during the course of your study, some candy or chocolate with a note saying "Thanks—we're halfway there," or a special lunch for those involved.

When the Unexpected Occurs

Sometimes the unexpected occurs. Things may happen in the middle of a study that were not planned for, such as a power outage due to a tremendous storm, a teacher walkout, major cuts in funding, participants who move in the middle of your study, or a data collector who quits before the study is completed. As a researcher, you cannot possibly plan for all of the issues that may arise which may affect the outcome of a study. Maruyama and Deno (1992) recommend that the best approach to handling these situations is to be flexible and think about ways to minimize factors that may lead to alternative explanations for your outcomes. Events may arise that will provide some impact on the results of a research study but may be explainable when writing up research results.

CONCLUSION

The purpose of this chapter was to outline the steps for the planning and implementation phases of the research process as well as to discuss obstacles that may arise during these phases. Steps that were detailed include gaining access to research sites, obtaining IRB approval, securing consent from participants, and marshalling resources to implement your study. The research process can often be difficult and unpredictable, but the rewards are many for those who persevere!

REFERENCES

Crone, D. A., Horner, R. H., & Hawken, L. S. (2004). *Responding to problem behavior in schools: The Behavior Education Program.* New York, NY: Guilford Press.

Elmes, D. G., Kantowitz, B. H., & Roediger, H. L. (2003). *Research methods in psychology* (7th ed.). Belmont, CA: Wadsworth/Thomson Learning.

Graziano, A. M., & Raulin, M. L. (2003). *Research methods: A process of inquiry* (4th ed.). Upper Saddle River, NJ: Allyn and Bacon.

Hemmeter, M. L., Doyle, P. M., Collins, B. C., & Ault, M. J. (1996). Checklist for successful implementation of field-based research. *Teacher Education and Special Education, 19*, 342–354.

Maruyama, G., & Deno, S. (1992). *Research in educational settings*. Newbury Park, CA: Sage Publications.

McIntyre, L. L., Gresham, F. M., DiGennaro, F. D., & Reed, D. D. (2007). Treatment integrity of school-based interventions with children in the *Journal of Applied Behavior Analysis* 1991–2005. *Journal of Applied Behavior Analysis. 40*, 659–672.

Penslar, R. L. (n.d.). *Institutional Review Board Guidebook*. Retrieved August 31, 2003, from http://ohrp.osophs .dhhs.gov/irb/irb_guidebook.htm.

Sieber, J. E. (1992). *Planning ethically responsible research: A guide for students and internal review boards*. Newbury Park, CA: Sage.

WITHDRAWAL AND REVERSAL DESIGNS

6

As described in Chapter 1, Baer, Wolf, and Risley (1968) delineated the important features of behavior analytic research. In doing so they described some of the basic experimental design options for demonstrating experimental control or functional relationships. One such major design approach involved comparison of a participant's performance during repeated alternations of baseline and intervention conditions (Parsonson & Baer, 1978). This approach is somewhat analogous to a group comparison design, in which one group receives an intervention and is then compared to a control or baseline group that did not receive the intervention. However, in this approach each participant serves as that participant's own control in comparing across baseline and intervention phases. As a simple example, suppose a father has a child who engages in yelling and grabbing behavior each time the father is on the phone, and the father is interested in seeing if he is reinforcing the behavior when it occurs by providing the attention (e.g., "Be quiet! I'm on the phone!"). For one series of phone calls the father could ignore the child while on the phone. In the next series of calls he could pay attention each time the child exhibits disruptive behavior. This two-step sequence could be repeated once more, and the father could then determine which situation appears to produce more yelling and grabbing. In actuality there are multiple variations of withdrawal and reversal designs that can be used to examine the effects of an intervention on a behavior. This chapter will describe the characteristics of these designs, outline the steps necessary to ensure successful implementation, and provide examples of how they have been used from the applied research literature.

CASE STUDY DESIGNS

The advantages of withdrawal and reversal designs are better understood if we begin by discussing the most basic single case research design available to researchers. This is the A-B design, which is also sometimes called a pre-experimental or case study design (Kazdin, 1981). Such designs include a single initial baseline phase (A) followed by a single intervention phase (B). Let's say for example that a supervisor in a residential home setting for adults with developmental disabilities collects data on the frequency of aggressive behaviors exhibited by one of the home's residents. After several days of baseline data collection the home staff implement an intervention procedure in which the resident is taught an alternative appropriate communication skill (e.g., using sign language to indicate the need for a break from activities). The staff simultaneously give the resident more tangible rewards for periods of time not engaging in aggressive behaviors (i.e., a differential reinforcement of other behavior, or DRO procedure). After the implementation of the intervention strategies the staff continues to collect data to determine if there is a decrease in the frequency of aggressive behavior. Let's suppose that after a couple of weeks of implementing the intervention the individual's aggressive behavior substantially decreases.

A real example of such a case study design was provided by Campbell and Skinner (2004). They conducted a study involving a classroom of 30 sixth-grade students whose teacher was concerned about the amount of time that was being consumed by transitions between activities (e.g., coming and going from recess and lunch). During the baseline phase the number of seconds required for these transitions was recorded, and a daily average was calculated. During the intervention phase the research staff worked with the teacher to implement the Timely Transitions Game (TTG), a procedure in which the class could qualify for steps toward rewards (e.g., popcorn party, class movie) for each transition that was accomplished in less time than a pre-specified criterion number of seconds. Figure 6.1 presents the average daily time for transitions (in seconds) during the baseline and intervention phases. There was a clear and consistent reduction in the amount of transition time during the intervention (TTG) phase.

Figure 6.1   Daily average time for transitions

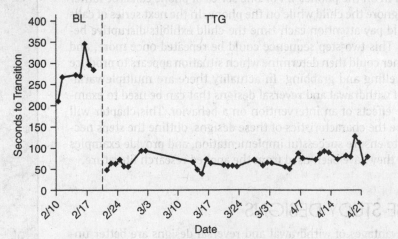

Source: Campbell, S., & Skinner, C. H. (2004). Combining Explicit Timing with an Interdependent Group Contingency Program to Decrease Transition Times: An Investigation of the Timely Transitions Game. *Journal of Applied School Psychology*, *20*, p. 21. Copyright 2004 by the Haworth Press. Reprinted with permission.

In both our hypothetical residential home example and in the Campbell and Skinner (2004) study, the data in the intervention phase were positive with regard to a desired reduction in problem behavior. However, it is not possible in either case to firmly conclude that the decrease was due to the intervention procedures. In Chapter 4 it was noted that the basic standard for demonstrating experimental control or a functional relationship is that a design must demonstrate a change in behavior at three different points in time (Horner et al., 2005). An A-B case study design can only document change at a single point in time. Therefore, such demonstrations are vulnerable to many of the possible threats to internal validity (e.g., historical events, maturation, measurement error). In our hypothetical example the resident in question may have experienced a change in medications or work setting leading to observed changes in behavior. Similarly, in the situation described by Campbell and Skinner (2004) the school principal may have implemented some type of school-wide behavioral program that might have impacted the students' behavior without the knowledge of the teacher or researchers.

Given that such A-B comparisons are likely (and hopefully) a common evaluation approach implemented in educational and clinical settings (Hayes, Barlow, & Nelson-Gray, 1999), it is worth considering what characteristics may enhance the internal validity of such investigations and our ability to draw conclusions from them. Kazdin (1981, 1982) described a set of factors, presented in Table 6.1, that should be considered in assessing the threats to validity of A-B or case study designs.

Table 6.1 Factors Influencing the Validity of A-B or Case Study Designs (Adapted from Kazdin, 1981, 1982).

1) Objectivity of Data
   - Do the data reported go beyond just testimony or anecdotal reports by researchers or participants that change has occurred (e.g., direct observation of overt behavior)?

2) Frequency and Duration of Assessment/Data Collection
   - Are data collected on a frequent and ongoing basis over a substantial period of time during both baseline and intervention conditions, as opposed to only single pre- and post-intervention measurements?

3) Stability of Data
   - Do the data (especially in the baseline phase) demonstrate a stable pattern of performance over a substantial period of time (see Chapter 4)?

4) Immediacy and Degree of Effect
   - As discussed in Chapter 4, the more substantial and immediate the effect produced by an intervention when it is first implemented, the less likely it is being produced by an alternative variable.

5) Replication Across Multiple Cases
   - As discussed in Chapter 4 experimental control or a functional relationship is demonstrated by change at multiple (3) points in time. Even if not "connected" in a single design, the more A-B case study examples which demonstrate a similar effect, the more convincing the argument that the intervention is responsible for that effect.

Based on these characteristics, case study investigations that involve more objective measures (e.g., direct observation), repeated measures over time, stable data in the baseline and intervention phases, immediate and substantial effects when intervention is implemented, and demonstration of effects across multiple participants will be considered less susceptible to concerns with threats to internal validity. Rickards-Schlichting, Kehle, and Bray (2004) reported a study in which they worked with six high school students who reported high levels of anxiety about public speaking. Direct observation data were collected from videotapes of the participants' public speaking behavior by trained observers using the Behavioral Assessment of Speech Anxiety measure (BASA; Mulac & Sherman, 1974). These measures were collected while the participants presented speeches to a peer audience. The researchers also collected self-report measures on both general and public speaking anxiety. The intervention involved a self-modeling procedure in which the participants periodically viewed edited videotapes of themselves demonstrating calm and effective speaking behavior. Figure 6.2 presents the pre- and post-intervention BASA data for four of the six participants. As can be seen, they all exhibited immediate and substantial reductions in behavioral manifestations of speech anxiety following the intervention. The objective nature of the data, repeated measurement occasions, stability of the data, immediate and substantial intervention effects, and replication across a number of cases help to rule out alternative explanations for the results.

The A-B design should allow us to predict with some certainty a participant's immediate future baseline performance. Once the intervention is implemented we can then compare the resulting performance to the predicted pattern. However, what if the intervention does not produce a change from the behavior pattern predicted by the baseline data? In such a case there are basically two options. First, since there was no apparent effect, we can simply treat the initial intervention data as an extension of the baseline data and go ahead and implement a modified or new intervention (see Figure 6.3). (Note that it would be very important to indicate to persons ultimately evaluating the data from such a study that there had been an initial intervention [as indicated in Figure 6.3] that is could not simply present all the data as all part of a single initial baseline phase; one rather, it would have to be divided into two phases on a graph). Once we do implement the modified or new intervention, however, we are confronted with the problem of multiple treatment interference (see Chapter 3). That is, we wouldn't be able to know for sure if any observed changes were due exclusively to the modified or new intervention, or to the *combination* of the initial *and* modified or new interventions.

An alternative strategy would be to first *withdraw* the initial intervention and return to a baseline data collection phase prior to implementing the modified or new intervention (see Figure 6.4). This helps to some extent to control the problem of multiple treatment interference by attempting to "wash-out" the effects of the initial intervention prior to implementing the modified or new intervention. Although even in this case it would be impossible to completely rule out the possibility of such intervention interaction effects, this approach may present a more viable alternative (Kazdin, 1982).

Figure 6.2 Self-reported speech anxiety scores of high school students

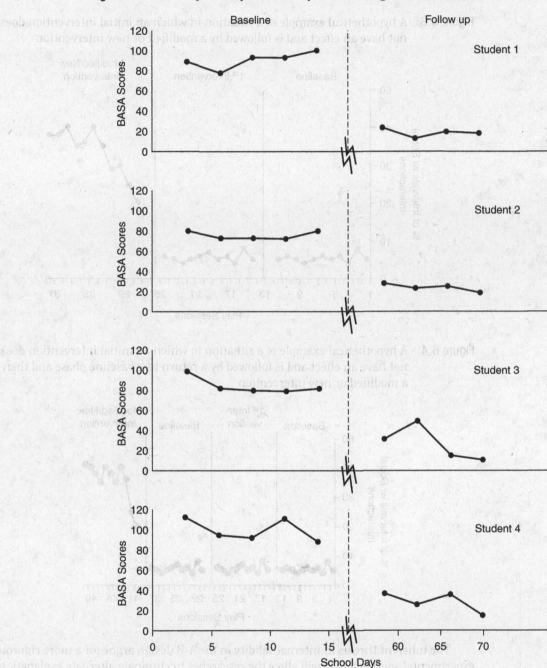

Source: Rickards-Schlichting, K. A., Kehle, T. J., & Bray, M. A. (2004). A self-modeling intervention for high school students with public speaking anxiety. *Journal of Applied School Psychology*, vol. 20, p. 56. Copyright the Haworth Press. Reprinted with permission.

Figure 6.3 A hypothetical example of a situation in which an initial intervention does not have an effect and is followed by a modified or new intervention

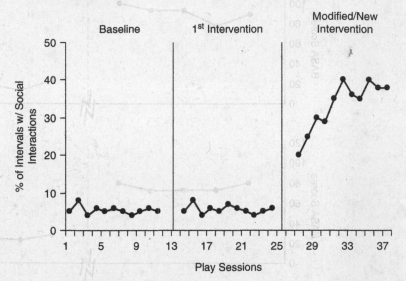

Figure 6.4 A hypothetical example of a situation in which an initial intervention does not have an effect and is followed by a return to a baseline phase and then a modified or new intervention

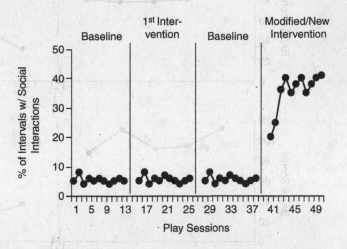

The inherent threats to internal validity in the A-B design argue for a more rigorous experimental approach that will allow the researcher to eliminate alternate explanations for changes in the target behavior. The easiest way to do this is to repeatedly contrast the study participants' behavior under baseline conditions (A) with their behavior during intervention (B). Withdrawal and reversal designs provide a mechanism for researchers to achieve this outcome.

WITHDRAWAL DESIGNS

The purpose of withdrawal designs is to document whether the introduction of the intervention consistently leads to a change in the study participant's behavior. Table 6.2 summarizes the key features of withdrawal designs. The most common withdrawal designs are the A-B-A and the A-B-A-B designs. The potential advantages and disadvantages for researchers of these designs are described in more detail below.

The A-B-A Design: Demonstrating Experimental Control

A substantial step toward a demonstration of experimental control or a functional relationship is gained by adding a second baseline phase to the A-B case study design, resulting in a baseline-intervention-baseline sequence (A-B-A). Such a sequence allows for the demonstration of a change in performance at a second point in time (i.e., the shift from intervention back to the baseline condition). This does not meet the proposed "gold standard" for demonstrating a functional relationship (3 points in time; Horner et al., 2005), but it is very helpful in going beyond the less controlled case study design approach. The addition of the intervention withdrawal and return to baseline helps to control for some of the threats to internal validity that have been discussed earlier (e.g., history, maturation, measurement problems).

An example of such a design approach was provided by Lavelle, Hovell, West, and Wahlgren (1992), who conducted a two-city study of the Colorado Occupant Protection Project (COPP). They collected initial baseline data on the frequency with which police issued citations to drivers for not using safety seats with child passengers. Then they

Table 6.2 Key Features of Withdrawal Designs.

Withdrawal Design	
Purpose	Verify a functional relationship between a behavior and an intervention.
General Characteristics	Repeated introduction and withdrawal of the intervention with a single study participant and target behavior.
Design Strengths	Allows the researcher to control the threats to internal validity inherent in A-B designs.
	Demonstration of experimental control can be achieved with a single study participant.
Design Weaknesses	Not appropriate for establishing new (nonreversible) behaviors.
	Withdrawal of the intervention may present ethical dilemmas to the researcher.
	Does not adequately control for effects by distal variables on the target behavior.

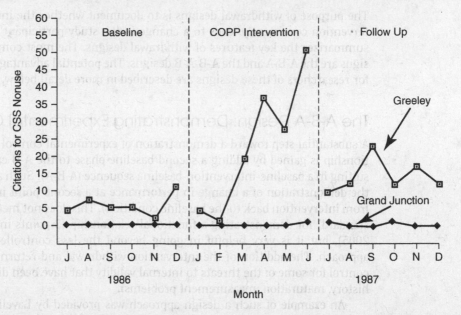

Figure 6.5 Frequency of tickets issued for nonuse of safety belts

Source: Lavelle, J. M., Hovell, M. F., West, M. P., & Wahlgren, D. R. (1992). Promoting law enforcement for child protection: A community analysis. *Journal of Applied Behavior Analysis*, vol. 25, p. 888. Copyright Society for the Experimental Analysis of Behavior. Reprinted with permission.

provided training to police officers in one city concerning the importance of safety seat use as well as data on how such use reduces injuries and fatalities. Officers were then provided with coupons they could give to drivers when issuing citations; these coupons were redeemable for a free safety seat and a waiver for the $50 fine. After several months of implementation, personnel changes in the city health and police departments resulted in the program being discontinued, thus providing an A-B-A comparison. The results of the program on the number of citations issued per month are presented in Figure 6.5. These data show a clear increase in the number of citations issued in the training city (Greeley) after the program was implemented and a rapid decline once it was discontinued. In addition, the number of citations issued in the non-program city (Grand Junction) remained low and stable throughout the study, providing an additional control comparison that gives additional confidence that the intervention was responsible for the increase seen in the number of citations issued in the training city.

Implementing an A-B-A Withdrawal Design Study

The fundamental considerations for designing and implementing an A-B-A withdrawal design are the same as those discussed in previous chapters for all single case research studies. Recommended steps for implementing an A-B-A design are similar to implementing an A-B-A-B design and will be presented in the following text. Although the A-B-A design helps address some of the problems of the case study design, it also has a unique set of problems that must be addressed when designing and implementing a study, including the reversibility of the behavior and the ethics of ending a study in a baseline condition.

Reversibility of Behavioral Performance

One of the critical questions with A-B-A designs (and by extension, A-B-A-B designs; see the following text) is whether the behavioral performance in question is *reversible* or not. That is, once the intervention is withdrawn in the second baseline (A) phase, is it likely that the participants' behavioral performance will change? As noted previously, to demonstrate experimental control (i.e., a functional relationship), changes in behavioral performance must be evident each time a change is made from a baseline to an intervention condition (or vice-versa). In some cases such a change may not be very likely to occur. For example, consider a situation in which a group of fifth grade students are being taught a strategy to solve long division problems. Once they are trained to do this fluently, it is unlikely that they will suddenly not be able to solve such problems just because the training is stopped or withdrawn. In such cases where the targeted behavior(s) involve the acquisition of such skills, other design options would be more suitable (e.g., multiple baseline designs; see Chapter 7).

It is interesting to note that the demonstration of experimental control required by withdrawal designs is in a sense counter to what we would like to see from an applied perspective. That is, it would be clinically beneficial if the effects of an intervention continued to be evident in a participant's performance even when that intervention was withdrawn. However, decades of behavioral research have demonstrated that such generalization and maintenance effects are unlikely to occur unless they are carefully programmed and planned for (Horner, Dunlap, & Koegel, 1988; Stokes & Baer, 1977).

Ethical Issues with Regard to Ending in a Withdrawal Phase

From clinical and ethical perspectives it would obviously not be a good thing to end an investigation in a baseline phase, or in a situation in which a participant or participants were no better off than when the study started. Most likely this accounts in large parts for why such designs are infrequently reported in the applied literature. One can assume that most teachers, parents, or participants would not want to end a study/intervention no better off, so to speak, than where they began. It has been argued that clinical or applied researchers have a moral and ethical obligation to ensure that participants ultimately be provided with the intervention once research activity has been completed, if that intervention has proven to be beneficial (Bailey & Burch, 2005; Barlow & Hersen, 1984).

The A-B-A-B Withdrawal Design: A Complete Experimental Design

In the A-B-A-B design, the researcher implements an additional intervention condition (B) in the experimental sequence in order to replicate the effects of the first intervention on the target behavior. As discussed previously, most single case studies involve small groups of participants. However, the use of an A-B-A-B sequence allows for the demonstration of a functional relationship within a single individual, assuming that a clear change is evident each time the intervention is implemented or withdrawn. Achieving a complete experimental design that demonstrates experimental control at three different points in time can be achieved by withdrawing the intervention during a third baseline phase, followed by final reintroduction of the intervention (A-B-A-B-A-B; Horner et al., 2005).

An example of such a design was provided by Yarbrough, Skinner, Lee, and Lemmons (2004). They evaluated another application of the Timely Transitions Game (TTG) described earlier (Campbell & Skinner, 2004). They conducted their study in a second grade classroom with 15 students, focusing on transitions back to class after lunch time. The procedures involved a group contingency to provide rewards when the students met criterion for making a transition. Figure 6.6 presents data on the number of seconds spent in transition each day. The data during the B phases demonstrate a substantial decrease in transition times when the TTG program was in effect. In this case the authors extended the study by implementing an additional A and B phase replication, resulting in an A-B-A-B-A-B sequence.

Another example of an A-B-A-B design was provided by Rasmussen & O'Neill (2006). This study involved three elementary school students attending a classroom in a psychiatric day treatment setting. They engaged in verbally disruptive behavior (e.g., talking out without raising their hands), which interfered with instruction for them and their classmates. An initial functional behavioral assessment (O'Neill et al., 1997) indicated that the students were doing this to obtain social attention, particularly from their teacher. During the initial baseline phases, data were collected on the percentage of intervals during which verbal disruptions occurred. The intervention involved *noncontingent* or *fixed-time* reinforcement schedules (Arnzen, Brekstad, & Holth, 2005). In such a procedure, the participant's desired reinforcement is provided on an ongoing periodic basis, regardless of behavior, in an attempt to *preempt* the need to

Figure 6.6   Daily transition times

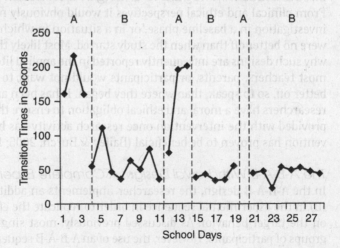

Source: Yarbrough, J. L., Skinner, C. H., Lee, Y. J., & Lemmons, C. (2004). Decreasing transition times in a second grade classroom: Scientific support for the Timely Transitions Game. *Journal of Applied School Psychology*, vol. 20, p. 97. Copyright the Haworth Press. Reprinted with permission.

engage in problem behavior to obtain the reinforcement. Initially, reinforcement is provided on a more frequent schedule than the participant appears to want according to the participant's baseline rate of problem behavior (Rasmussen & O'Neill, 2006).

The data in Figure 6.7 represent the percentage of intervals with verbal disruptions for the three students. During the initial baseline phases all three students were exhibiting

Figure 6.7 The percentage of 10 second intervals with occurrence of verbal disruptions

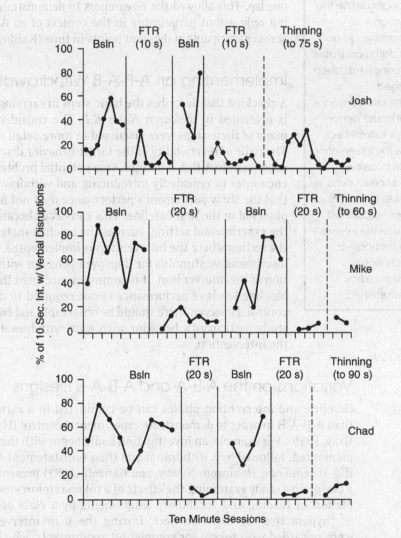

Source: Figure 1 from Rasmussen & O'Neill, The Effects of Fixed-time reinforcement schedules on problem behavior of children with emotional and behavioral disorders in a day-treatment setting—JABA, 2006, vol. 39, p. 455. Reprinted with permission.

verbal disruptions at a high rate. When fixed-time reinforcement (FTR) was provided in the form of social attention and interaction from the classroom teacher, the rate of verbal disruptions substantially decreased. The baseline and FTR phases were repeated with similar results. In the final phase the frequency of the fixed-time reinforcement was gradually decreased (i.e., every 60–90 seconds, versus every 10–20 seconds), and the low rates of behavior were maintained until the students left the day treatment program. One aspect of this study worth noting is that the three students attended the day treatment program at different times; that is, their stays in the program did not overlap. This allowed the researchers to demonstrate a replication of effects not only within participants in the context of an A-B-A-B design, but also across participants at different points in time (Kazdin, 1982).

Implementing an A-B-A-B Withdrawal Design

A checklist that describes the basic steps in carrying out an A-B-A-B design is presented in *Research Notes 6.1*. The considerations in carrying out many of these steps were discussed in more detail in Chapters 1 though 5. The issue of reversibility of the target behavior discussed previously is also of concern to A-B-A-B designs. One potential problem that researchers may encounter in repeatedly introducing and withdrawing the intervention is that the study participant's performance does not fully return to the levels observed in the first baseline. This can occur because irrelevant stimuli in the experimental setting, such as the teacher, materials, or the location in the setting where the intervention is implemented, may begin to serve as a discriminative stimulus for improved behavior with repeated implementation of the intervention. It is commonly accepted that a complete return to baseline levels of performance is not required to document experimental control. However, there should be observable and consistent changes in the study participant's behavior with each withdrawal and reintroduction of the intervention.

Variations on the A-B-A and A-B-A-B Designs

Baseline and intervention phases can be conducted in a variety of sequences other than A-B-A-B in order to demonstrate experimental control (Hayes, Barlow, & Nelson-Gray, 1999). For example, an investigation could begin with the intervention being implemented, followed by a withdrawal and then reinstatement of the intervention in a B-A-B sequence. Robinson, Newby, and Ganzell (1981) presented an example of such a design in a study examining the effects of a token reinforcement system on the completion of reading and vocabulary assignments by a class of 18 students identified as "hyperactive" by their teachers. During the B or intervention phases students were rewarded with tokens for completing assignments, which they could then cash in for time spent playing pinball and electronic "pong" games (remember, this was awhile ago!). The graph in Figure 6.8 presents data on the number of assignments completed by the class as a whole. The token reinforcement program clearly had an impact in increasing the amount of completed work during the B phases. Notably, the authors also presented data from several individual students, which indicated that the program had a more substantial impact for some than others.

The B-A-B sequence is somewhat problematic, in that it doesn't allow for the desired display of changes in behavior at three points in time (Horner et al., 2005), as there are only two shifts between baseline and intervention phases. Therefore, it does not provide as powerful a demonstration of experimental control. However, as previously discussed, replication of such effects with multiple participants within and across separate investigations would reduce concerns about threats to validity. Also, this type of approach has the ethical advantage of ending in an intervention phase, which would presumably be of greater benefit to the participants.

Figure 6.8 Number of completed class assignments

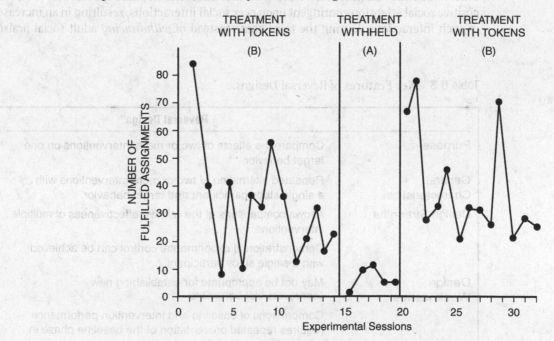

Source: Robinson, P. W., Newby, T. J., & Ganzell, S. L. (1981). A token system for a class of underachieving hyperactive children. *Journal of Applied Behavior Analysis*, vol. 14, p. 311. Copyright The Society for the Experimental Analysis of Behavior. Reprinted with permission.

THE REVERSAL DESIGN

Characteristics of the Reversal Design

The terms *withdrawal* and *reversal* are often used interchangeably in textbooks and other professional literature. However, withdrawal and reversal designs are distinctly different from one another and are structured to allow the researcher to answer different research questions. In contrast to the withdrawal design, a true *reversal* design is structured to compare the effects of two or more interventions by alternating them in the experimental sequence and observing their differential impact on the target behavior. Table 6.3 presents the key features of reversal designs. In the initial phase (baseline or A), repeated measures are taken of the behavior(s) of interest. In the second phase the first intervention (B) is implemented on the target behavior until a stable pattern of performance is established. In the next phase the second intervention (C) is introduced and measurement of the target behavior continues. Ideally, the first and second interventions would be alternated again in order to establish any differential effect they might have on the behavior. This design was used in an early study by Allen, Hart, Buell, Harris, and Wolf (1964) examining the influence of adult social attention on a young child's peer social interactions in a preschool classroom (see Figure 6.9). An initial baseline established the initial rates of interactions the child had with peers. During the first intervention phase the teachers provided positive social attention contingent upon peer social interactions, resulting in an increase in such interactions. During the third phase instead of *withdrawing* adult social praise

Table 6.3   Key Features of Reversal Designs.

	Reversal Design
Purpose	Compare the effects of two or more interventions on one target behavior.
General Characteristics	Repeated alternation of two or more interventions with a single study participant and target behavior.
Design Strengths	Allows comparisons of the relative effectiveness of multiple interventions.
	Demonstration of experimental control can be achieved with a single study participant.
Design Weaknesses	May not be appropriate for establishing new (nonreversible) behaviors.
	Comparisons of baseline and intervention performance requires repeated presentation of the baseline phase in adjacent phases to all interventions.
	May require the researcher to control for sequence and carry over effects.

Figure 6.9   Percentage of time spent in social interaction during approximately
2 hours of each morning session

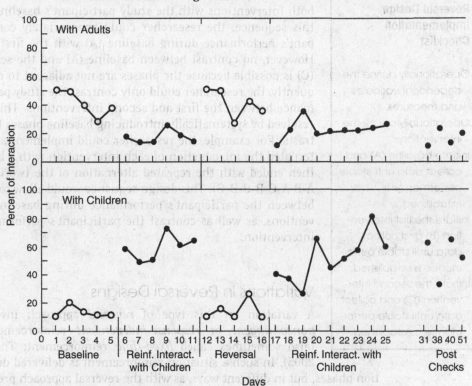

Source: Allen, K. E., Hart, B., Buell, J. S., Harris, F. R., & Wolf, M. M. (1964). Effects of social reinforcement
on isolate behavior of a nursery school child. *Child Development*, vol. 35, p. 515. Copyright Society for
Research in Child Development. Reprinted with permission.

altogether, it was instead provided when the child exhibited proximity and attention to
adults. This resulted in an increase in adult-directed interactions, and a decrease in peer-
to-peer interactions. During the fourth phase the teachers then *reversed* the contingencies once again so that social praise was provided contingent upon interactions with peers,
which then increased once again. These types of manipulations provided strong evidence
that the adult social praise was the effective variable in influencing the child's peer-related
social behavior.

Implementing a Reversal Design

Research Notes 6.2 presents an implementation checklist for designing and carrying
out a reversal design. It is important to note that a design sequence that begins with

Research Notes 6.2

Reversal Design Implementation Checklist

Operationally define the dependent variables and measures.

Operationally define the interventions.

Initiate baseline (A) and collect data until stable performance is established.

Initiate the first intervention (B) and collect data until stable performance is established.

Initiate the second intervention (C) and collect data until stable performance is established.

a baseline and is followed by repeated alternations of the two interventions under study (i.e., A-B-C-B-C) does not allow the researcher to contrast both interventions with the study participant's baseline performance. In this sequence, the researcher could appropriately contrast the participant's performance during baseline (A) with the first intervention (B). However, no contrast between baseline (A) and the second intervention (C) is possible because the phases are not adjacent to each other. Consequently, the researcher could only contrast the study participant's performance between the first and second interventions. This situation can be resolved by systematically introducing baseline phases to allow such contrasts. For example, the researcher could implement a sequence that alternated the introduction of each intervention with a baseline phase and then ended with the repeated alternation of the two interventions (i.e., A-B-A-C-B-C-B-C). This design sequence would allow for a direct contrast between the participant's performance during baseline and both interventions, as well as contrast the participant's performance during each intervention.

Variations in Reversal Designs

A variation on this type of *reversal* approach involves the use of *noncontingent* or *response-independent* reinforcement contingencies (also sometimes called *fixed-time* reinforcement; Thompson & Iwata, 2005). In such a situation reinforcement is delivered during all intervention phases, but in different ways, as with the reversal approach previously described. Such an approach was described in another early research report by Hart, Reynolds, Baer, Brawley, and Harris (1968), who studied the cooperative peer play behavior of Martha, a child in a preschool classroom setting (see Figure 6.10). They conducted an initial baseline phase to assess the child's typical rate of peer play. In the next phase teachers delivered social attention and approval, but on a periodic random basis; that is, it was not delivered contingent on any particular play behavior. In the next phase they continued to deliver attention and approval, but only *contingent* upon Martha being engaged in cooperative play with peers. The final two phases repeated the noncontingent and contingent reinforcement procedures. The data clearly demonstrated that only the *contingent* reinforcement procedures produced increases in Martha's play behavior.

Figure 6.10 Percent of time engaged in proximity and social interaction

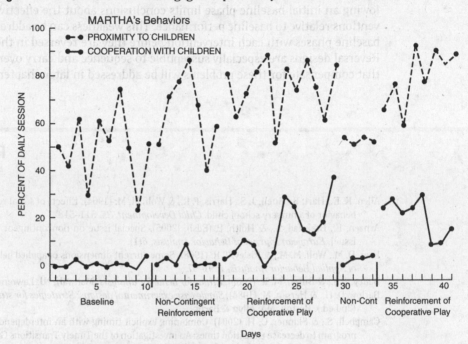

Source: Hart, B. M., Reynolds, N. J. Baer, D. M., Brawley, E. R. & Harris, F. R. (1968). Effect of contingent and non-contingent social reinforcement on the cooperative play of a preschool Child. *Journal of Applied Behavior Analysis.* vol. 1, p. 75. Copyright Society for the Experimental Analysis of Behavior. Reprinted with permission.

SUMMARY

Withdrawal and reversal designs allow the researcher to compensate for the threats to internal validity inherent in the case study or A-B design. A withdrawal design (A-B-A-B) enables the researcher to contrast a study participant's behavior during baseline and intervention conditions. Demonstration of experimental control is achieved through the repeated introduction and withdrawal of the intervention across time. It is critical, following the withdrawal of the intervention, that target behavior returns to levels that approximate the initial baseline phase. Thus, withdrawal designs require that the target behavior be reversible.

The reversal design is structured to allow the researcher to compare the differential effects of two interventions on the same target behavior. The focus is on identifying the most effective intervention. A design sequence that only reverses the interventions following an initial baseline phase limits conclusions about the effectiveness of the interventions relative to baseline performance. This weakness can be addressed by alternating baseline phases with each intervention before they are reversed in the design sequence. Reversal designs are especially susceptible to sequence and carry over effects. Strategies that compensate for these problems will be addressed in later chapters.

REFERENCES

Allen, K. E., Hart, B., Buell, J. S., Harris, F. R., & Wolf, M. M. (1964). Effects of social reinforcement on isolate behavior of a nursery school child. *Child Development, 35,* 511–518.

Arnzen, E., Brekstad, A., & Holth, P. (Eds.). (2005). Special issue on noncontingent reinforcement [Special issue]. *European Journal of Behavior Analysis, 6*(1).

Baer, D. M., Wolf, M. M., & Risley, T. R. (1968). Some current dimensions of applied behavior analysis. *Journal of Applied Behavior Analysis, 1,* 91–97.

Bailey, J. S., & Burch, M. R. (2005). *Ethics for behavior analysts.* Mahwah, NJ: Lawrence Erlbaum.

Barlow, D. H., & Hersen, M. (1984). *Single case experimental designs: Strategies for studying behavior change* (2nd ed.). Boston, MA: Allyn & Bacon.

Campbell, S., & Skinner, C. H. (2004). Combining explicit timing with an interdependent group contingency program to decrease transition times: An investigation of the Timely Transitions Game. *Journal of Applied School Psychology, 20,* 11–27.

Hart, B. M., Reynolds, N. J., Baer, D. M., Brawley, E. R., & Harris, F. R. (1968). Effect of contingent and non-contingent social reinforcement on the cooperative play of a preschool child. *Journal of Applied Behavior Analysis, 1,* 73–76.

Hayes, S. C., Barlow, D. H., & Nelson-Gray, R. O. (1999). *The scientist practitioner: Research and accountability in the age of managed care* (2nd ed.). Boston, MA: Allyn & Bacon.

Horner, R. H., Carr, E. G., Halle, J., McGee, G., Odom, S., & Wolery, M. (2005). The use of single-subject research to identify evidence-based practice in special education. *Exceptional Children, 71,* 165–179.

Horner, R. H., Dunlap, G., & Koegel, R. L. (Eds.) (1988). *Generalization and maintenance: Life-style changes in applied settings.* Baltimore, MD: Paul H. Brookes.

Kazdin, A. E. (1981). Drawing valid inferences from case studies. *Journal of Consulting and Clinical Psychology, 49,* 183–192.

Kazdin, A. E. (1982). *Single-case research designs: Methods for clinical and applied settings.* New York, NY: Oxford University Press.

Lavelle, J. M., Hovell, M. F., West, M. P., & Wahlgren, D. R. (1992). Promoting law enforcement for child protection: A community analysis. *Journal of Applied Behavior Analysis, 25,* 885–892.

Mulac, A., & Sherman, A. R. (1974). Behavioral assessment of speech anxiety. *Quarterly Journal of Speech, 60,* 134–143.

O'Neill, R. E., Horner, R. H., Albin, R. W., Sprague, J. R., Storey, K., & Newton, J. S. (1997). *Functional assessment and program development for problem behavior: A practical handbook* (2nd ed). Belmont, CA: Wadsworth.

Parsonson, B. S., & Baer, D. M. (1978). The analysis and presentation of graphic data. In T. R. Kratochwill (Ed.), *Single subject research: Strategies for evaluating change* (pp. 101–165). New York, NY: Academic Press.

Rasmussen, K., & O'Neill, R. E. (2006). The effects of fixed-time reinforcement schedules on problem behavior of children with emotional and behavioral disorders in a day treatment classroom setting. *Journal of Applied Behavior Analysis, 39,* 453–457.

Rickards-Schlichting, K. A., Kehle, T. J., & Bray, M. A. (2004). A self-modeling intervention for high school students with public speaking anxiety. *Journal of Applied School Psychology, 20,* 47–60.

Robinson, P. W., Newby, T. J., & Ganzell, S. L. (1981). A token system for a class of underachieving hyperactive children. *Journal of Applied Behavior Analysis, 14,* 307–315.

Stokes, T. F., & Baer, D. M. (1977). An implicit technology of generalization. *Journal of Applied Behavior Analysis, 10,* 349–367.

Thompson, R. H., & Iwata, B. A. (2005). A review of reinforcement control procedures. *Journal of Applied Behavior Analysis, 38,* 257–278.

Yarbrough, J. L., Skinner, C. H., Lee, Y. J., & Lemmons, C. (2004). Decreasing transition times in a second grade classroom: Scientific support for the Timely Transitions Game. *Journal of Applied School Psychology, 20,* 85–107.

MULTIPLE BASELINE AND MULTIPLE PROBE DESIGNS

Susan M. Johnston, *University of Utah*

Chapter 6 provides information regarding the use of withdrawal and reversal (A-B-A-B) designs. However, in some instances, withdrawal or reversal designs are not appropriate or may be unlikely to effectively demonstrate changes in behavior. One instance in which these designs may not be appropriate is when acquisition of new skills is intended (Alberto & Troutman, 1995; Cuvo, 1979; Datillo, Gast, Lowy, & Malley, 2000; Hersen & Barlow, 1976; Kratochwill, 1978; Martella, Nelson, & Marchand-Martella, 1999; Murphy & Bryan, 1980; Tawney & Gast, 1983). For example, consider an investigation by Johnston, McDonnell, Nelson, and Magnavito (2003) in which the researchers examined the impact of an intervention strategy on teaching functional communication skills using augmentative and alternative communication in inclusive preschool settings. If the researchers had chosen to use a withdrawal (A-B-A-B) design, they probably would not have demonstrated the effectiveness of the intervention strategy because the target behaviors, once acquired, would not have returned to baseline rates during the withdrawal phase.

Other situations in which a withdrawal or reversal design may not be preferred would be where a return to baseline rates is unethical or unsavory (Alberto & Troutman, 1995; Cuvo, 1979; Datillo et al., 2000; Hersen & Barlow, 1976; Kratochwill, 1978; Martella et al., 1999; Murphy & Bryan, 1980; Tawney & Gast, 1983). For example, Vaughn, Clarke, and Dunlap (1997) examined the impact of an assessment-based intervention on the challenging behaviors engaged in by an 8-year-old boy with disabilities. If the researchers had chosen to use a withdrawal (A-B-A-B) design, it would have been necessary to remove the intervention during the withdrawal phase. It is likely that removing the intervention would have resulted in an increase in the participant's rate of challenging behavior. In many instances, creating a situation where challenging behaviors increase may be uncomfortable and perhaps unethical. Furthermore, in applied settings it is likely that teachers, parents, and other caregivers will balk at a request to return to situations where the rates of challenging behavior increase once they have seen the frequency of those behaviors decrease.

When faced with instances where acquisition of skills is likely or when a return to baseline is objectionable, a researcher may consider alternatives to the A-B-A-B design. Included among these alternatives are multiple baseline designs and several variants. This chapter discusses the characteristics of these designs, outlines the steps required to implement them, and presents examples of these designs as used from the applied research literature.

CHARACTERISTICS OF MULTIPLE BASELINE DESIGNS

Multiple baseline designs avoid many of the problems inherent in withdrawal designs because the researcher does not need to return to baseline. Instead, the intervention is introduced across time and across separate conditions such as individuals, behaviors, or settings. In multiple baseline designs, the baselines start at the same time but intervention is introduced at a different point in time for each condition. Table 7.1 summarizes the key features of multiple baseline designs. Figure 7.1 illustrates the staggered introduction of intervention across three different behaviors for the same study participant. Baseline begins at the same time for all three behaviors and data collection continues until stable performance is established. At this point, the intervention is initiated for behavior 1. However, the baseline phase for behaviors 2 and 3 continues. Once the impact

Table 7.1 Key Features of Multiple Baseline Designs.

	Multiple Baseline Designs
Purpose	Verify a functional relationship between a behavior and an intervention through the replication of effects across different conditions (e.g., behaviors, people, or contexts).
General Characteristics	Baseline data are collected simultaneously across three conditions and the intervention is systematically introduced in each condition after stable performance has been established.
Design Strengths	Does not require the intervention to be withheld or reversed and therefore is appropriate for establishing new behaviors.
	Allows for the documentation of experimental control across a variety of conditions.
Design Weaknesses	Requires concurrent measurement across all conditions.
	Extended baseline and interventions may threaten the demonstration of experimental control.
	Does not allow immediate intervention on potentially harmful behaviors.

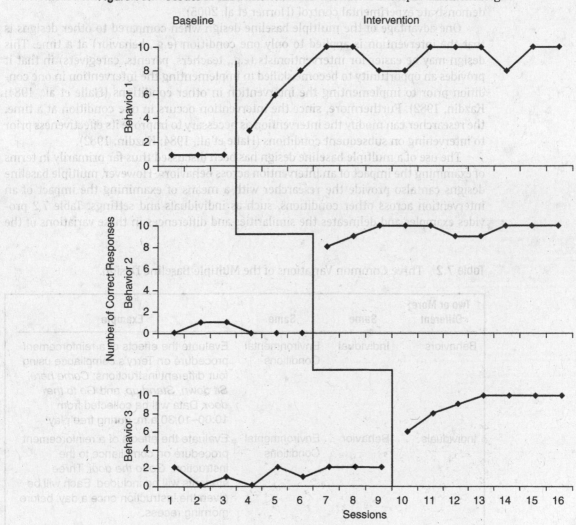

Figure 7.1 Model of the basic characteristics of a multiple baseline design

of the intervention is established for behavior 1 intervention is then initiated for behavior 2 and baseline continues for behavior 3. Similarly, when the impact of the intervention is established for behavior 2 the intervention is then initiated with behavior 3. When implementing a multiple baseline design, it is important for the data to show that change occurs only when the intervention is introduced. Thus, the baseline rates for the second and third conditions must remain stable until intervention is introduced (Cuvo, 1979; Drew & Hardman, 1985; Halle, Stoker, & Schloss, 1984; Kazdin, 1982; Kratochwill, 1978; Rubin & Babbie, 1993; Tawney & Gast, 1983). Successive introduction of the intervention with three different behaviors at three different points in time allows the researcher to demonstrate experimental control (Horner et al, 2005).

One advantage of the multiple baseline design when compared to other designs is that the intervention is applied to only one condition (e.g., behavior) at a time. This design may be easier for interventionists (e.g., teachers, parents, caregivers) in that it provides an opportunity to become skilled in implementing the intervention in one condition prior to implementing the intervention in other conditions (Halle et al., 1984; Kazdin, 1982). Furthermore, since the intervention occurs in one condition at a time, the researcher can modify the intervention as necessary to improve its effectiveness prior to intervening on subsequent conditions (Halle et al., 1984; Kazdin, 1982).

The use of a multiple baseline design has been discussed thus far primarily in terms of examining the impact of an intervention across behaviors. However, multiple baseline designs can also provide the researcher with a means of examining the impact of an intervention across other conditions, such as individuals and settings. Table 7.2 provides examples and delineates the similarities and differences in these variations of the

Table 7.2   Three Common Variations of the Multiple Baseline Design.

Two or More Different	Same	Same	Example
Behaviors	Individual	Environmental Conditions	Evaluate the effects of a reinforcement procedure on Terry's compliance using four different instructions: *Come here, Sit down, Stand up,* and *Go to the door.* Data will be collected from 10:00–10:30 a.m. during free play.
Individuals	Behavior	Environmental Conditions	Evaluate the effects of a reinforcement procedure on compliance to the instruction, *Go to the door.* Three students will be included. Each will be given the instruction once a day, before morning recess.
Environmental Conditions	Behavior	Individual	Evaluate the effects of a reinforcement procedure on Jerry's compliance to the instruction, *Go to the door.* The teacher will give the instruction at three different times throughout the day: before morning recess, before afternoon recess, and just before school ends.

Source: Halle, J., Stoker, R., & Schloss, P. (1984). Facilitating teacher-conducted research: A tutorial on single-subject design—the multiple baseline. *The Volta Review, 86*(2), 89–101.

multiple baseline design. A multiple baseline across behaviors design examines the impact of the intervention across two or more behaviors by the same individual and under the same environmental conditions. A multiple baseline across individuals design examines the impact of the intervention across two or more individuals while the target behaviors and the environmental conditions remain constant. Finally, a multiple baseline across environmental conditions design examines the impact of the intervention across two or more environmental conditions while the target behavior and the individual remains constant.

IMPLEMENTING A MULTIPLE BASELINE DESIGN

Although investigations that use multiple baseline designs can vary in terms of the interventions, the participants, the behaviors, or the settings, the steps that are addressed when implementing a study using a multiple baseline design are fairly consistent. *Research Notes 7.1* presents the basic steps in designing and implementing a multiple baseline design study. However there are also several unique issues that researchers must take into consideration in designing and implementing such a study.

Independence of the Conditions

As previously discussed, multiple baseline designs are well suited for situations where the same intervention can be implemented across conditions (e.g., behaviors, individuals, environmental contexts). When identifying the conditions, it is important to ensure that they are independent of each other (Cuvo, 1979). If the behaviors, individuals, or environmental contexts are not independent, the researcher runs the risk of having the impact of the intervention generalize to untreated conditions.

For example, consider a situation where the researcher is interested in teaching an individual with disabilities how to order three different food items (e.g., hamburger, French fries, milk) by pointing to pictures on a communication board. In this instance, the researcher might discover that once the student learns how to order a hamburger, his skill generalizes, and he is able to point to pictures to request the other food items (e.g., French fries, milk) that did not receive the intervention. Generalization to untreated conditions can also occur across individuals. For example, consider a situation where a researcher is interested in teaching three students with moderate cognitive delays to raise their hands in order to obtain the attention of the teacher during class. In this instance, the researcher may discover that prompting and reinforcing the hand-raising behavior for one student results in increases in the hand-raising behavior of the other students who observed, but did not receive, the intervention. Finally, generalization to untreated conditions can also occur across environmental contexts (e.g., time, settings). Consider a situation where a researcher is interested in teaching an individual with Attention Deficit Disorder (ADD) to wait in line across three different environmental contexts (e.g., at lunch, at the bus stop, at a movie theater) without knocking into nearby people. In this instance, the researcher may discover that instruction that decreases the behavior in one context (e.g., at lunch) results in decreases in other contexts (e.g., at the bus stop, at a movie theater).

All of these examples of generalization are considered positive outcomes from an educational perspective; however, generalization to untreated conditions is not useful to the researcher's goal of demonstrating a clear relationship between the intervention and the behavior change. Thus, in order to demonstrate experimental control, it is critical for the researcher to identify behaviors, individuals, or environmental contexts that are independent of each other.

Functionally Related Conditions

While it is critical to select conditions that are independent of one another, a primary assumption underlying the principle of the multiple baseline design is that conditions selected by the researcher are similar enough to allow the replication of the intervention effects. Unfortunately, there are no empirically validated strategies to ensure this outcome; the way it is achieved will vary based on the type of conditions to which the intervention is applied. For example, in a multiple baseline design across subjects, the researcher will want to select subjects that have similar learning and behavioral characteristics. This can be accomplished by establishing specific subject selection criteria for including participants in a study. Similarly, in a multiple baseline design across behaviors the researcher needs to select behaviors that are topographically similar to each other and of comparable difficulty. For instance, in examining the effects of an instructional strategy on the acquisition of sight word reading, the researcher would want to select stimulus materials that were similar in terms of reading levels and complexity. This could be established by selecting sight words from a specific grade-level reading list.

Extended Experimental Phases

A final, and very important, issue to consider when implementing a multiple baseline design is that the design necessitates withholding intervention for some conditions for extended periods of time and/or continuously implementing an intervention for extended periods of time. Several authors have suggested that extended baselines create a situation in which the participant's behavior is essentially in extinction (Cuvo, 1979; Horner & Baer, 1978). For example, consider an investigation where the researchers are interested in examining the impact of an intervention package that includes antecedent prompts (e.g., modeling, verbal prompts) as well as consequences (e.g., social praise) on increasing an individual's participation in three different activities (e.g., lunch, math, social studies). Since the provision of social praise is one component of the intervention package, it would be necessary for the researchers to refrain from providing social praise contingent on participation during baseline. Thus, if the participant did happen to participate in one or more of the activities during the baseline phase, this behavior would, in essence, be placed on extinction. Furthermore, in the third (or fourth, or fifth) condition, this extinction is likely to be in place for an extended amount of time. Therefore, in this example, the intervention package under investigation must not only be powerful enough to change the target behavior (e.g., participation), but also powerful enough to reverse the extinction that occurred during baseline.

A different problem occurs when participants are exposed to interventions for long periods of time while waiting for the intervention to be lagged into other conditions. In this case, the participant's performance may begin to decelerate because they have satiated on the intervention. Consider for example a study in which the researcher was examining the impact of an intervention in teaching sight word reading to students with developmental disabilities. The three conditions in the study included three sets of sight words selected from the third-grade Dolch word list. Following the typical design structure, the participant would be exposed to the intervention for the first word set for an extended period while waiting for the remaining conditions to be lagged in. It would not be surprising, or uncommon, for the participants' performance to decrease or become variable because they were bored with repeated presentation of material that they had already mastered. This problem might be avoided by designing the study so that target behavior is acquired rapidly by controlling the difficulty, complexity, and amount of behavior that the participant must learn. In some cases, this may prove difficult and the researcher may have to consider alternate designs that can accommodate these problems.

VARIATIONS IN THE MULTIPLE BASELINE DESIGN

A multiple probe design is a variation of the multiple baseline design that can address the difficulties associated with extended baseline and intervention phases (Horner & Baer, 1978, Murphy & Bryan, 1980). As previously discussed, when implementing a multiple baseline design study, the researcher collects data simultaneously across all conditions. This means that the researcher will collect a great deal of baseline data for condition 2 and even more baseline data for condition 3 prior to intervention. This also means that the researcher will collect a great deal of data demonstrating effectiveness of the intervention for condition 1 (while collecting baseline and intervention data for conditions 2 and 3). In addition to the issues previously discussed, these extended data collection phases can be problematic in applied settings and may take more time than is warranted.

Unlike data in a multiple baseline design, in a multiple probe design data are not continuously collected across all conditions. Instead, probe data are collected intermittently to document performance during the baseline and intervention phases and to allow the researcher to contrast performance across conditions. The key features of multiple probe designs are presented in Table 7.3. These designs are particularly well suited for situations where the researcher can make an assumption of baseline stability, including when (a) baseline levels are low, (b) there is no opportunity for the target behavior to occur

Table 7.3   Key Features of Multiple Probe Designs.

Multiple Probe Designs	
Purpose	Verify a functional relationship between a behavior and an intervention through the replication of effects across different conditions (e.g., behaviors, people, or contexts).
General Characteristics	Baseline data are collected simultaneously across three conditions and the intervention is systematically introduced in each condition after stable performance has been established.
Design Strengths	Does not require the intervention to be withheld or reversed and therefore is appropriate for establishing new behaviors.
	Allows for the documentation of experimental control across a variety of conditions.
	Does not require continuous measurement and therefore avoids the problems associated with extended experimental phases.
Design Weaknesses	Intermittent probes may not provide sufficient data to document experimental control.
	Intermittent probes may increase the problems associated with observer reactivity.
	Does not allow immediate intervention on potentially harmful behaviors.

without intervention, or (c) the dependent measures typically would only improve contingent upon training (Cuvo, 1979; Horner & Baer, 1978).

Figure 7.2 illustrates a common structure for the multiple probe design. Initially, the researcher conducts a baseline probe across all three conditions. Baseline probes continue with condition 1 until a stable pattern of performance is established. However, no additional baseline probes are conducted on condition 2 or 3. The intervention is then introduced in condition 1 and the researcher conducts another baseline probe in conditions 2 and 3. The researcher continues to regularly probe (but with less frequency) the participant's performance in the intervention phase in condition 1 in order to determine if the participant's performance maintains across time. Baseline probes continue with condition 2 until a stable pattern of performance is established but no additional probes are conducted in condition 3. At this point, the intervention is introduced into the second condition and the researcher conducts a baseline probe in condition 3 and intervention probes are continued in condition 1. This pattern is followed until the intervention has been introduced in all conditions. It is recommended that the researcher conduct a minimum of three baseline probes prior to the introduction of the intervention in a condition in order to establish a stable pattern of baseline performance. This increases the likelihood that the researcher will be able to document a functional relationship

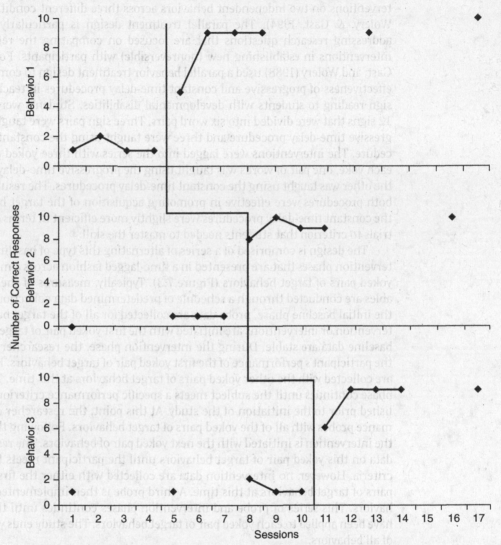

Figure 7.2 Model of the basic characteristics of a multiple probe design

Source: Halle, J. W., Stocker, R. G., & Schloss, P. J. (1984), Facilitating teacher-conducted research: A tutorial on single subject design—the multiple baseline. *The Volta Review*, vol. 86(2), p. 97. Reprinted with permission from the Alexander Graham Bell Association for the Deaf and Hard of Hearing (www.agbell.org).

between the intervention and the change in the participant's behavior. It is also important that probes are conducted concurrently across all three tiers prior to the introduction of the intervention in each condition. This will allow the researcher to contrast the participant's performance across the conditions under study.

Another variation of the multiple probe design is referred to as the parallel treatment design (Gast & Wolery, 1988). This design is conceptualized as two concurrent parallel multiple probe designs and it is structured to examine the effectiveness of one or more interventions on two independent behaviors across three different conditions (Holcombe, Wolery, & Gast, 1994). The parallel treatment design is particularly well suited for addressing research questions that are focused on comparing the relative efficacy of interventions in establishing new (nonreversible) with participants. For example, Ault, Gast, and Wolery (1988) used a parallel behavior treatment design to compare the relative effectiveness of progressive and constant time-delay procedures in teaching community sign reading to students with developmental disabilities. Students were taught to read 12 signs that were divided into six word pairs. Three sign pairs were taught using the progressive time-delay procedure and three were taught using the constant-time delay procedure. The interventions were lagged into the series with three yoked pairs of signs. In each yoke, one pair of words was taught using the progressive time-delay procedures and the other was taught using the constant time-delay procedures. The results indicated that both procedures were effective in promoting acquisition of the target behavior but that the constant time-delay procedures were slightly more efficient in terms of the number of trials to criterion that students needed to master the skill.

The design is comprised of a series of alternating this type of baseline probe with intervention phases that are presented in a time-lagged fashion across a minimum of three yoked pairs of target behaviors (Figure 7.3). Typically, measures of the dependent variables are conducted through a schedule of predetermined data collection probes. During the initial baseline phase, probe data are collected for all of the target behaviors. The intervention or interventions are initiated with the first yoked pair of target behaviors once baseline data are stable. During the intervention phase, the researcher collects data on the participant's performance of the first yoked pair of target behaviors. However, no data are collected with the other yoked pairs of target behaviors at this time. The intervention phase continues until the subject meets a specific performance criterion that was established prior to the initiation of the study. At this point, the researcher conducts performance probes with all of the yoked pairs of target behaviors. Following the second probe, the intervention is initiated with the next yoked pair of behaviors. The researcher collects data on this yoked pair of target behaviors until the participant meets the pre-specified criteria. However, no intervention data are collected with either the first or third yoked pairs of target behaviors at this time. A third probe is then implemented with all six behaviors. This series of probe and intervention phases continues until the interventions have been applied to each yoked pair of target behaviors. The study ends with a final probe of all behaviors.

Implementing Multiple Probe Designs

The steps in designing and carrying out multiple probe designs are essentially the same as those required for multiple baseline designs. Multiple probe designs are also subject to the same issues that were addressed previously in relation to multiple baseline designs. However, multiple probe designs also have two unique problems that researchers must address.

Figure 7.3 Illustration of a parallel treatment design

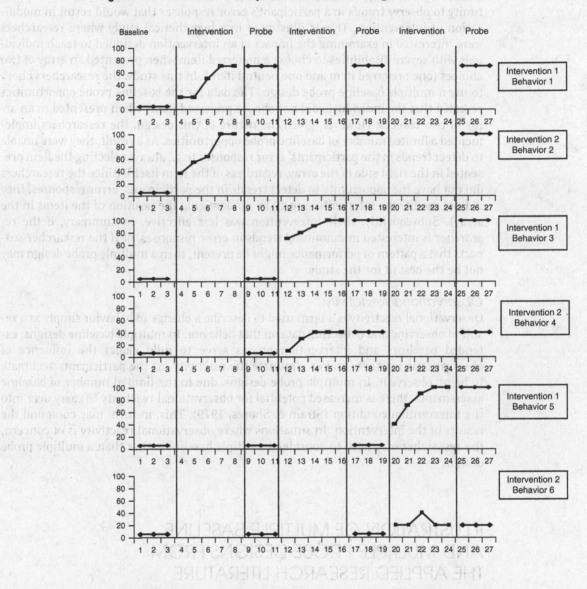

Limited Baseline Data

Although multiple probe designs were developed as a means of decreasing the frequency of baseline data collection, the presence of only limited baseline data may be problematic in that it may not provide the researcher with an opportunity to establish stable patterns of performance during the baseline phase (Strain & Shores, 1979). For example, when using a multiple probe design, the researcher may not have the opportunity to observe trends in a participant's error responses that would result in modification of intervention. This is illustrated in a hypothetical study where researchers were interested in examining the impact of an intervention designed to teach individuals with severe disabilities to choose a preferred item when presented an array of two choices (one preferred item and one neutral item). In this study, the researchers chose to use a multiple baseline probe design. The data for the baseline probe opportunities revealed that the individuals did not choose preferred items when presented in an array of two choices. However, given the nature of this design, the researchers implemented a limited number of baseline probe opportunities. As a result, they were unable to detect trends in the participants' error responses (e.g., always selecting the item presented in the right side of the array, regardless of the item itself). Since the researchers did not have the opportunity to detect trends in the participants' error responses, they did not modify the intervention (e.g., by randomizing the position of the items in the array). Subsequently, their intervention was less effective. In summary, if the researcher is interested in examining trends in error responses, or if the researcher suspects that a pattern of performance might be present, then a multiple probe design may not be the best fit for the study.

Observational Reactivity

Observational reactivity is a term used to describe a change in behavior simply as a result of observing and collecting data on that behavior. In multiple baseline designs, extended baselines and intervention phases serve to fully depict the influence of observational reactivity and/or eliminate the reactivity (as the participants acclimate to being observed). In multiple probe designs, due to the limited number of baseline assessments, there is increased potential for observational reactivity to carry over into the intervention condition (Strain & Shores, 1979). This, in turn, may confound the results of the intervention. In situations where observational reactivity is of concern, the researcher may need to consider a multiple baseline rather than a multiple probe design.

ILLUSTRATION OF MULTIPLE BASELINE AND MULTIPLE PROBE DESIGNS FROM THE APPLIED RESEARCH LITERATURE

Multiple Baseline Design

A study conducted by Vaughn et al. (1997) illustrates the use of a multiple baseline design. In this study, the investigators conducted functional assessments and assessment-based interventions with Andrew, an 8-year-old boy with severe disabilities who engaged in challenging behaviors (aggression, property destruction, whining,

Figure 7.4   Illustration of a multiple baseline design

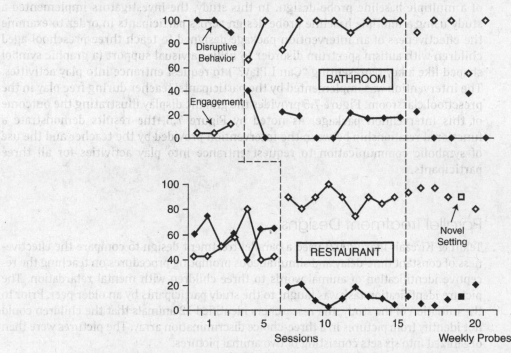

Source: Vaughn, B., Clarke, S., & Dunlap, G. (1997). Assessment-based intervention for severe behavior problems in a natural family context. *Journal of Applied Behavior Analysis*, vol. 30(4), p. 715. Reprinted with permission.

collapsing on the floor, attempting to run away). After developing hypotheses regarding the function of Andrew's challenging behaviors, the investigators implemented a study using a multiple baseline design across environmental contexts in order to examine the effectiveness of an intervention package which consisted of supplementary rewards and visual schedules. The intervention was implemented by Andrew's mother during bathroom and restaurant routines. Figure 7.4 provides the graphic display illustrating the outcome of this intervention package across each environmental context (e.g., bathroom and restaurant routines). As noted by Figure 7.4, the results reveal a functional relationship between the intervention package and the percentage of intervals when challenging behaviors occurred. The results also reveal a functional relationship between the intervention package and the percentage of intervals in which Andrew was engaged in the routine (e.g., following the natural sequence of the routine).

Multiple Probe Design

A study conducted by Johnston, Nelson, Evans, and Palazolo (2003) illustrates the use of a multiple baseline probe design. In this study, the investigators implemented a study using a multiple baseline probe design across participants in order to examine the effectiveness of an intervention package designed to teach three preschool-aged children with autism spectrum disorder to utilize a visual support (a graphic symbol shaped like a key representing "Can I Play?") to request entrance into play activities. The intervention was implemented by the participants' teacher during free play in the preschool classroom. Figure 7.5 provides the graphic display illustrating the outcome of this intervention package. As noted by Figure 7.5, the results demonstrate a functional relationship between the intervention provided by the teacher and the use of symbolic communication to request entrance into play activities for all three participants.

Parallel Treatment Designs

Tekin & Kircaali-Iftar (2002) used a parallel treatment design to compare the effectiveness of constant time-delay and simultaneous prompting procedures on teaching the receptive identification of animal words to three children with mental retardation. The picture identification task was taught to the study participants by an older peer. Prior to the initiation of the study, the researchers identified 12 animals that the children could not identify from pictures in a three-choice discrimination array. The pictures were then organized into six sets consisting of two animal pictures.

The siblings taught three of the animal sets using a four second constant time-delay procedure and three of the animal sets using simultaneous prompting procedures. Instruction under both conditions was carried out in a one-to-one instruction format. All instructional procedures were held constant except for the type of response prompting procedure used by the siblings.

The primary dependent variable included the percentage of animals correctly identified by the children during probe sessions. In addition, the researchers collected several measures of efficiency, including the number of sessions to criterion, the number of trials to criterion, the number of errors made by subjects, and the total amount of time required for subjects to meet criterion. Finally, the researchers also conducted pre-post generalization probes on nontrained animal pictures and maintenance probes at one, four, and five weeks after the child met criterion.

Figure 7.6 presents an illustrative graph for one of the study participants. Based on their analysis of the data, the researchers concluded that siblings could be taught to reliably implement both of the response prompting strategies, that both strategies led to the acquisition of the identification task but that simultaneous prompting produced fewer errors during instruction, and that the constant time-delay procedure resulted in better generalization to nontrained stimuli.

Figure 7.5 Illustration of a multiple probe design

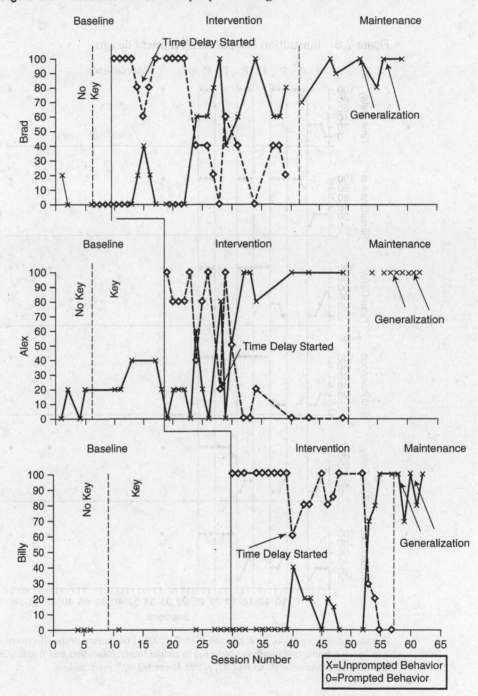

Source: Johnston, S., Nelson, C., Evans, J., & et al (2003). The Use of Visual Supports in Teaching Young Children with Autism Spectrum Disorders to Initiate Interactions. *Augmentative and Alternative Communication,* vol. 19(2), pp. 86–103. Reprinted with permission.

Figure 7.6 Illustration of a parallel treatment design

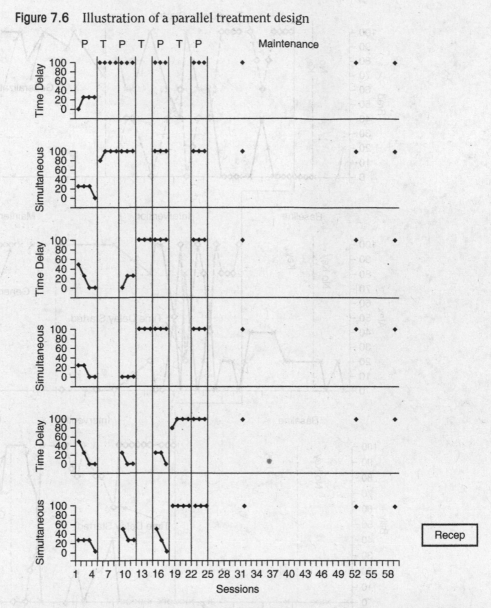

Source: Figure from Tekin, E., & Kircaali-Iftar, G. (2002). Comparison of the effectiveness and efficiency of two response prompting prcedures delivered by sibling tutors, *Education and Training in Mental Retardation and Developmental Disabilities*, vol. 37, p. 292. Reprinted with permission.

SUMMARY

Multiple baseline, multiple probe, and parallel treatment designs involve the sequential introduction of intervention across conditions (e.g., behaviors, individuals, or environmental conditions). The effectiveness of an intervention is demonstrated when the dependent measures only change contingent upon the introduction of the intervention. This chapter has provided information regarding the characteristics and steps for implementing multiple baseline and multiple probe designs. Furthermore, this chapter has provided examples from the literature and has discussed frequently encountered issues and strategies for interpreting outcomes of multiple baseline and multiple probe design studies. The next chapter will discuss yet another strategy for evaluating the effects of intervention, the changing criterion design.

REFERENCES

Alberto, P. A., & Troutman, A. (1995). *Applied behavior analysis for teacher* (4th ed.). Englewood Cliffs, NJ: Merrill.

Ault, M. J., Gast, D. L., & Wolery, M. (1988). Comparison of progressive and constant time-delay procedures in teaching community-sign word reading. *American Journal on Mental Retardation, 93,* 44–56.

Barlow, C. H., & Hersen, M. (1984). *Single case experimental design: Strategies for studying behavior change* (2nd ed.). Tarrytown, NJ: Pergamon Press.

Bloom, M., & Fischer, J. (1982). *Evaluating practice: Guidelines for the accountable professional.* Englewood Cliffs, NJ: Prentice Hall.

Cuvo, A. (1979). Multiple-baseline design in instructional research: Pitfalls of measurement and procedural advantages. *American Journal of Mental Deficiency, 84*(3), 219–228.

Datillo, J., Gast, D., Lowy, D., & Malley, S. (2000). Use of single-subject research designs in therapeutic recreation. *Therapeutic Recreation Journal, 34*(3), 253–270.

Drew, C., & Hardman, M. (1985). *Designing and conducting behavioral research.* Boston, MA: Allyn & Bacon.

Gast, D. L., & Wolery, M. (1988). Parallel treatment design: A nested single subject design for comparing instructional procedures. *Education and Treatment of Children, 11,* 270–285.

Halle, J., Stoker, R., & Schloss, P. (1984). Facilitating teacher-conducted research: A tutorial on single-subject design – the multiple baseline. *The Volta Review, 86*(2), 89–101.

Hersen, M., & Barlow, D. H. (1976). *Single case experimental designs: Strategies for studying behavior change.* New York, NY: Pergamon Press.

Holcombe, A., Wolery, M., & Gast, D. L. (1994). Comparative single-subject research: Descriptions of designs and discussion of problems. *Topics in Early Childhood Education, 14,* 119–145.

Horner, R., & Baer, D. (1978). Multiple-probe technique: A variation of the multiple baseline. *Journal of Applied Behavior Analysis, 11*(1), 189–196.

Horner, R. H., Carr, E. G., Halle, J., McGee, G., Odom, S., & Wolery, M. (2005). The use of single-subject research to identify evidence-based practice in special education. *Exceptional Children, 71,* 165–179.

Johnston, S., Nelson, C., Evans, J., & Palazolo, K. (2003). The use of visual supports in teaching young children with autism spectrum disorders to initiate interactions. *Augmentative and Alternative Communication, 19*(2), 86–103.

Johnston, S., McDonnell, A., Nelson, C., & Magnavito, A. (2003). Implementing augmentative and alternative communication intervention in inclusive preschool settings. *Journal of Early Intervention, 25*(4), 263–280.

Kazdin, A., & Kopel, S. (1975). On resolving ambiguities of the multiple-baseline design: Problems and recommendations. *Behavior Therapy, 6,* 601–608.

Kazdin, A. (1982). *Single-case research designs: Methods for clinical and applied settings.* New York, NY: Oxford University Press.

Kratochwill, T. (1978). *Single subject research: Strategies for evaluating change.* New York, NY: Academic Press.

Martella, R., Nelson, R., & Marchand-Martella, N. (1999). *Research methods: Learning to become a critical research consumer.* Boston, MA: Allyn & Bacon.

Murphy, R., & Bryan, A. (1980). Multiple-baseline and multiple-probe designs: Practical alternatives for special education assessment and evaluation. *The Journal of Special Education, 14*(3), 325–335.

Rubin, A., & Babbie, E. (1993). *Research methods for social work* (2nd ed.). Monterey, CA: Brooks/Cole.

Strain, P., & Shores, R. (1979). Additional comments on multiple-baseline designs in instructional research. *American Journal of Mental Deficiency, 84*(3), 229–234.

Tawney, J., & Gast, D. (1983). *Single subject research in special education.* Columbus, OH: Merrill.

Tekin, E., & Kircaali-Iftar, G. (2002). Comparison of the effectiveness and efficiency of two response prompting procedures delivered by sibling tutors. *Education and Training in Mental Retardation and Developmental Disabilities, 37,* 283–299.

Vaughn, B., Clarke, S., & Dunlap, G. (1997). Assessment-based intervention for severe behavior problems in a natural family context. *Journal of Applied Behavior Analysis, 30*(4), 713–716.

Changing Criterion Designs

8

Felix F. Billingsley, *University of Washington*

The changing criterion design is a unique variation of the A-B-A design that can be used to examine the impact of an intervention that is applied in graduated steps to a target behavior (Hall & Fox, 1977; Hartmann & Hall, 1976). It is useful in situations in which expectations of immediate changes in the target behavior are unrealistic and in situations that will require the study of participant's behavior to be shaped to a desired level of performance. Although the changing criterion design has not been widely reported in the research literature it has many potential applications in educational or community service programs (e.g., increasing oral reading rates, decreasing time spent watching television).

For example, consider the case of Leon, a high school student who, unfortunately, is quite overweight; therefore, as part of his physical education class, he is involved in a speed walking program. Leon, however, is less than a speed walker; in fact, he moves at a snail's pace regardless of the encouragement that he receives from his peers and the coach. The coach decides that he needs to be more systematic in his program and that he should build Leon's speed in small increments, starting with a relatively slow walking speed and moving through several steps in which speed is steadily increased. He fits Leon with a pedometer and begins collecting baseline data on his steps per minute. After about six days, when the baseline data are relatively stable, the coach sets a steps-per-minute criterion for Leon that is 15% above his average baseline speed. He picked that criterion based on his professional judgment regarding what he felt Leon could likely achieve in a first effort. He then implements the intervention with subphase 1 in which he tells Leon that, whenever the criterion is met, he can have 10 minutes to engage in one of his highly preferred activities, hitting the punching bag. Leon fails to meet the criterion on the first day of the intervention, but meets it on the following three days. Next, the coach introduces subphase 2, in which he increases the criterion by 15% of the average of Leon's speed in subphase 1. When Leon has met that criterion for three consecutive days, the criterion is once again increased for subphase 3. This procedure is continued through a total of six subphases where Leon's criterion speed during subphase 6 is the walking speed goal that the coach had in mind when he initially developed the program for Leon.

We see that the coach wanted to change Leon's performance by gradually shaping a behavior (steps per minute) toward an ultimate walking speed aim. This is exactly the kind of situation in which an investigator might wish to use the changing criterion design: where participants have the behavior at some level in their repertoire and where the intent is to increase or decrease the behavior in incremental steps in successive approximations to the desired terminal level by using the presentation of contingencies. In fact, it was the use of such methods in educational programs for students with disabilities that stimulated early statements of the rationale for, and the requirements of, the changing criterion design as a tool for applied research (e.g., Hall & Fox, 1977; Hartmann & Hall, 1976). Those early statements described applications of the design to investigate techniques related to improving mathematics performance, decreasing cigarette smoking, and increasing the number of workbook pages completed. Prior to and since the work of Hall and Fox (1977) and Hartmann and Hall (1976), the design has been used to examine functional relationships between interventions and behavior in a wide variety of areas. Some of those areas include, for example, self-monitoring (Martella, Leonard, Marchand-Martella, & Agran, 1993), self-feeding (Luiselli, 2000), undesired classroom behaviors (Deitz & Repp, 1973), vocational performance (Davis, Bates, & Cuvo, 1983), exercise (Fitterling, Martin, Gramling, Cole, & Milan, 1988), safety (Bigelow, Huynen, & Lutzker, 1993) and addictive behaviors (e.g., caffeinism: Foxx & Rubinoff, 1979; smoking: Friedman & Axelrod, 1973). This chapter will describe the characteristics, design, implementation steps, and design variations of the changing criterion design and will also provide illustrations of how it has been used in applied research.

CHARACTERISTICS OF CHANGING CRITERION DESIGNS

The logic underlying the changing criterion design is that the target behavior changes in the desired direction each time the criterion changes. Experimental control is demonstrated through the replication of these changes across time. The basic structure of the changing criterion design consists of baseline and intervention phases. However, the intervention phase is further divided into a series of subphases that reflect the stepwise increase or decrease in the performance criterion for the study participant. The key features of the changing criterion are outlined in Table 8.1 and an illustration of the design structure is presented in Figure 8.1.

Note that the design bears a relationship to some other designs we have previously considered. It could be conceptualized as a series of A-B designs in which each subphase acts as "B" for the condition it follows and as an "A" for the condition it precedes. Similarities to the multiple baseline design have also been identified, in that "changes in the criterion function like the sequential changes in the behavior, situation, or person to

Table 8.1 Features of Changing Criterion Designs.

	Changing Criterion Designs
Purpose	Document a functional relationship between stepwise changes in a performance criterion and the target behavior.
General Characteristics	The design consists of baseline and intervention phases. The intervention phase is further divided into subphases that correspond to changes in the performance criteria established for the study participant.
Design Strengths	Appropriate for target behaviors in which immediate and dramatic changes are unrealistic and must be shaped across time.
	Requires only one target behavior.
	Does not require a withdrawal or reversal of the intervention.
Design Weaknesses	Limited to interventions that manipulate the consequences for the target behavior.
	Establishing criterion levels is often subjective and not data driven.

Figure 8.1 Model of a changing criterion design

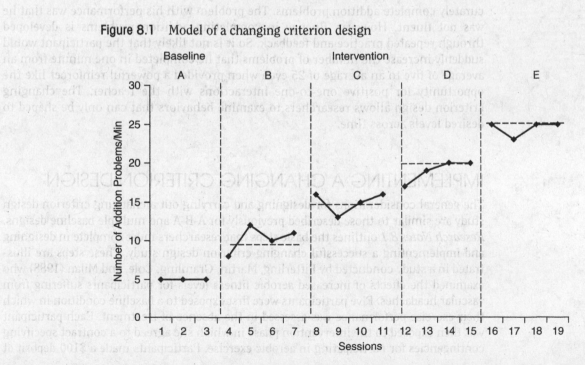

119

which treatment is applied with traditional variants of the multiple baseline design" (Hartmann & Hall, 1976, p. 530). However, the changing criterion design does not require a withdrawal of the intervention to demonstrate experimental control as would be necessary in extending the A-B design to document a functional relationship, nor does it require more than one behavior (or situation, or person) as in the multiple baseline design (Hartmann & Hall, 1976; Kazdin, 1982).

Figure 8.1 shows the sequence of experimental phases for a hypothetical study examining the effects of the participant's social interaction with the participant's teacher as a consequence for increasing fluency in completing addition problems. The desired terminal level of performance for the participant is 25 problems per minute. The researcher begins by collecting baseline data until stable performance of the target behavior is established. The intervention phase is initiated beginning with the first subphase. In this example, the first criterion level was set at 10 problems per minute on two consecutive sessions. Once the participant met this criterion, the researcher increased the criterion to 15 problems per minute on two consecutive sessions. This process would continue until the participant met the terminal performance level of 25 problems per minute. Experimental control is demonstrated through the replication of immediate and stable behavior change with each successive change in the criterion level.

One of the key advantages of the changing criterion design is that it can be used with target behaviors in which significant changes in the target behavior are unrealistic. In the example, the participant had already acquired the skills necessary to accurately complete addition problems. The problem with his performance was that he was not fluent. However, fluency in completing addition problems is developed through repeated practice and feedback. So it is not likely that the participant would suddenly increase the number of problems that he completed in one minute from an average of five to an average of 25 even when provided a powerful reinforcer like the opportunity for positive one-to-one interactions with the teacher. The changing criterion design allows researchers to examine behaviors that can only be shaped to desired levels across time.

IMPLEMENTING A CHANGING CRITERION DESIGN

The general considerations for designing and carrying out a changing criterion design study are similar to those described previously for A-B-A and multiple baseline designs. *Research Notes 8.1* outlines the basic steps that researchers must complete in designing and implementing a successful changing criterion design study. These steps are illustrated in a study conducted by Fitterling, Martin, Gramling, Cole, and Milan (1988) who examined the effects of increased aerobic fitness levels for participants suffering from vascular headaches. Five participants were first exposed to a baseline condition in which their exercise performance was assessed in the absence of treatment. Each participant was then exposed to the intervention phase in which she agreed to a contract specifying contingencies for participating in aerobic exercise. Participants made a $100 deposit at the beginning of training that was refunded in payments of $5.00 on each occasion that they adhered to an exercise criterion. If participants exercised below the criterion, or above it, the refund was forfeited. At the termination of training, if a participant had earned a refund of at least $85.00, she was allowed to keep the pedometer that had been issued to her and was offered alternative headache treatment at no cost. Other components of the program package included instructions, modeling, stimulus control, performance feedback and praise, shaping, and verbal strategies. Exercise criteria were set in terms of "Cooper Points"; a Cooper point "is a standardized measure of the amount of aerobic benefit derived from different exercise topographies, intensities, and durations" (Fitterling et al., 1988, p. 11). Figure 8.2 provides data for one of the participants, Cathy, throughout baseline, the intervention phase consisting of 10 subphases, and follow-up phases at three and six months following the conclusion of intervention.

Although the structure of the changing criterion design is relatively simple there are a number of issues that researchers must take into consideration when designing and implementing it. These include the need to clearly define the behavior and set a terminal performance goal, systematically implementation of the subphases, and thereby ensuring compliance of performance with the criterion.

Defining the Behavior and Setting a Terminal Goal

As in all single case studies, the target behavior must be operationally defined so that it can be accurately measured across the experimental phases. However, a key element of the changing criterion design is that the researcher needs to establish the terminal level of performance prior to the initiation of the study. For example, Fitterling et al. (1988) defined aerobic exercise behavior in terms of Cooper Points achieved on each session. Cooper (1977) suggested a weekly minimum of 24 Points for women in order to achieve and maintain an adequate aerobic fitness level; therefore, a terminal goal of 24 Points per week was established (8 Points for each of three weekly sessions; see tenth subphase, Figure 8.2). The terminal goal specified in this study is of the nature of all goals specified for changing criterion designs; that is, it indicated a desired *degree* or *level* of performance. It did not indicate a behavior that was different topographically from behaviors that preceded it in previous subphases, or that was not initially in the individual's repertoire to some extent (see Cooper, Heron, & Heward, 1987). Hence, goals might be identified in terms of rate, frequency, accuracy, duration, latency, intensity, or magnitude (as in number of Cooper Points).

The specific goal established for any particular behavior will depend on judgments regarding the level of performance that will provide adequate educational, social, health, or other benefits to the individual and/or to others in the school or community.

Figure 8.2 Changing criterion design showing aerobic exercise in Cooper Points for Cathy during baseline, aerobic training, and 3- and 6-month follow-ups. Points connected by solid lines indicate her aerobic exercise performance and the heights of shaded areas indicate the exercise performance criterion levels

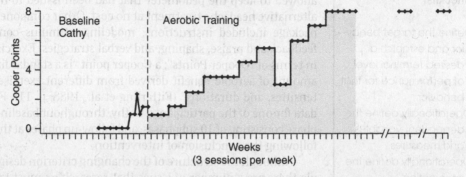

Source: Figure 1 from Fitterling, Martin, Gramling, Cole & Milan, Behavioral management of exercise training in vascular headache patients: An examination of exercise adherence and headache activity, JABA, 1988, vol. 21, p. 14. Reprinted with permission.

Therefore, to assist in setting a goal for academic or social performance in educational programs, some questions that one might ask are: (a) what level of performance is required to help the student move to the next step in the curriculum; (b) what level is likely to promote generalization and maintenance of performance; (c) what level will be acceptable to others in school and community settings; (d) what level will reduce disruptions in the classroom learning environment; (e) what level do "successful" peers achieve; (f) what level will reduce a burden on caregivers; (g) what level might be necessary to make further participation in similar activities interesting to, or fun for, the student; and (h) what level might increase positive interactions with peers and other members of the school and community?

Systematic Implementation of the Subphases

Experimental control is demonstrated in changing criterion designs through the replication of changes in the target behavior as each successive criterion level or subphase is introduced in the design sequence. In the Fitterling et al. (1988) study, the criterion for Cathy for the first intervention subphase was set at 1 Cooper Point and, thereafter, was increased by 0.5 to 1 Cooper Point until the goal of 24 Points per week was achieved in the tenth subphase. One exception to this process may be noted, however; in the seventh subphase, Cathy was given a less intense exercise criterion (3 Points per session) than in the previous week (6 Points per session). Her data, therefore, reflect *bidirectional* changes. In addition, although most of her subphases were only 1 week (3 sessions) long, others (the fourth and tenth subphases) were twice as long. Some questions related to what we observe in Cathy's graph might include: (a) what guidelines exist for the size of changes in criterion levels; (b) how long should subphases last and why would some be longer than others; (c) how many subphases should be included in the intervention phase, and (d) what is the purpose of using bidirectional criterion changes? These questions highlight some of the critical issues that researchers must address in designing the changing criterion design.

Size of Changes

The size of criterion changes has been determined through a variety of methods. In Fitterling et al. (1988), no indication was provided regarding the manner by which the magnitude of the steps was determined, but the investigators' comments seem to suggest that it was based on the "exercise tolerance" (p. 12) of the participants. In other words, step size was apparently determined by clinical judgment. Although professional or clinical judgment should not be abandoned (in fact, this may be the only method available if the baseline level is zero [Alberto & Troutman, 2003]), other methods have been suggested. Kazdin (1982), for example, indicated that an initial criterion level might be set at the level of the lowest or near lowest baseline data point, or at a level 10% or 15% below the mean of the baseline. For subsequent steps, Kazdin suggested two general guidelines.

First, the criterion should be changed gradually to maximize the probability that the individual can successfully attain the criterion. Kazdin (1982) notes that, "Abrupt and large shifts in the criterion may mean that relatively stringent performance demands are placed on the client" (p. 167). If those demands are too stringent, the individual may fail to access the consequences specified by the program and, as a result, performance may worsen rather than improve and stabilize at criterion levels. Worsening would, of course, certainly be an undesirable outcome from an educational, as well as from an experimental, perspective. On the other side of the coin, very large changes might result in the individual reaching the terminal goal in so few phases that experimental control is questionable (Cooper et al., 1987; Richards, Taylor, Ramasamy, & Richards, 1999).

Second, although the criterion should be changed at a modest level to maximize success, changes must be large enough so that the correspondence of changes in the criterion and performance can be observed over the course of the intervention phase. It has been repeatedly noted in the literature that the degree of day-to-day variability in the target behavior will influence the size of criterion changes. Where the data are relatively stable, as in each of the subphases of Figure 8.2, small changes in behavior will be discernable and criterion changes could, if desired, be relatively small. However, as data increase in variability, larger criterion changes will be necessary (as well as longer subphases) in order for changes in the target behavior to be identified.

Additional guidelines for determining the magnitude of criterion changes include:

1. Set the initial criterion at the mean of the stable portion of the baseline data and then increase it by that amount in subsequent subphases (Alberto & Troutman, 2003). Using this method, the first criterion level for a student who averaged two correct answers to reading comprehension questions during baseline would be two. The criterion level for each subsequent subphase would then be increased by two until the goal was attained.

2. If using the mean of the baseline data rendered the task too difficult for the student during the first subphase, then the changes in the criterion could be increased by half the baseline mean. On the other hand, if the student performed higher than the criterion during the first subphase, the following subphases could be set at twice the mean of the baseline (Alberto & Troutman, 2003).

As indicated by guideline 2 above, criterion changes are not required to be in equal steps throughout the intervention phase (Kazdin, 1982). "In the beginning, smaller changes in the criteria may be needed to maximize opportunities for the client's success in earning the consequence. As progress is made, the client may be able to make larger steps in reducing or increasing the behavior" (Kazdin, 1982, p. 168). In fact, Cooper et al. (1987) have suggested that varying the sizes of criterion changes provides a more convincing demonstration of experimental control than if all changes are of the same magnitude. Constant shifts in the magnitude of changes where the participant's performance fails to meet criterion levels, however, may produce serious questions regarding experimental control (Kazdin, 1982).

Length of Subphases

As in the case of the magnitude of criterion changes, subphase length will also be determined, at least in part, by the degree of variability in performance. Stability is required after performance changes occur and before the next change in criterion is introduced in order to establish a functional relationship. Therefore, "each treatment phase must be long enough to allow the rate of the target behavior to restabilize at a new and changed rate" (Hartmann & Hall, 1976). It is preferable that changes in behavior are immediate, and that performance remains stable at the criterion level as long as that level is maintained (Cooper et al., 1987). In Figure 8.2, we see that Cathy's data in each subphase are quite stable, with close correspondence to the specified criterion, and that changes in her exercise behavior occurred rapidly when criteria were modified. Therefore, subphases for Cathy could be relatively brief, usually only three sessions in length. Where changes occur relatively slowly, longer phases are required in order to allow behaviors to stabilize at the criterion level.

Although most subphases for Cathy were only three sessions long, some (subphases 4 and 10) were twice as long (Figure 8.2). The increased length in this case, however, was not due to the fact that performance changes occurred slowly; obviously, they occurred quite rapidly. Where behaviors match criterion levels quickly, researchers may vary the length of some subphases in order to strengthen internal validity. Cooper et al. (1987) maintained that, "When the target behavior closely follows successively more demanding criteria that are held in place for varied periods of time, the likelihood is reduced that the observed changes in behavior are a function of some factor other than the independent variable (e.g., maturation, practice effects)" (p. 220). Hartmann and Hall (1976) suggested that, if treatment subphases do not differ in length, then the baseline phase should be longer than each subphase. This difference in length between the baseline phase and intervention subphases is, once again, to ensure that changes in performance are a function of the treatment variable and not some other variable that occurs naturally at the same time as criterion changes.

Figure 8.3 Work production rate for worker with profound mental retardation

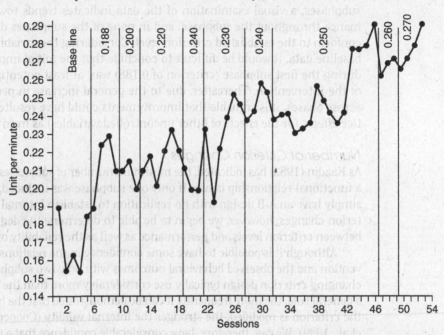

Source: Renzaglia, A., Wehman, P., Schutz, R., & Karan, O. (1978). Use of cue redundancy and positive reinforcement to accelerate production in two profoundly retarded workers. *The British Journal of Social & Clinical Psychology*, vol. 17, pp. 183–187. Reprinted with permission from the British Journal of Clinical & Social Psychology, © The British Psychological Society.

Where performance does not stabilize following criterion changes, then increased phase length is necessary to ascertain that the data are simply "bouncing" around the criterion level and are not reflecting some improving or worsening trend. Where increasing subphase length does not reveal relative stability in the data, internal validity is seriously compromised. Figure 8.3 (Renzaglia, Wehman, Schultz, & Karan, 1978) provides an example in which data were highly variable and where stability at, or near, the criterion level was never obtained. Further, improving trends tended to permeate many of the subphases. Figure 8.3 data indicate the production rate of a worker with substantial cognitive challenges in response to a contingency system in which pennies that could be exchanged for back-up reinforcers were made available for improvements in performance. Following baseline, according to Renzaglia et al. (1978), "target criterion rates were initially increased by 0.02 tasks per minute for the first three changes. The remaining target criterion rates were increased in increments of 0.01 tasks per minute. These target criterions had to be met across three consecutive days before the required rates were increased" (p. 185). The size of criterion changes was modified from 0.02 to 0.01 tasks per minute due to the fact that the worker's performance dropped markedly in the subphase requiring 0.24 tasks per minute and it was noted thereafter that consistent improvements in performance were observed. Unfortunately, in seven out of the nine subphases, a visual examination of the data indicates trends toward improved performance throughout the subphase, and in none of the subphases did the data set closely conform to the established criterion level. Considering the variability that existed in the baseline data, it would be difficult to conclude that the initial improvement in behavior during the first subphase (criterion of 0.188) was, at least potentially, due to the effects of the intervention. Thereafter, due to the general increase in performance within and across phases, it is arguable that improvements could have resulted as much from practice effects (or the effects of other uncontrolled variables) as from intervention effects.

Number of Criterion Changes
As Kazdin (1982) has indicated, the minimum number of subphases necessary to establish a functional relationship is two. If only one subphase was included, the researcher would simply have an A-B design with no replication to establish internal validity. With two criterion changes, however, we begin to be able to determine the degree of correspondence between criterion levels and performance as well as the reliability of that correspondence.

Although it is possible to have some confidence in the relationship between the intervention and the observed behavioral outcomes with only two subphases, studies using the changing criterion design typically use considerably more than the minimum number. As a general rule, the more frequently it can be demonstrated that the behavior changes when the criterion is modified, the stronger the internal validity (Cooper et al., 1987; Richards et al., 1999). We can, therefore, have considerable confidence that a functional relationship exists between the intervention and Cathy's exercise performance (Figure 8.2). Not only does her behavior closely correspond to the established criterion levels but also correspondence is demonstrated across a series of 10 intervention subphases.

Cooper et al. (1987) have pointed out, however, that it would typically be impossible to "simply add any desired number of subphases to the design" (p. 221) since the number of subphases is interrelated with both phase length and the magnitude of criterion changes (Hartmann & Hall, 1976). If, for example, only a relatively short period of time is available during which to conduct an investigation, long subphase length could reduce the number of possible criterion shifts to a number that weakens confidence in the presence of a functional relationship. Similarly, larger criterion changes reduce the number of subphases that can be introduced before the participant achieves the terminal goal.

Correspondence of Performance with Response Criterion
The final consideration in implementing research using the changing criterion design involves assessing correspondence between the performance of participants and the response criterion associated with each subphase. Kazdin (1982) has contended, "The strength of the demonstration depends on showing a close correspondence between the criterion and behavior over the course of the intervention phase" (p. 160). Figure 8.2 data for Cathy show an exact match between her behavior and the criterion for each subphase of the intervention. This, then, is a demonstration of a very strong relationship. In many cases, however, the correspondence is not as perfect and there are no widely accepted standards by which

an acceptable degree of correspondence may be judged; however, investigators sometimes articulate their own standards. Fitterling et al. (1988), for example, considered a consistent correspondence to have occurred "when at least the last three data points did not vary more than 20% from the criterion and visual inspection of the data indicated no trend" (p. 14).

Where performance does not closely match criterion levels, Kazdin (1982) has observed that authors may suggest the existence of a functional relationship because: (a) the mean levels of performance change in a stepwise fashion when changes in the criterion level occur, even though performance does not conform to the criterion levels, or (b) "performance fell at or near the criterion in each subphase on all or most of the occasions" (p. 161). In other words, an adequate demonstration of experimental control is considered achieved when it is obvious that changes in performance are associated with changes in criterion levels, even in the absence of an exact performance-criterion match. Nonetheless, deviation from criterion levels produces ambiguities in interpretation (Barlow & Hersen, 1984; Kazdin, 1982) and, in general, the greater that deviation, the greater will be the ambiguity.

It has been suggested that one way to reduce the ambiguities that may arise from a lack of close correspondence between performance and criterion levels, or where stability has not been clearly achieved in successive subphases, is to introduce "bidirectional" rather than simply "unidirectional" changes in the criterion (Barlow & Hersen, 1984; Kazdin, 1982; Richards et al., 1999). Bidirectional changes are those in which criterion levels are changed in both more and less stringent directions. Changes in direction of performance (e.g., increasing performance following decreasing performance) may be easier to achieve than an exact correspondence between criterion levels and performance and, therefore, permit a more confident evaluation of experimental control (Kazdin, 1982) than would otherwise be possible.

As in the case of including both longer and shorter subphases within the intervention phase, bidirectional changes also strengthen internal validity by further reducing the potential confounding effect of variables such as history, maturation, or measurement factors (Hartmann & Hall, 1976). Criterion changes in Figure 8.2 are of a bidirectional nature. Cathy's exercise behavior changed in correspondence with steadily increasing shifts in the criterion for six subphases, at which point she was exposed to a less stringent criterion. Her behavior also followed that shift closely and then improved immediately when the criterion level was increased once again. It is clear that her performance was under the control of the contingency arrangement.

Bidirectional changes in the response criterion amount to a form of reversal, similar to the reversal phases that are found in some ABA-type designs. The reversals in the changing criterion design, however, are reversals in the direction of the criterion change and do not typically involve total elimination of treatment with the intent that the learner's performance should revert to near-baseline levels. (However, total withdrawals of treatment are sometimes used; [e.g., DeLuca & Holborn, 1992]). It is much more common that the treatment remains in place and that the criterion level is simply changed to a former one that is less stringent. For Cathy (Figure 8.2), that meant a change in the criterion from six to three Cooper Points. An advantage of these "mini reversals" is that they require neither a cessation of the treatment that produced improvement nor a dramatic reduction in improved performance. In other words, the learner can continue to receive the intervention, albeit with a less stringent criterion, and respond at a level that constitutes improvement relative to baseline. Further, the "mini-reversals" are typically brief, and the participant is quickly returned to a more stringent criterion.

In seeking to ensure correspondence between performance and changes in criterion levels, it is critical that the participant's freedom to respond is not limited by the experimental arrangement (Cooper et al., 1987). That is, the experiment must be arranged in such a way that any ceiling or floor on the participant's ability to respond considerably exceeds the criterion currently in place. By way of example, during the first subphase of an investigation in which the intent was to teach a previously non-ambulatory student to increase the distance she walked independently, a table with some preferred items on it might be placed 3 feet in front of the student. When the student walked that distance, she would gain access to the items for a given amount of time. In the next subphase, the table might be placed 6 feet in front of her, then, in the next, 9 feet, and so forth. In this case, it could be found that the student's performance matched the specified criterion levels exactly. Even so, it could not be concluded that experimental control had been demonstrated because the position of the table had imposed a ceiling (i.e., it limited her ability to walk further than the criterion distance). The student was not free to demonstrate the nature of the progress she might have made had the table not blocked her way and artificially constrained her to conform to the criterion level.

Another example would be giving a student a worksheet containing five math problems when the criterion level for reinforcement is five (Cooper et al., 1987). As Cooper et al. (1987) noted, "Although the student could complete fewer than five problems, the possibility of exceeding the criterion has been eliminated, resulting in an impressive-looking graph, perhaps, but one that is badly affected by poor experimental procedure" (p. 221). The observation that the student must have the freedom to respond above and below criterion levels suggests one of the limitations of the changing criterion design. That is, not only is the design inappropriate for the study of antecedent instructional conditions that might dictate performance levels, it is also typically inappropriate for investigations in which the positive or negative consequences being examined are administered (or withdrawn) immediately following the achievement of criterion levels. This is because administration or withdrawal immediately following criterion level performance could act to interrupt or terminate responding at that level, thereby acting as a kind of "artificial" ceiling or floor. For this reason, consequences for criterion achievement are often delivered following performance for some period of time, such as a class session. For example, in their study of math performance by a student with behavior disorders, Hall and Hartmann (1976) provided access to recess and the opportunity to play basketball after a 45-minute session in which the student met the established criterion for correctly solving problems. Consequences are also frequently provided following completion of some activity without regard to time. Using that method, Luiselli (2000) instructed parents to provide to a child who chronically refused food "reward time" following lunch and supper meals whenever the child attained the specified criterion level for self-feeding responses during those meals. Similarly, for Cathy (the exerciser whose data are included in Figure 8.2), $5 of the $100 that she had deposited was refunded after she completed her exercise activities on each exercise occasion.

The previous comments are not meant to imply that *all* consequences need to be delayed until the end of a period of time or the end of an activity. Frequently, consequences that do not interrupt the flow of responding are provided following behaviors that are considered appropriate. Cathy, for example, received praise while she exercised (Fitterling et al., 1988). In a similar fashion, in Luiselli's (2000) self-feeding investigation, praise followed each self-feeding response. In yet another example, points were given to obese and nonobese boys on a changing variable ratio schedule for peddling exercise bicycles at a speed consistent with the specified schedule (DeLuca & Holborn, 1992). In that investigation, a ringing bell and the illumination of a light signaled the award of each point.

VARIATIONS IN THE CHANGING CRITERION DESIGN

Sometimes, intervention data are so highly variable, so far from established criterion levels, or reflect such a pronounced trend toward improvement throughout most or all of the intervention phase (e.g., Renzaglia et al., 1978) that internal validity cannot be established by simply manipulating design elements. In those cases, more is needed than, for instance, varying the length of subphases or introducing mini-reversals. Where such extreme departures from design requirements exist, or where it is feared that they *may* exist, the answer to strengthening internal validity may lie in the use of a design variation that employs features of other designs such as a changing criterion with a multiple baseline, changing criterion with a return to baseline, or component analysis.

Changing Criterion with a Multiple Baseline

Where more than one participant, behavior, or setting is available for study, and where carryover between participants, behaviors, or settings is unlikely, combining a multiple baseline design with the changing criterion design can strengthen presumptions of a functional relationship (Schloss & Smith, 1994). Such a mixed design can even allow such a presumption to be made where it might otherwise be impossible.

An example of combining a changing criterion with a multiple baseline design is provided in Figure 8.4. The figure presents the data obtained by Martella et al. (1993) in an investigation of a self-monitoring program designed to reduce the negative statements of Brad, a middle school student with mild mental retardation. The intervention included self-monitoring of negative statements, the opportunity to earn "small reinforcers" for being at or below the criterion level for any given day, and "large" reinforcers for being at or below criterion for four consecutive sessions.

Intervention subphases were implemented following baseline data collection in a changing criterion format during each of two classroom periods. Consistent with the multiple baseline design requirements, subphases were introduced first in Period 2 and then sequentially introduced in Period 1 (top and bottom frames of Figure 8.4, respectively). The intervention phase in both periods was followed by a phase ("partial-sequential withdrawal") in which the training components were gradually withdrawn across three subphases and then by follow-up assessments in which the only intervention component

Figure 8.4   Example of combined changing criterion and multiple baseline

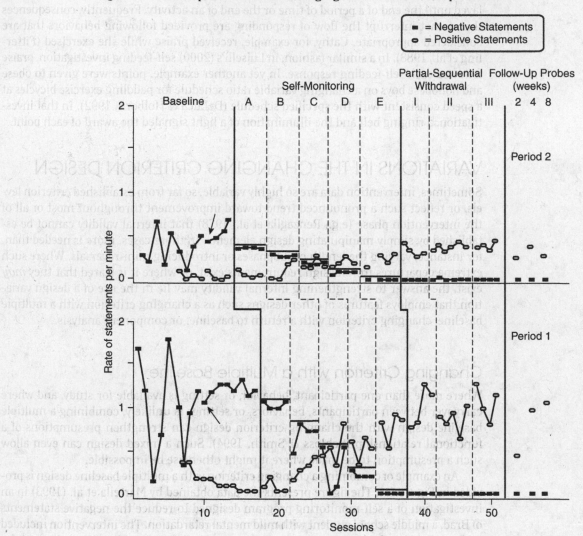

Source: Figure 1 from Martella, Leonard, Marchand-Martella, & Agran-Self-Monitoring negative statements. *Journal of Behavioral Education*, 1993, vol. 3, p. 84. Reprinted with permission.

that was used was a self-monitoring form. Data for both negative and positive statements were collected and are included in Figure 8.4. Note, however, that intervention was applied only to the negative statements (solid rectangles on both panels of the chart) and it will be data regarding those statements in which we will be interested for purposes of this discussion.

During Period 2 (top panel), the baseline for negative statements is variable with some tendency toward increasing numbers of such statements across time. With introduction of the intervention subphases following the time lag required in multiple baseline designs, responding follows the criterion changes closely and reflects a high degree of stability just below criterion levels. During Period 1 (bottom panel), baseline data reflect even more variability than during Period 2 and, during intervention subphases, responding is neither as stable as we observed during Period 2, nor did it approximate criterion levels as closely until the final subphase (subphase E) of the intervention. Data are particularly variable and often disparate from criterion levels in subphases B and C. In both periods, Brad's rate of negative statements remained at zero with one exception throughout partial-sequential withdrawal subphases and during the follow-up probes.

The variable performance noted in the Period 1 intervention phase renders conclusions regarding functional relationships somewhat ambiguous. However, conclusions regarding reliable intervention effects need not be based solely on the changing criterion design employed for that period. Because the data are also presented as part of a multiple baseline design across Periods 2 and 1, the effect of the intervention can be clearly established. During both periods, performance improved only after treatment was introduced and, in Period 1, the treatment was applied in a time-lagged manner in order to control for threats to internal validity. The result of this combined design is a strong demonstration of the positive effects of the intervention on Brad's negative statements.

Changing Criterion with Return to Baseline

We indicated earlier that, sometimes, bidirectional changes in criterion levels (i.e., minireversals) are implemented during the intervention phase in order to strengthen internal validity. Strengthening, in such cases, is achieved without requiring the substantial deterioration in performance that is necessary in designs of the A-B-A type where return to baseline phases are used to provide a replication of effect. In some investigations, however, a complete return to baseline conditions is employed as either an interim subphase (e.g., De Luca & Holborn, 1992) or following the intervention phase. This is a particularly attractive option where the intent is to achieve extreme changes in behavior, where it seems unlikely that the change could be made in a single large step, and where difficulty might be foreseen in achieving a close match between responding and the criterion level. Such a difficulty is not uncommon; as Kazdin (1982) stated, "If the behavior is not easy for the client to monitor, it may be difficult for him or her to perform the behavior at the exact point that the criterion is met" (p. 164). For example, it might be much more difficult for a worker with developmental disabilities to tell when she was close to achieving "rate per minute" criterion levels for some vocational task than it would be for a student to observe that she had met the criterion for completing a specified number of math problems on math worksheets.

Deitz and Repp (1973) used a combined changing criterion/withdrawal design in a study that explored the use of differential reinforcement of low rates of responding (DRL) to eliminate changes of subject from "the ongoing academic discussion to another, usually social, topic" (p. 460) by a class of 15 high school senior girls. The data for this investigation were collected during a 50-minute class period and are included in

Figure 8.5   Example of a changing criterion with a return to baseline conditions

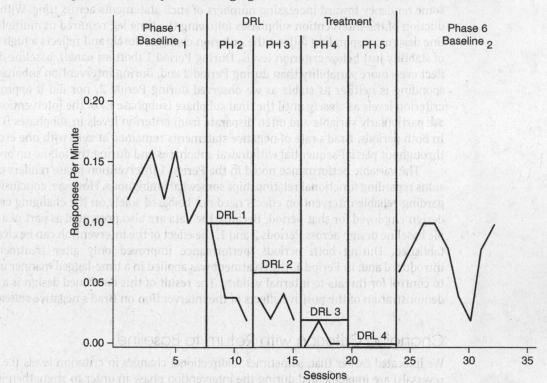

Source: Figure 3 from Deitz & Repp, Decreasing classroom misbehavior through the use of DRL schedules of reinforcement, JABA, 1973, vol. 6, p. 461. Reprinted with permission.

Figure 8.5. During baseline assessments, it was found that the girls averaged a rate of 0.13 subject changes per minute. Successively more stringent DRL schedules were then introduced across four intervention subphases. In the first subphase, an initial criterion level of 0.10 subject changes per minute was established. If the rate of subject changes fell at or below the criterion for the first 4 days of the week, Friday was designated as a "free" day and the class could use the time as they pleased. That same contingency was in effect for the remaining three subphases in which criterion levels were successively lowered to 0.06, 0.02, and zero rates of responding. When changes were made, they were explained to the class, but the girls were never informed of their ongoing accumulation of responses during the class session. Finally, baseline conditions were reinstituted for nine sessions in which the DRL contingencies were withdrawn.

The baseline data for this study were variable, with a drop in subject changes in the last two sessions (see Figure 8.5, Phase 1). During the first intervention subphase (PH 2), a rapidly decelerating trend in the data may be observed. In PH 3, the data were somewhat variable, but with no noticeable trend. During PH 4, three of four datum points fell at zero responses. During none of those subphases did the data closely and consistently match the established DRL criterion levels. Finally, in PH 5 (the fourth subphase), responding matched the zero criterion set for that subphase. If the investigation had ended at that point, it would have been questionable whether the reduction in subject changes was a result of the steadily decreasing DRL schedule or of extraneous variables. This ambiguity is a result of both the sharply decelerating trend during PH 2 that could have been a continuation of the drop in responding in the last two baseline sessions and the lack of a consistent match between performance and criterion levels during all subphases until PH 5, the final subphase. However, following the final subphase, return to baseline conditions were implemented in Phase 6 and, although the class's subject-change behavior did not revert to baseline levels, their responding was far above that in the preceding subphase and, generally, above that in the other intervention subphases. The effects of reinstituting baseline conditions as the final phase of the study, therefore, greatly increases our confidence in the presence of a functional relationship between the independent and dependent variables in this investigation. It should be noted that an additional use of a return to baseline phase, or a phase in which most treatment components are withdrawn, might be to provide follow-up data to examine maintenance effects as in the case of Cathy (Figure 8.2) and Brad (Figure 8.4).

Component Analyses

It is seldom that the interventions examined with changing criterion designs involve only a contingency arrangement. Typically, interventions consist of a treatment package that may include such elements as instructions, interim reinforcers and/or feedback, self-observation, self-recording, self-charting, and visual or oral cues regarding the contingency arrangement associated with changing subphases. It is seldom, however, that a component analysis is conducted on such training packages and, as a result, the contributions of individual program components usually go unknown. As indicated by Hartmann and Hall (1976), additional design features are required in order to tease out the role played by the individual parts of an intervention. Those additional features involve the omission of one or more of the intervention components. Hall and Fox (1977) provided a good example.

In their descriptions of three experiments using the changing criterion design, Hall and Fox (1977) included one study that focused on task completion by a 10-year-old boy (John) with mental retardation and spina bifida. The goal was to increase the number of assigned pages John completed during work on programmed academic tasks. Data indicating the number of assigned pages that John completed each day throughout the study are included in Figure 8.6.

In the 10-day baseline, the teacher gave John assistance as needed before starting an assignment and then recorded the number of pages completed out of the first 10 assigned. John was awarded one point for each page. The points, however, could not be exchanged for any additional items or activities. The intervention phase was then begun in which John was provided with a token for every page of work he completed. The tokens could be used daily to access an activity in which he had shown interest (cafeteria duty)

Figure 8.6 Example of a changing criterion design with a component analysis

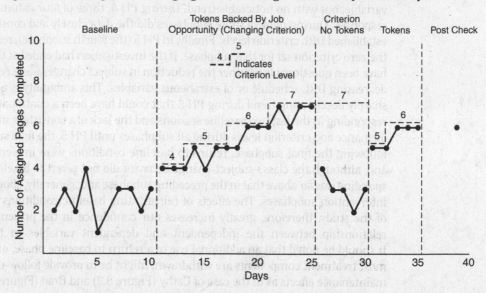

Source: Figure from Hall & Fox—Changing-criterion design: An alternate applied behavior analysis procedure. In Etzel, LeBlanc, & Baer (Eds.)—New developments in behavioral research—Theory, methos, and application—1977—p. 161. Reprinted with permission.

contingent upon the completion of the requisite number of pages. During the first subphase, the criterion level was set at four completed pages. Across the next three subphases, criterion levels were sequentially increased to five, six, and then seven pages. Figure 8.6 data show that John's performance closely matched the established criterion levels during each intervention subphase; he completed exactly the number of pages required by the changing criterion levels on 12 out of 15 days. The data, then, seem clear in suggesting that the treatment applied during the intervention phase bore a functional relationship to John's behavior. However, the effect on performance of simply stating the desired criterion level in the absence of the token system remained unknown.

To examine the effects of criterion setting without the token system components, the investigators withdrew those components on the 26th day of the study and instituted a phase in which John was simply instructed to continue working at the previous criterion level of seven tasks. The data for this "Criterion No Tokens" phase, shown in Figure 8.6, indicate that John's performance quickly worsened and trended downward during the 5 days of the phase. During that time, the number of pages he completed ranged from two to four. However, with the reinstitution of the token system with criterion levels of five and then six pages, John's performance immediately followed the criterion changes and matched criterion levels exactly. It, therefore, appears that the token system was essential to the success of the intervention package.

SUMMARY

Many educational and therapeutic programs seek gradual, stepwise improvement in performance. That is, in the case of desired behaviors, such as reading, mathematics, cooperative social behaviors, etc., the intent is to shift levels of performance from a relatively low to a relatively high level. In the case of undesirable behaviors, such as inappropriate social behaviors, addictive behaviors, behaviors that are disruptive in the classroom, etc., the goal is to gradually reduce levels of performance from those that are relatively high to those that are relatively low, or to eliminate them altogether. The changing criterion design is highly compatible with the intent of such programs and, therefore, may often provide an attractive alternative to other design options. It may be of particular interest to both researchers and practitioners that, following baseline assessments, the design typically allows students to continue movement toward the ultimate instructional goal without discontinuing the benefits of intervention.

A limitation of the design is that it is most useful for testing interventions which use consequences—reinforcers or punishers—as their primary behavior change component. Of course, such interventions are frequently used in one form or the other in many instructional situations; therefore, this limiting factor is certainly not universal. Another limitation is that the design is not designed for programs in which shaping is applied to changes in behavioral topography rather than to changes in level. Where an attempt is made to change the topographical features of behavior (e.g., improving a particular tumbling maneuver in gymnastics, or shaping increasingly sophisticated verbal responses), Cooper et al. (1987) have suggested that a more appropriate design might be the multiple probe design (discussed in Chapter 7 of this text).

Replication to establish internal validity is achieved through repeatedly achieving a match between performances and changing criterion levels (Alberto & Troutman, 2003). Where a failure to precisely achieve such matches occurs, tactics such as mini-reversals may be used to increase confidence in functional relationships. In addition, the design is adequately flexible so that it may be combined with other designs to confirm the effects of the treatment, to examine maintenance, or to evaluate the contribution of intervention components.

REFERENCES

Alberto, P. A., & Troutman, A. C. (2003). *Applied behavior analysis for teachers* (6th ed.). Upper Saddle River, NJ: Merrill Prentice Hall.

Barlow, D. H., & Hersen, M. (1984). *Single case experimental designs: Strategies for studying behavior change* (2nd ed.). New York, NY: Pergamon.

Bigelow, K. M., Huynen, K. B., & Lutzker, J. R. (1993). Using a changing criterion design to teach fire escape to a child with developmental disabilities. *Journal of Developmental and Physical Disabilities, 5*, 121–128.

Cooper (1977). *The aerobics way.* New York: Bantam Books.

Cooper, J. O., Heron, T. E., & Heward, W. L. (1987). *Applied behavior analysis.* Columbus, OH: Merrill.

Davis, P., Bates, P., & Cuvo, A. J. (1983). Training a mentally retarded woman to work competitively: Effect of graphic feedback and a changing criterion design. *Education and Training in Mental Retardation, 18,* 158–163.

Deitz, S. M., & Repp, A. C. (1973). Decreasing classroom misbehavior through the use of DRL schedules of reinforcement. *Journal of Applied Behavior Analysis, 6,* 457–463.

De Luca, R. V., & Holborn, S. W. (1992). Effects of a variable-ratio reinforcement schedule with changing criteria on exercise in obese and nonobese boys. *Journal of Applied Behavior Analysis, 25,* 671–679.

Fitterling, J. M., Martin, J. E., Gramling, S., Cole, P., & Milan, M. A. (1988). Behavioral management of exercise training in vascular headache patients: An investigation of exercise adherence and headache activity. *Journal of Applied Behavior Analysis, 21,* 9–19.

Foxx, R. M., & Rubinoff, A. (1979). Behavioral treatment of caffeinism: Reducing excessive coffee drinking. *Journal of Applied Behavior Analysis, 12,* 335–344.

Friedman, J., & Axelrod, S. (1973). The use of a changing-criterion procedure to reduce the frequency of smoking behavior. Unpublished manuscript, Temple University, Philadelphia, PA.

Hall, R. V., & Fox, R. G. (1977). Changing-criterion designs: An alternate applied behavior analysis procedure. In B. C. Etzel, J. M. LeBlanc, & D. M. Baer (Eds.), *New developments in behavioral research: Theory, method and application. In honor of Sidney W. Bijou* (pp. 151–166). Hillside, NJ: Lawrence Erlbaum.

Hall & Hartman (1976). The changing criterion design. *Journal of Applied Behavior Analysis, 9,* 527–532.

Kazdin, A. E. (1982). *Single-case research designs: Methods for clinical and applied settings.* New York, NY: Oxford.

Luiselli, J. K. (2000). Cueing, demand fading, and positive reinforcement to establish self-feeding and oral consumption in a child with chronic food refusal. *Behavior Modification, 24,* 348–358.

Martella, R. C., Leonard, I. J., Marchand-Martella, N. E., & Agran, M. (1993). Self-monitoring negative statements. *Journal of Behavioral Education, 3,* 77–86.

Renzaglia, A., Wehman, P., Schultz, R., & Karan, O. (1978). Use of cue redundancy and positive reinforcement to accelerate production in two profoundly retarded workers. *British Journal of Clinical Psychology, 17,* 183–187.

Richards, S. B., Taylor, R. L., Ramasamy, R., & Richards, R. Y. (1999). *Single subject research: Applications in educational and clinical settings.* San Diego, CA: Singular.

Schloss, P. J., & Smith, M. A. (1994). *Applied behavior analysis in the classroom.* Boston, MA: Allyn and Bacon.

MULTIPLE TREATMENT DESIGNS

John J. McDonnell and Timothy Riesen,
University of Utah
Shamby Polychronis, *Westminster College*

9

Previous chapters have presented several different designs that can be used to document the effects of a specific intervention (or treatment condition) on a target behavior. In some cases, however, the researcher is interested in comparing the effects of two or more interventions across behaviors or study participants. The Multiple Treatment Design (MTD) enables the researcher to accomplish this goal (Barlow & Hersen, 1984; Holcombe, Wolery, & Gast, 1994; Tawney & Gast, 1984). This design is also referred to as the changing conditions design, the ABC design, or the multiple treatment with reversal design (Alberto & Troutman, 2009; Cooper, Heron, & Heward, 2007). It can be used to address research questions such as: (a) Is intervention 1 more effective than intervention 2? (b) Is an intervention more effective under condition A than under condition B? or (3) Is an intervention more effective at level A or level B? (Holcombe et al., 1994). Since the primary purpose of the MTD is to evaluate the relative efficacy of two interventions (or variations in a single intervention), these studies commonly focus on strategies that were previously validated using other withdrawal/reversal or multiple baseline designs. This chapter will describe the general characteristics of the MTD, discuss several common variations in the MTD, outline several key procedural issues in implementing an MTD study, and provide illustrations of how the MTD has been used in the applied research literature.

CHARACTERISTICS OF THE MTD

The MTD enables the researcher to compare the relative effects of two or more interventions (or treatment conditions) on a single target behavior. The MTD is an extension of the A-B-A-B reversal design. Consequently, the interventions that are being compared are repeatedly reversed in successive experimental phases in order to document intervention effects. Table 9.1 presents a summary of the critical features of the MTD. The MTD has two common design structures (Figure 9.1). The first is the MTD

Table 9.1 Features of the MTD.

	Multiple Treatment Design (MTD)
Purpose	Compare the effects of two or more interventions or treatment conditions on one behavior.
General Characteristics	Repeatedly reversing the presentation of the interventions or treatment conditions with individual participants or groups.
Design Strengths	Can be used to compare the impact of multiple interventions.
	Some design variations allow for more immediate implementation of the intervention or treatment because (a) a baseline phase is not required and/or (b) the interventions do not have to be "lagged" in across behaviors or participants.
Design Weaknesses	May not be appropriate for establishing new (nonreversible) behaviors.
	Repeated reversal of the treatments or conditions may not mesh with the typical structure of schools or other service settings.
	Requires that the researcher control for sequence and carry over effects.

Figure 9.1 Two common structures for the MTD

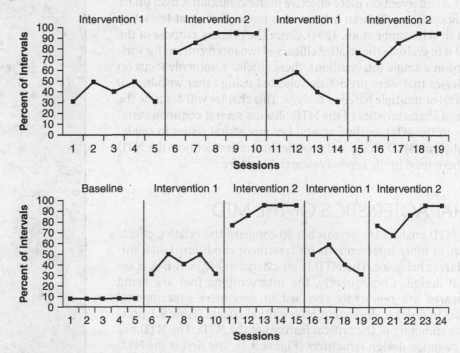

without baseline (B-C-B-C). In this design, the interventions are reversed at least two times during the study. However, the researcher can reverse the intervention phases as many times as necessary to document the differential effects of the interventions on the target behavior.

The second common structure is the MTD with baseline (A-B-C-B-C). In this structure, the researcher begins with a baseline phase designed to establish pretreatment levels of performance of the target behavior by the study participant. Once stable baseline performance has been established, the first intervention is implemented for several sessions followed by the second intervention. The interventions are reversed at least twice during the study but can be reversed repeatedly until a differential effect is observed. While this design allows for direct comparisons between the two interventions, it does not allow for comprehensive comparisons between the participant's performance during baseline and the intervention phases. This occurs because such comparisons can legitimately only be made between adjacent phases within the study. So, while the participant's performance during baseline (A) could be contrasted with the first intervention (B), it could not be compared to the second intervention (C).

The MTD is an extremely flexible design that allows researchers to compare any number of interventions or combinations of interventions. Some of the more common variations in the MTD will be discussed in more detail below.

The independent variables in an MTD are the interventions (or treatment conditions) that are being compared. The dependent variable is a measure of the change in the target behavior. Data collected during each experimental phase are plotted separately on the graph. The researcher uses the guidelines for visual analysis of the data described in Chapter 4 to determine whether differential effects are observed between the interventions in adjacent experimental phases. The researcher can conclude that one intervention is more effective than the other for a participant when it consistently has a differential effect on the target behavior.

For example, an MTD could be used to compare the impact of teacher-delivered social reinforcement with student self-monitoring on the academic engagement of 4 students with disabilities during regularly scheduled math periods. The researcher would gather baseline data on the rates of the students' academic engagement until stable performance was established. The social reinforcement phase would be introduced and implemented for a predetermined number of sessions. The researcher would track the amount of time that the students were engaged in the academic tasks presented by the classroom teacher during each session and plot it on the graph. Then, the researcher would introduce the self-monitoring phase and implement it for a predetermined number of sessions. The two interventions would be reversed at least twice during the study. The intervention that consistently produced the highest level of academic engagement by the students would be considered the most effective treatment.

The MTD is a good option when the researcher is interested in comparing the effects of two or more interventions on target behaviors that are "reversible" (Holcombe et al., 1994). Traditionally, these are recognized as behaviors that are likely to return to pretreatment levels when an intervention is removed or withdrawn (Gast & Wolery, 1988; Holcombe et al., 1994; Sindelar, Rosenberg, & Wilson, 1985). Examples of reversible behaviors that have been used in applied research studies include on-task behavior, social interactions between peers, self-stimulatory behaviors, and postural alignment. However, unlike other reversible designs, the MTD does not require the researcher to return to baseline. Instead, the design is structured to focus on the differential effects of one intervention on the target behavior with another intervention in successive adjacent experimental phases (A-B-C-B-C-B-C). The assumption underlying the MTD is that each intervention will have a consistent and differential effect on the target behavior every time the interventions are reversed within the study. This unique feature of the MTD limits its potential utility in studying the effects of interventions on behaviors that are not reversible such as reading, math, or communication skills. For example, once participants learned to correctly complete single digit addition problems it is highly unlikely that they would return to previous performance levels.

In addition, the characteristics of the MTD make it vulnerable to two common threats to internal validity. These are sequence effects and carry over effects. Sequence effects result from the order in which interventions are presented to the participant within the study. For example, in our illustrative study, if social reinforcement and self-monitoring were presented in the same order to all participants, it would be difficult for the researcher to assess whether observed changes in the target behavior were the result of the interventions or simply their order of implementation.

Carry over effects are the impact that one intervention may have on the effectiveness of the other. When two interventions are implemented successively it is possible that the effects of one intervention may "carry over" to the next experimental phase (Barlow & Hersen, 1984; Holcombe et al., 1994; Tawney & Gast, 1984). In our illustrative study, it is possible that any number of aspects of the social reinforcement condition could "carry over" to the self-monitoring condition. For example, the teacher's physical proximity to the participants could become a power conditioned reinforcer during the social reinforcement condition that would influence the participants' performance during the self-monitoring condition. This interaction between the interventions can have one of two possible impacts on the target behavior. First, the implementation of one intervention leads to a reduction in the effectiveness of the second intervention being studied. This phenomenon is referred to as contrast effects. A second possibility is that one intervention improves the effectiveness of the second intervention. This is referred to as induction effects. The potential for carry over effects are high in MTD studies because of the repeated reversal of the interventions during the study. The steps that researchers can take to control for sequence and carry over effects in MTD studies will be discussed in more detail below.

IMPLEMENTING AN MTD STUDY

The general guidelines for implementing single case research studies were discussed earlier (see Chapters 1–4). A checklist of the general steps required to successfully implement a MTD study is presented in *Research Notes 9.1*. The unique structure of the MTD requires the researcher to address several methodological challenges in designing and implementing a successful study. These include: (a) ensuring sufficient replication of the effects of the interventions to demonstrate experimental control, (b) scheduling the presentation of the interventions to control for possible sequence effects, (c) assuring procedural equivalence between the interventions, and (d) demonstrating the reliability of the dependent measures and the fidelity of treatment.

Replicating Intervention Effects

The purpose of an MTD is to examine the efficacy of one intervention compared to another or to assess the efficacy of a specific intervention under different conditions. As indicated earlier, this is accomplished by repeatedly reversing the implementation of the interventions with a single behavior and participant. One intervention is considered to be more effective than the other if its effect on the target behavior is replicated across the adjacent experimental phases. However, simply replicating the effects of the interventions with a single behavior and participant is insufficient to allow the researcher to draw firm conclusions about their relative effectiveness. As discussed earlier in this text, it is generally accepted that the effects of an intervention must be replicated across at least three different participants, behaviors, and/or conditions to clearly demonstrate experimental control.

One option for addressing this issue in an MTD study is to implement concurrent baselines with several participants, behaviors, or conditions (Figure 9.2). In this alternative, the sequence of experimental phases is implemented independently and in parallel fashion across the baselines. The second option is to use a multiple baseline design structure to lag in the sequence of experimental phases across participants, behaviors, or conditions (Figure 9.3). Generally, multiple baseline designs are considered to be more effective in controlling for threats to internal validity than concurrent designs. However, multiple baseline designs can be problematic in many study settings because they often require (a) significant amounts of resources to collect data across several participants, behaviors, or conditions and (b) prolonged baseline conditions that can create a negative experience for participants. In addition, delaying the implementation of the interventions may at times put the participant at-risk.

Develop an Intervention Schedule to Control for Sequence Effects

As discussed earlier, the MTD is highly susceptible to sequence effects. Consequently, the researcher must take steps to control for this possible threat to internal validity. One way of addressing this issue is to counterbalance the introduction of the interventions across participants, behaviors, or conditions. For example, in our illustrative study, the researcher might implement the social reinforcement condition first, followed by the self-monitoring condition, with Participants 1 and 3. To control for possible sequence effects, the researcher would counterbalance the schedule of implementation with

Research Notes 9.1

MTD Study Implementation Checklist

Operationally define the dependent variables and measures.

Operationally define the interventions, ensuring that they are procedurally equivalent.

Counterbalance the introduction of the interventions across participants or groups as necessary to control for sequence effects.

Initiate baseline and collect data until stable performance is established.

Implement the first intervention until stable performance is established.

Implement the second intervention until stable performance is established.

Reverse the interventions at least twice during the study.

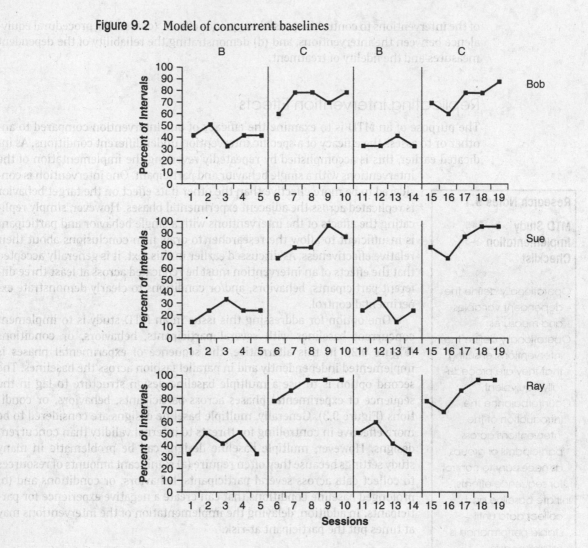

Figure 9.2   Model of concurrent baselines

Participants 2 and 4 by implementing the self-monitoring condition first, followed by the social reinforcement condition. This process allows the researcher to reduce the likelihood that the order in which interventions are implemented with the participants leads to changes in the target behavior. A similar structure can be used to counterbalance the order of presentation across behaviors or conditions.

Ensure Procedural Equivalence

Researchers must design the study methods so the interventions that are being compared differ only on their relevant components. Other variables should be held constant to the

Figure 9.3 Model of a multiple baseline

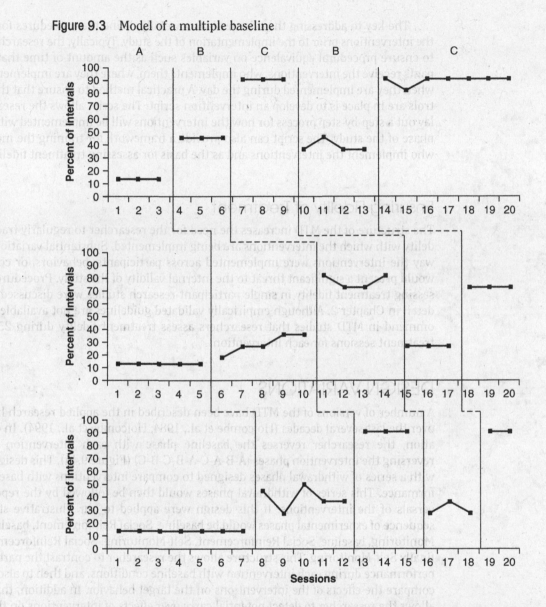

maximum extent possible. Without these controls it may become difficult for the researcher to determine whether changes in the target behavior occurred because of the intervention or because of other factors. For example, in our illustrative study, if the length of the treatment session were longer under the social reinforcement condition than under the self-monitoring condition, it would be impossible to assess whether improvements in the participant's academic engagement occurred because of the effectiveness of social reinforcement or simply due to differences in the length of the intervention sessions.

The key to addressing these issues is to carefully define the procedures for each of the interventions prior to the implementation of the study. Typically, the researcher needs to ensure procedural equivalence on variables such as the amount of time that participants receive the interventions, who implements them, where they are implemented, and when they are implemented during the day. A practical method to ensure that these controls are in place is to develop an intervention script. The script allows the researcher to lay out a step-by-step process for how the interventions will be implemented within each phase of the study. The script can also provide a framework for training the individuals who implement the interventions and as the basis for assessing treatment fidelity.

Ensuring Fidelity of Treatment

The structure of the MTD increases the need for the researcher to regularly track the fidelity with which the interventions are being implemented. Substantial variations in the way the interventions were implemented across participants, behaviors, or conditions would present a significant threat to the internal validity of the study. Procedures for assessing treatment fidelity in single participant research studies were discussed in more detail in Chapter 2. Although empirically validated guidelines are not available, we recommend in MTD studies that researchers assess treatment fidelity during 25% of all treatment sessions for each intervention.

DESIGN VARIATIONS

A number of versions of the MTD have been described in the applied research literature over the last several decades (Holcombe et al., 1984; Holcombe et al., 1994). In one variation, the researcher reverses the baseline phase with each intervention prior to reversing the intervention phases (A-B-A-C-A-B-C-B-C) (Figure 9.4a). This design begins with a series of withdrawal phases designed to compare interventions with baseline performance. This series of withdrawal phases would then be followed by the repeated reversals of the interventions. If this design were applied to our illustrative study, the sequence of experimental phases would be baseline, Social Reinforcement, baseline, Self-Monitoring, baseline, Social Reinforcement, Self-Monitoring, Social Reinforcement, and finally Self-Monitoring. This structure allows the researcher to contrast the participants' performance during each intervention with baseline conditions, and then to also directly compare the effects of the interventions on the target behavior. In addition, this design allows the researcher to detect potential carry over effects of interventions on the target behavior. During the initial experimental phases, the researcher would expect the participants' performance to return to baseline levels following the withdrawal of each intervention. If this did not occur, it would suggest that carry over effects were present.

A second variation in the MTD enables the researcher to compare the effects of single interventions with various packages of interventions (A-B-BC-C-BC) (Figure 9.4b). For example, in our illustrative study, in addition to examining the unique effects of social reinforcement and self-monitoring in isolation, the researcher might also be interested

Figure 9.4 Variations in the MTD

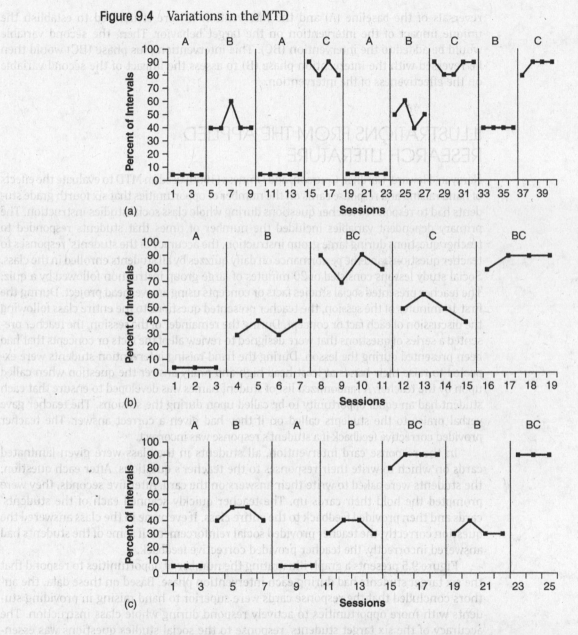

in assessing the effect that combining the two interventions might have on the students' academic engagement. This comparison would be accomplished through a series of reversals in which each intervention (B or C) was compared with the combination (BC).

A final variation enables the researcher to assess the impact of a second variable on the effectiveness of an intervention (A-B-A-B-BC-B-BC) (Figure 9.4c). The first two reversals of the baseline (A) and the intervention (B) are structured to establish the unique impact of the intervention on the target behavior. Then, the second variable would be added to the intervention (BC). This intervention plus phase (BC) would then be reversed with the intervention phase (B) to assess the impact of the second variable on the effectiveness of the intervention.

ILLUSTRATIONS FROM THE APPLIED RESEARCH LITERATURE

Narayan, Heward, Gardner, Courson, and Omness (1990) used an MTD to evaluate the effects of hand raising and response cards on the number of opportunities that six fourth grade students had to respond to teacher questions during whole class social studies instruction. The primary dependent variables included the number of times that students responded to teacher questions during large group instruction, the accuracy of the students' responses to teacher questions, and the performance on daily quizzes by all students enrolled in the class. Social study lessons consisted of 20 minutes of large group instruction followed by a quiz. The teacher presented social studies facts or concepts using an overhead project. During the first 10 minutes of the session, the teacher presented questions to the entire class following the discussion of each fact or concept. During the remainder of the session, the teacher presented a series of questions that were designed to review all of the facts or concepts that had been presented during the lesson. During the hand raising intervention students were expected to raise their hands at least head high and orally answer the question when called upon by the teacher. A randomized list of student names was developed to ensure that each student had an equal opportunity to be called upon during the sessions. The teacher gave verbal praise to the students called on if they had given a correct answer. The teacher provided corrective feedback if a student's response was incorrect.

In the response card intervention, all students in the class were given laminated cards on which to write their responses to the teacher's questions. After each question, the students were asked to write their answers on the card. After five seconds, they were prompted the hold their cards up. The teacher quickly scanned each of the students' cards and then provided feedback to the entire class. If everyone in the class answered the question correctly, the teacher provided social reinforcement. If some of the students had answered incorrectly, the teacher provided corrective feedback.

Figure 9.5 presents a graph illustrating the number of opportunities to respond that the six target students had during each intervention phase. Based on these data, the authors concluded that the response cards were superior to hand raising in providing students with more opportunities to actively respond during whole class instruction. The accuracy of the six target students' response to the social studies questions was essentially the same under both conditions, in spite of the high rates of responding demanded during the response card condition. Finally, the data suggested that the mean daily quiz scores improved for all students in the class under the response card condition.

In a more recent study, Patel, Piazza, Martinez, Volkert, and Santana (2002) used a multiple treatment design to assess the effects of differential reinforcement with a preferred activity and differential reinforcement plus escape extinction on food refusal by three young

Figure 9.5 Illustration of a MTD study

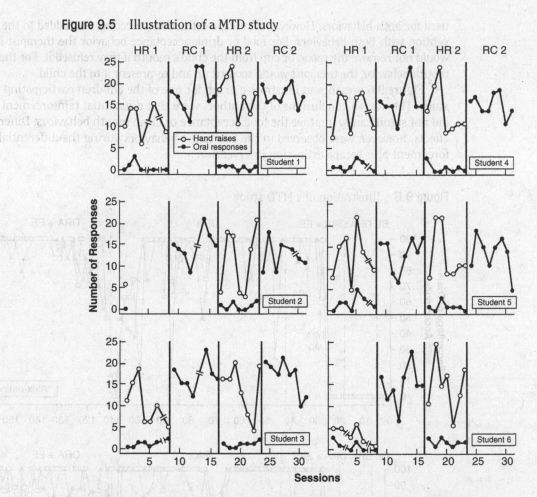

Source: Narayan, J. S., Heward, W. L., Gardner III, R., Courson, F. H., & Omness, C. K. (1990). Using response cards to increase student participation in an elementary classroom. *Journal of Applied Behavior Analysis,* vol. 23, pp. 483–490. Reprinted with permission.

children with pediatric feeding disorders. The dependent variables for the study were the percent of trials in which the child accepted food or drink in their mouth when it was offered by a therapist and the percent of trials in which the child had a "clean mouth" (i.e., did not spit out the food). The acceptance and clean mouth behaviors were treated in alternating sessions within each intervention phase. In the first intervention, the child was allowed to interact with a preferred toy on their high chair tray or the table for 20 seconds if they accepted the food or drink from the therapist. If the child refused the food or drink (e.g., crying, batting, head turning) the spoon or cup was simply removed for 30 seconds. The same differential reinforcement procedure was used during the sessions focused on the clean mouth behavior. No differential consequences were provided to the child for expulsion of or vomiting the bite of food or drink. In the second intervention, differential reinforcement was used for both behaviors. However, an escape extinction procedure was added to the intervention with both behaviors. For food or drink acceptance behavior the therapist simply would not remove the spoon or cup from the child's mouth if they refused it. For the clean mouth behavior, the therapist would scoop it up and re-present it to the child.

Figure 9.6 presents an illustrative graph for one of the children participating in the study. The overall conclusions of the authors were that differential reinforcement alone did not significantly improve the food acceptance or clean mouth behaviors. Differential effects, however, were observed in the two target behaviors during the differential reinforcement plus escape extinction intervention.

Figure 9.6   Illustration of a MTD study

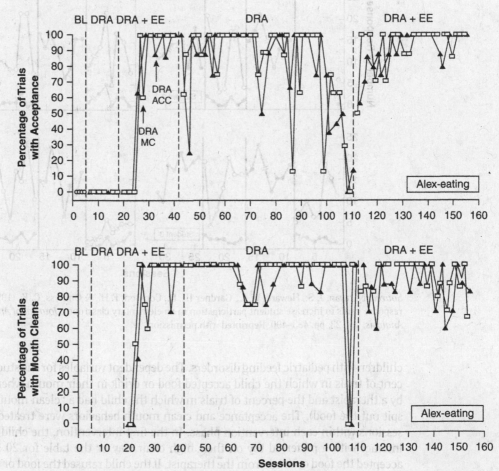

Source: Patel, M. R., Piazza, C. C., Martinez, D. J., Volkert, V. M., & Santana, C. M. (2002). An evaluation of two differential reinforcement procedures with escape extinction to treat food refusal. *Journal of Applied Behavior Analysis,* vol. 35, pp. 363–374. Reprinted with permission.

SUMMARY

The MTD enables researchers to compare two or more interventions with a single behavior. In the MTD, the relative effectiveness of the interventions is compared through the repeated reversal of the interventions during the study. Consequently, the MTD can only be used to study behaviors that are reversible. Like all withdrawal or reversal designs, the MTD is particularly susceptible to sequence and carry over effects. The researcher must design the study procedures to control for these possible threats to the internal validity of the study. In spite of these limitations, the MTD provides researchers with a good alternative when they are interested in comparing the effectiveness of interventions in applied settings. The MTD has a flexible structure that enables researchers to design experimental phases to carry out any number of possible comparisons. Further, there are several variations of the MTD that eliminate the need for a baseline phase.

REFERENCES

Alberto, P. A., & Troutman, A. C. (2009). *Applied behavior analysis for teachers* (8th ed.). Upper Saddle River, NJ: Merrill.

Barlow, D. H., & Hersen, M. (1984). *Single case experimental designs*. Boston, MA: Allyn & Bacon.

Cooper, J. O., Heron, T. E., & Heward, W. L. (2007). *Applied behavior analysis* (2nd ed.). Upper Saddle River, NJ: Merrill.

Gast, D. L., & Wolery, M. (1988). Parallel treatment design: A nested single participant design for comparing instructional procedures. *Education and Treatment of Children, 11,* 270–285.

Holcombe et al. (1994)

Holcombe, A., Wolery, M., & Gast, D. L. (1994). Comparative single-participant research: Descriptions of designs and discussion of problems. *Topics in Early Childhood Education, 14,* 119–145.

Narayan, J. S., Heward, W. L., Gardner III, R., Courson, F. H., & Omness, C. K. (1990). Using response cards to increase student participation in an elementary classroom. *Journal of Applied Behavior Analysis, 23,* 483–490.

Patel, M. R., Piazza, C. C., Martinez, D. J., Volkert, V. M., & Santana, C. M. (2002). An evaluation of two differential reinforcement procedures with escape extinction to treat food refusal. *Journal of Applied Behavior Analysis, 35,* 363–374.

Sindelar, P. T., Rosenberg, M. S., & Wilson, R. J. (1985). An adapted alternating treatments design for instructional research. *Education and Treatment of Children, 8,* 67–76.

Tawney, J. W., & Gast, D. L. (1984). *Single participant research in special education.* New York, NY: Merrill.

SUMMARY

The MTD enables researchers to compare two or more interventions with a single behavior. In the MTD, the relative effectiveness of the interventions is compared through the repeated reversal of the interventions during the study. Consequently, the MTD can only be used to study behaviors that are reversible. Like all withdrawal or reversal designs, the MTD is particularly susceptible to sequence and carry over effects. The researcher must design in the study procedures to control for these possible threats to the internal validity of the study. In spite of these limitations, the MTD provides researchers with a good alternative when they are interested in comparing the effectiveness of interventions in applied settings. The MTD has a flexible structure that enables researchers to design experimental phases to carry out any number of possible comparisons. Further, there are several variations of the MTD that eliminate the need for a baseline phase.

REFERENCES

Alberto, P. A., & Troutman, A. C. (2006). Applied behavior analysis for teachers (6th ed.). Upper Saddle River, NJ: Merrill.

Barlow, D. H., & Hersen, M. (1984). Single case experimental designs. Boston, MA: Allyn & Bacon.

Cooper, J. O., Heron, T. E., & Heward, W. L. (2007). Applied behavior analysis (2nd ed.). Upper Saddle River, NJ: Merrill.

Gast, D. L., & Wolery, M. (1988). Alternating treatment design: A rested single participant design for comparing instructional procedures. Education and Treatment of Children 11, 270–275.

Holcomb et al. (1994).

Holcombe, A., Wolery, M., & Gast, D. L. (1994). Comparative single subject research: Description of designs and discussion of problems. Topics in Early Childhood Education 14, 119–145.

Mace, F. C., Hock, M. L., Lalli, J. S., West, B. J., Belfiore, P., Pinter, E., & Brown, D. K. (1988). Behavioral momentum in the treatment of noncompliance. Journal of Applied Behavior Analysis, 21, 123–141.

Neef, N. A., Iwata, B. A., & Page, T. J. (1980).

Piazza, C. C., Fisher, W. W., Hanley, G. P., LeBlanc, L. A., Worsdell, A. S., Lindauer, S. E., & Keeney, K. M. (1998).

Singh, N. N., Dawson, M. J., & Gregory, P. R. (1980).

Sidman, M. (1960). Tactics of scientific research. New York: Basic Books.

Tawney, J. W., & Gast, D. L. (1984). Single subject research in special education. New York, NY: Merrill.

ALTERNATING TREATMENT DESIGNS

John J. McDonnell and Matthew Jameson,
University of Utah
Tessie Rose, *American Institutes for Research*

Alternating Treatment Designs (ATD) were developed to allow researchers to compare the efficacy of several interventions (or treatment conditions) within a single study participant or group of participants (Barlow & Hersen, 1984; Holcombe, Wolery, & Gast, 1994; Tawney & Gast, 1984). This design has also been referred to as the multielement design (Ulman & Sulzer-Azaroff, 1975), multiple schedule design (Barlow & Hersen, 1984), concurrent schedule design (Barlow & Hersen, 1984), and the simultaneous treatment design (Kazdin & Hartmann, 1978). Unlike the Multiple Treatment Design (MTD), in which interventions or treatments are implemented successively with participants during the study, this group of designs allows the researcher to implement the interventions simultaneously. Consequently, they offer a number of practical advantages to researchers in carrying out comparison studies. This chapter will describe the key characteristics of these designs, outline the procedural considerations for using them, and provide illustrations of how they have been used in the applied research literature.

THE ALTERNATING TREATMENT DESIGN (ATD)

Characteristics of the ATD

The ATD is structured to allow researchers to compare the effects of two or more interventions on one behavior. This is accomplished by rapidly alternating the application of the interventions (or treatment conditions) with a participant or group of participants across treatment sessions. The interventions under study can be presented to study participants alternately, in rotation, or randomly (Alberto & Troutman, 2009; Cooper, Heron, & Heward, 2007). For example, in comparing two interventions a researcher could alternate them weekly (e.g., intervention 1 (B) the first week and intervention 2 (C) the second week), daily (e.g., B on Monday and C on Tuesday, B on Wednesday, etc.), between sessions on the same day (e.g., B in the morning and C in the afternoon), or between portions of the same session (e.g., B the first 15 minutes of the session and C the last 15 minutes of the session). When studying three or more treatments the researcher could develop a block rotation schedule that predetermines the order that each treatment is presented to the study participants (e.g., B-C-D; C-D-B; D-C-B). Finally, the treatments could be presented randomly to the participants (e.g., B-C-C-C-B-B-C-B).

Table 10.1 presents a summary of the critical features of the ATD. The ATD has two common design structures (Figure 10.1). In the first and perhaps most commonly used option, the interventions are introduced to the participant without a baseline phase. The second option includes a baseline phase, a comparison phase, and a return to baseline (Holcombe et al., 1994). There are, however, other variations in the design structure that do not require the researcher to return to the baseline phase but do allow the researcher to add a third phase in which the "best" intervention is used alone. These variations will be discussed in more detail in the following text.

The independent variables in an ATD study are the interventions or treatment conditions being compared. The primary dependent variables include measures of the level of changes in the target behavior and how quickly those changes occurred. The effects of

Table 10.1   Features of the ATD.

Alternating Treatment Design (ATD)	
Purpose	Compare the effects of two or more interventions or treatment conditions on one behavior.
General Characteristics	Rapid, alternating presentations of the interventions or treatment conditions with individual participants or groups.
Design Strengths	Can be used to compare the impact of multiple interventions.
	Allows for more immediate intervention or treatment because interventions do not have to be "lagged" in across behaviors or participants.
	Does not require a baseline phase.
Design Weaknesses	May not be appropriate for establishing new (nonreversible) behaviors.
	Alternation of treatments or conditions may not mesh with the typical structure of schools or other service settings.
	Requires that the researcher control for a number of potential threats to internal validity such as amount of exposure to intervention or treatment condition, the individuals carrying out the intervention or treatment, or location of the intervention or treatment.

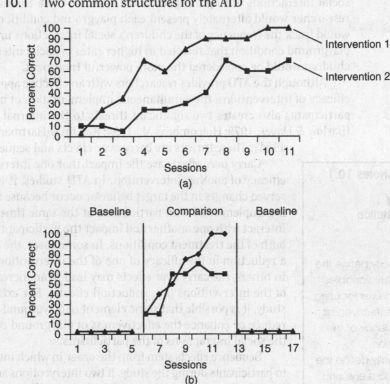

Figure 10.1   Two common structures for the ATD

the interventions on the target behavior are continuously tracked across treatment sessions and the data for each intervention are plotted in a separate data path on the graph.

Unlike other single case designs which are based on establishing a stable level of performance in each phase before experimental conditions are changed, the treatments in an ATD are manipulated independent of the study of the participant's level of responding. Experimental control is determined by examining the differences between each treatment's data path. In making a decision about whether experimental control has been demonstrated, the researcher must consider the trend and variability of each data path, as well as the overlap between or among the data paths. An intervention is considered to be superior (a) if it consistently produces more change, or more rapid change, in the target behavior across individual participants or groups; (b) if stable levels of performance have been established; and (c) if the majority of the data points for the intervention fall outside of the range of the values of the data points of the other interventions being studied.

For example, a researcher might be interested in comparing the frequency of social interactions of four children with intellectual disabilities and their peers under two different playground conditions at one elementary school. Prior to implementing the interventions, the researcher would gather baseline data on the frequency of the children's social interactions during a regular recess period. Once baseline data were stable, the researcher would alternately present each playground condition across school days and would track the frequency of the children's social interactions under each condition. The playground condition that resulted in higher rates of social interactions across all of the children would be considered the more powerful treatment.

Although the ATD provides researchers with an effective approach for comparing the efficacy of interventions, the simultaneous implementation of multiple treatments with participants also creates two significant threats to the internal validity of these studies (Barlow & Hayes, 1979; Holcombe et al., 1994; Kazdin & Hartmann, 1988; Tawney & Gast, 1984). These threats are carry over effects and sequence effects.

Carry over effects are the impact that one intervention may have on the efficacy of another intervention. In ATD studies, it is quite possible that observed changes in the target behavior occur because the interventions are being implemented with participants at the same time. The interventions may interact with one another and impact the participant's performance in one or both of the treatment conditions. In some cases, the carry over effects lead to a reduction in the efficacy of one of the interventions (i.e., contrast effects). In others, the carry over effects may lead to an increase in the efficacy of one of the interventions (i.e., induction effects). For example, in our illustrative study, it is possible that some element of playground condition 1 could either reduce or enhance the effectiveness of playground condition 2 in improving the social interactions of the participants.

Sequence effects stem from the order in which interventions are presented to participants during the study. If two interventions are presented to all participants in the same order it is possible that any differential effects they have on the target behavior are simply a result of the sequence in which they were presented. In our illustrative study, if the two playground conditions were presented in the same order to all participants it would be difficult to judge whether observed differences in the two interventions were the result of their overall efficacy or simply due to the order in which they were presented to the participants.

In order to minimize the possible impact of carry over and sequence effects, as well as other threats to internal validity, the researcher must select an appropriate design option and carefully plan and implement the study methods. The following sections will discuss some of the key issues in completing these two steps with an ATD.

Implementing an ATD Study

Many of the general guidelines for implementing single participant research studies have been discussed earlier. A checklist of the general steps for carrying out an ATD study is presented in *Research Notes 10.1*. The unique structure of the ATD requires that researchers address several methodological challenges in designing and implementing a successful study. These include

---

Research Notes 10.1

ADT Study Implementation Checklist

Operationally define the dependent variables and measures focusing on both effectiveness and efficiency of the intervention.

Operationally define the interventions ensuring that they are procedurally equivalent.

Counterbalance the introduction of the interventions across participants or groups.

If a baseline condition is used, collect data until stable performance is established.

Initiate the comparison phase until a differential effect is observed between the interventions.

Collect reliability data on data collection procedures during baseline and comparison phases.

the need to (a) establish a schedule for controlling the presentation of the interventions across participants, (b) control the exposure of participants or groups to each intervention, (c) achieve procedural equivalence across the interventions, and (d) assure the reliability of the participant performance measures and the fidelity of the interventions.

Scheduling the Presentation of the Interventions

As we noted earlier, ATD studies are susceptible to sequence effects. Several authors have argued that the likelihood of sequence effects is reduced in an ATD study by rapidly alternating presentation of the interventions within or across treatment sessions (Barlow & Hersen, 1984; Holcombe et al., 1994; Tawney & Gast, 1984). The assumption is that the brief exposure of the participants to each intervention reduces the probability that their performance during one intervention will be influenced by the other.

However, researchers can take additional steps to reduce the likelihood that sequence effects will occur by developing a schedule that controls the order in which the interventions are presented to participants during the study. One option is to counterbalance the presentation of the interventions across participants. In other words, a study would begin with one participant by presenting intervention 1 followed by intervention 2. The presentation of these interventions would be alternated in this order throughout the duration of the study. The order of introduction of the interventions would be reversed for a second participant, with intervention 2 being presented first, followed by intervention 1. In our illustrative study examining the effects of two playground conditions, the researcher would counterbalance the introduction of the conditions across the study participants. For instance, the comparison phase for participants 1 and 3 might begin with playground condition 1 followed by playground condition 2. The order of introduction of the two conditions would be reversed for participants 2 and 4.

A second option is to develop a randomized schedule of presentation. In our illustrative study, the researcher would develop an intervention schedule for participant 1 using a randomized numbers table to determine the order in which playground conditions 1 and 2 were presented. A separate randomized schedule would be developed for each of the remaining participants using the same process. This option may help reduce the potential for sequence effects because the participants would not be able to predict which intervention they receive across sessions. However, randomized schedules may also prove to be incompatible with the schedules or organization of many schools or other service settings.

Controlling Exposure to the Interventions or Conditions

Another key procedural consideration in using an ATD is to ensure that the study participants have an equal amount of exposure to each intervention during the study. This is critical because without these controls it is impossible to determine whether any differential effects on the target behavior are due to the efficacy of the intervention or due to differences in the amount of intervention that participants received. For example, if children in our illustrative study participated in playground condition 1 for 30 days, and playground condition 2 for only 20 days, it would be impossible to determine whether any differences were due to the interventions or due to the amount of time they spent in each intervention. The researcher would run into the same problem if the number of treatment days were held constant but the treatment sessions were longer in playground condition 1 than playground condition 2 (e.g., 20 minutes versus 15 minutes). To address this issue, the researcher must ensure that participants receive the same number of treatment days in each intervention (e.g., 20 days in playground condition 1 and 20 days in playground condition 2). Second, and equally important, the researcher must ensure that other aspects of the interventions such as the amount of time or the number of instructional trials that participants receive are indistinguishable from one another.

Procedural Equivalence

Researchers must design the study methods so that other procedural elements of the interventions are controlled. This includes issues such as who implements the interventions, where they are implemented, time of day they are implemented, and so on. The objective is to ensure that these elements of the interventions do not vary significantly from one another. For example, in our illustrative study, if playground condition 1 was implemented by one teacher across all four children and playground condition 2 was implemented by another teacher, then it would be difficult to flesh out the impact of the interventions from the impact of who implemented them. The researcher would have a similar problem if playground condition 1 was implemented in one section of the school yard and playground condition 2 was implemented in a different section. Ideally, the researcher would design the study methods to ensure that these kinds of procedural elements are held constant across all of the interventions and participants. However, the logistical constraints of many study settings may prevent this from occurring and the researcher will have to use other strategies to eliminate these kinds of confounding factors as explanations for changes in the target behavior. The counterbalancing strategy described previously can be a useful tool to address many of these issues. For example, in our illustrative study, the playground conditions could be counterbalanced across the sections of the school yard and participants.

Reliability of Participant Performance Measures and Fidelity of Treatment

The unique structure of the ATD demands that researchers (a) regularly assess the reliability of the data collection procedures used to quantify the participants' performance and (b) continuously evaluate the fidelity of the implementation of the interventions throughout the comparison phase. In developing these assessment procedures it is critical that the researcher equally distributes the observations across each phase of the study, dependent variable, interventions, and participants. A researcher's failure to address these issues will jeopardize the researcher's ability to assess experimental control and to eliminate alternate explanations for observed changes in the target behavior.

Design Variations

The basic ATD is comprised of a single comparison phase (see Figure 10.1 above). The interventions that are being compared are simultaneously introduced with each participant and are rapidly alternated within or across treatment sessions. The comparison phase continues until one of the interventions has a differential effect on the target behavior.

However, in the second most common design option, the researcher implements a baseline phase to establish stable performance of the target behavior. In the comparison phase, the interventions being studied are rapidly alternated within or across treatment sessions. The comparison phase continues until one intervention produces a differential effect on the target behavior. Once the most effective intervention is identified for a participant, the researcher initiates a second baseline phase. As in other withdrawal designs the expectation is that the target behavior will return to baseline levels. This enables the researcher to clearly document experimental control by the interventions.

ATD with a No-treatment Control Condition

One potential alternative design option that allows the researcher to eliminate the need to return to baseline is to insert a no-treatment control condition in the treatment schedule during the comparison phase (Figure 10.2a). For example, in the illustrative

Figure 10.2 Variations in the ATD

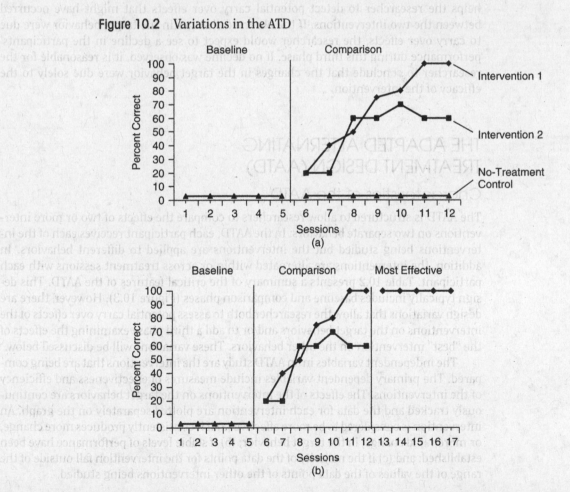

study on social interactions, the researcher might develop a treatment schedule in which a no-treatment session was implemented every third school day with the participants. This option allows the researcher to directly compare the impact of the interventions with baseline continuously throughout the study and provide the evidence necessary to document experimental control. Equally important, however, is that the addition of a no-treatment session within the comparison phase increases the ability of the researcher to detect carry over effects. If the participant's performance during the no-treatment sessions changes across time, this would alert the researcher to the possibility of carry over effects.

ATD with a Best Treatment Phase

A second variation in the ATD is to add a third experimental phase in which the researcher implements the most effective intervention alone (Figure 10.2b). This additional phase allows the researcher to assess whether the changes in the target behavior that are produced by the "best" intervention maintain across time. In addition, this third phase also helps the researcher to detect potential carry over effects that might have occurred between the two interventions. If the observed changes in the target behavior were due to carry over effects, the researcher would expect to see a decline in the participants' performance during this third phase. If no decline was observed, it is reasonable for the researcher to conclude that the changes in the target behavior were due solely to the efficacy of the intervention.

THE ADAPTED ALTERNATING TREATMENT DESIGN (AATD)

Characteristics of the AATD

The AATD is structured to allow researchers to compare the effects of two or more interventions on two separate behaviors. In the AATD, each participant receives each of the interventions being studied but the interventions are applied to different behaviors. In addition, the interventions are alternated within or across treatment sessions with each participant. Table 10.2 presents a summary of the critical features of the AATD. This design typically includes baseline and comparison phases (Figure 10.3). However, there are design variations that allow the researcher both to assess potential carry over effects of the interventions on the target behaviors and/or to add a third phase examining the effects of the "best" intervention on the other behaviors. These variations will be discussed below.

The independent variables in an AATD study are the interventions that are being compared. The primary dependent variables include measures of effectiveness and efficiency of the interventions. The effects of the interventions on the target behaviors are continuously tracked and the data for each intervention are plotted separately on the graph. An intervention is considered to be more effective (a) if it consistently produces more change, or more rapid change, in the target behavior; (b) if stable levels of performance have been established; and (c) if the majority of the data points for the intervention fall outside of the range of the values of the data points of the other interventions being studied.

Table 10.2   Features of the AATD.

	Adapted Alternating Treatment Design (AATD)
Purpose	Compare the effects of two or more interventions or treatment conditions on separate behaviors.
General Characteristics	Alternating presentations of the interventions or treatment conditions with individual participants or groups.
Design Strengths	Can be used in examining the effects of interventions or treatment conditions on new (nonreversible) behaviors.
	Can be used to compare the impact of multiple interventions.
	Allows for more immediate intervention or treatment because interventions do not have to be "lagged" in across behaviors or participants.
Design Weaknesses	Alternation of treatments or conditions may not mesh with the typical structure of schools or other service settings.
	Requires that the researcher control for a number of potential threats to internal validity such as amount of exposure to intervention or treatment condition, the individuals carrying out the intervention or treatment, or location of the intervention or treatment.

For example, a researcher might be interested in comparing the effects of two response-prompting strategies (i.e., constant time delay and the system of most-to-least prompts) on the acquisition of sight word reading skills with four children with disabilities. Prior to the study, the researcher would identify a set of sight words that each student could not read. The sight words would be organized into two instructional sets consisting of the same number of words. Then each of the sight word sets would be taught using either constant time delay or the system of most-to-least prompts. The researcher would conduct baseline and establish stable performance on each set of sight words for each child. The researcher would then implement a comparison phase in which the assistance strategies were alternated across school days during the children's regular reading period. The researcher would record each student's performance under each assistance condition during each session. The comparison phase would continue until the student could read each set of sight words at a predetermined performance criteria. The assistance strategy that produced the fastest rate of acquisition across students would be determined to be the most effective.

In contrast to the Multiple Treatment Design (MTD) and the Alternating Treatment Design (ATD), the AADT is a good option when the researcher is interested in studying the effects of two or more interventions on the development of new behaviors (or nonreversible behaviors). The Multiple Treatment Design (MTD) and the Alternating Treatment Design (ATD) are structured to assess the effects of two or more interventions on single target behavior that is likely to return to baseline levels when the treatments are

Figure 10.3   Common structure of the AATD

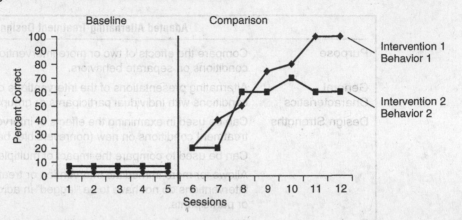

withdrawn. This feature of the MTD and the ATD creates significant problems for researchers in addressing questions that focus on target behaviors that do not have this characteristic. Consequently, the MTD or the ATD would not be an appropriate design for our illustrative study comparing the effects of constant time delay and the system of most-to-least prompts on children's acquisition of sight word reading skills. For example, it would impossible to differentiate the effects of the prompting strategies on the acquisition of sight word reading if both interventions were applied to the same set of sight words. In addition, it is unlikely that, having learned to read the sight words, a participant's performance would return to baseline levels if the interventions were withdrawn.

Although the AATD provides an effective approach for comparing the efficacy of interventions in teaching new behaviors, it is particularly susceptible to carry over and sequence effects. In addition, the structure of the AATD creates additional challenges for the researcher in ensuring that the target behaviors selected for the study are equally difficult and are functionally independent of one another (Gast & Wolery, 1998; Romer, Billingsley, & White, 1988; Sindelar, Rosenberg, & Wilson, 1985). In implementing a study using the AATD, the researcher must ensure that the target behaviors identified for the study are equally difficult for the participants. Without this control, it is impossible to determine if differences in a participant's performance are due to the relative efficacy of the interventions or to the fact that one behavior is "easier" for the participant than the other. In our illustrative study, if the two sets of sight words differed significantly from one another in terms of reading level, it would be impossible for the researcher to draw any valid conclusions about the relative efficacy of the two response prompting strategies.

AATD studies also require that the target behaviors be functionally independent of one another. In other words, the researcher must ensure that the acquisition of one of the target behaviors does not lead to improved performance of the other behavior. For example, brushing one's teeth and writing one's name could be understood as functionally independent, because it is extremely unlikely that learning to do one of the behaviors would result in improved performance of the other behavior. In our illustrative study, the researcher would attempt to identify sight words that reduced the likelihood that these kinds of carry over effects would occur. For example, the instructional sets might not include sight words such as MEN and WOMEN because they are frequently paired with one another in many school and community settings. In addition, the similarity in their structure might increase the likelihood that the participant could read one word after learning to read the other. These kinds of cross over effects between the target behaviors would seriously limit the researcher's ability to document clear experimental control by the interventions.

Implementing an AATD Study

Research Notes 10.2 presents a checklist of the steps necessary to successfully implement an AATD study. The procedural considerations for the AATD are essentially the same as for the ATD. The researcher must (a) counterbalance the introduction and presentation sequence of the interventions across participants or develop a randomized presentation sequence; (b) control the exposure of participants or groups to each intervention; (c) ensure that the interventions are procedurally equivalent; and (d) regularly track the reliability of data collection procedures and the fidelity of implementation of the interventions. However, the structure of the AATD requires the researcher to consider several other procedural issues in order to minimize the threats to internal validity previously discussed and to document experimental control. These include (1) identifying dependent variables and measures that will assess both the effectiveness and efficiency of the interventions, (2) establishing a criterion for evaluating the relative efficacy of the interventions, (3) ensuring that the target behaviors are equally difficult for the participants, and (4) ensuring that the behaviors are functionally independent.

Identifying Multiple Dependent Variables and Measures

The purpose of the ATD is to enable the researcher to determine whether one intervention is "better than" another. In order to achieve this goal, the researcher must examine both the *effectiveness* and the *efficiency* of the interventions. *Effectiveness* refers to the extent to which the interventions produced meaningful changes in the target behavior. Measures of effectiveness often include percent of correct responses, number of behaviors demonstrated within a specified period of time, the amount of time the participant engages in the target behavior, and so on. *Efficiency* refers to how quickly the interventions produced meaningful changes in the target behavior. Measures of efficiency typically include the number of trials or sessions that participants require to achieve a specified level of performance that is established prior to the initiation of the study. In order to make a clear determination of which intervention works the best, the researcher must use measures that assess both

---

Research Notes 10.2

AADT Study Implementation Checklist

Operationally define the dependent variables and measures, focusing on both effectiveness and efficiency of the intervention.

Identify target behaviors that are equally difficult and functionally independent.

Operationally define the interventions, ensuring that they are procedurally equivalent.

Counterbalance the introduction of the interventions across participants or groups.

Initiate baseline and collect data until stable performance has been established.

Initiate the comparison phase, implementing the treatment schedule until each participant meets the predetermined performance with one or more of the interventions.

their effectiveness and efficiency. It is quite possible that all of the interventions being compared in a study could produce significant changes in the target behavior across all participants or groups. When this occurs, the relative efficacy of an intervention can only be determined by analyzing how fast it produced the desired changes.

Establish a Performance Criterion

It is highly recommended that researchers establish a predetermined criterion for assessing whether meaningful changes in the target behavior have occurred (Gast & Wolery, 1984; Holcombe et al., 1994; Romer et al., 1988; Tawney & Gast, 1984). For example, in our illustrative study the researcher might establish a criterion that required participants to correctly read 90% of the sight words on two consecutive treatment sessions in each intervention to end the comparison phase. This would allow the researcher to not only establish whether the response prompting strategies had produced meaningful changes in the participant's sight word reading skills but to directly compare how quickly the strategies produced these changes. This could be done, for example, by counting the number of instructional trials that participants required to meet the criterion in each intervention condition.

Identify Target Behaviors that Are Equally Difficult

Although empirical methods for establishing the equivalence of target behaviors have been proposed in the literature (Romer et al., 1988), the more widely used approach is based on a two-step process described by Gast and Wolery (1988). These authors suggest that establishing the equivalence of two behaviors can be done by first matching the target behaviors on the complexity of the discriminations and movements that must be completed by the participants. Next, the researcher assesses the actual differences in the participant's performance of the target behaviors during baseline.

In the first step, the researcher conducts an analysis of the relative difficulty of the discriminations and movements that are embedded within the potential target behaviors. In some areas, such as reading and mathematics, measures of the relative difficulty of material are readily available and widely used (i.e., "readability" scores, grade-equivalence scores). For example, in the illustrative study described previously the researcher selected sight words for each instructional set based on their grade-level equivalence scores. However, such standards may not exist for all behaviors. This is especially true when researchers are interested in studying behaviors that occur naturally in home, school, or community settings. In these situations, Gast and Wolery (1988) suggest that behaviors must be matched based on the number and complexity of the discriminations and movements that participants are required to complete.

For example, McDonnell and McFarland (1988) compared the effects of two chaining strategies in teaching Laundromat skills to four high school students with moderate to profound mental retardation using an AATD. The students were taught to load and start a washing machine and to purchase "Tide" from a commercial soap dispenser in a Laundromat located near their school. To successfully use the washer, the students needed to complete six steps including locating an empty machine, measuring and inserting laundry soap, loading the clothes, setting the wash cycle, inserting four quarters into the coin slot, activating the machine, and removing the clothes from the machine. The soap dispenser also required the students to complete six steps including locating the machine, identifying the correct laundry soap, moving the selection bar to the correct position, inserting one quarter and one dime into the coin slot, activating the dispenser, and retrieving the soap. Based on the initial analysis of the specific discriminations and movements necessary to complete these steps, the researchers concluded that the two behaviors were likely to be equally difficult for the participants in the study.

Once behaviors of comparable difficulty have been identified, the researcher must document that there are no differences in the participant's ability to complete the behaviors prior to implementation of the interventions. This is accomplished by demonstrating that the participant's performance during baseline is stable (i.e., no significant variation across data points) and that the mean value of the participant's performance on both behaviors is equal or nearly equal. In the illustrative sight word study, the researcher would examine the baseline data to see if the percentage of words read correctly by the participants in each instructional set was approximately the same across all of the data points. Similarly, in their study, McDonnell & McFarland (1988) found that the percentage of correct steps completed by the participants during baseline was identical across the two behaviors. Given this, they argued that it was reasonable to assume that the two behaviors had the same level of difficulty for the participants in the study.

Of course, it is impossible to determine definitively whether two behaviors are equally difficult for a participant. The best that researchers can do is to reduce the likelihood that any changes in the target behaviors can be attributed to such differences. The process proposed by Gast & Wolery (1988) provides a reasonable and thoughtful approach to addressing this problem.

Identify Target Behaviors that Are Functionally Independent

Carry over effects between target behaviors are a unique threat to the internal validity of AATD studies. In typical educational settings, carry over effects, or the generalization of interventions to nontrained behaviors, is considered a positive outcome for students. For example, it would be considered a benefit if a student was able to purchase items in a fast food restaurant after he was taught to purchase items in a grocery store. However, this phenomenon in AATD studies seriously limits the ability of the researcher to document the differential effects of the interventions being studied. While the problem of the functional independence of target behaviors is widely recognized, specific strategies for resolving it have not been developed or validated. At this point, researchers must rely on a logical analysis of the target behavior to identify features of the response or the materials used during intervention that would increase the likelihood of carry over effects. In addition, researchers can use the design variations described previously to detect carry over effects if the target behaviors may be prone to such influences.

Design Variations

The AATD typically includes baseline and comparison phases (see Figure 10.3 above). During baseline, the researcher simultaneously collects data on all target behaviors until stable performance has been established. In the comparison phase, the interventions are rapidly alternated within or across treatment sessions. In addition, the interventions are implemented following a predetermined presentation schedule that is designed to control for possible sequence effects. The comparison phase continues until one of the interventions is shown to be more effective than the other.

AADT with a No-treatment Control Condition

Figure 10.4a presents a design variation that helps the researcher to assess the potential carry over effects of the interventions being studied. In this option, a third behavior of equal difficulty is identified to serve as a no-treatment behavior, and is tracked across the baseline and comparison phases for each participant (Holcombe et al., 1994; Romer et al., 1988). For example, in the illustrative study on sight words, the researcher would develop a third set of sight words at the same reading level that would serve as a "control" set. For each participant, two of the three word sets would be randomly assigned to the response prompting strategies. The third set of words would serve as the no-treatment control.

Figure 10.4   Variations on the AATD

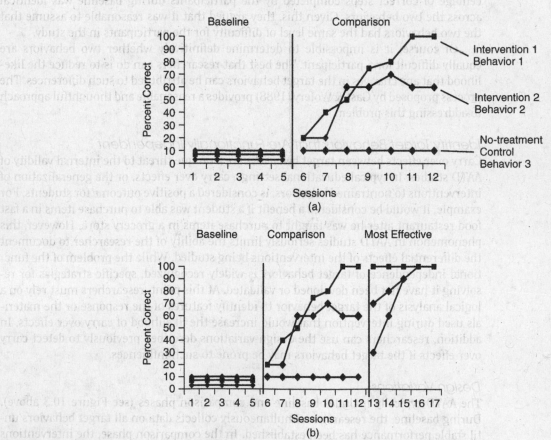

The researcher would assess the participant's performance on all three sets of sight words throughout the course of the study and would record the data for each set separately on the graph. Carry over effects would be suspected if the participant's performance on the control behavior improved during the comparison phase of the study. If the change in the control behavior was significant, then it would be difficult for the researcher to clearly differentiate the unique effects of the interventions on the target behaviors.

AADT with a Best Treatment Phase

A second variation in AATD is to add a third experimental phase in which the most effective treatment is applied to all target behaviors selected for the study (Figure 10.4b). This phase allows for the replication of the effects of the "best" intervention on additional behaviors. The participant's improved performance on the second target behavior and/or no-treatment control behavior would strengthen the demonstration of experimental control.

EXAMPLES FROM THE APPLIED RESEARCH LITERATURE

Alternating Treatment Design (ATD)

Reinhartsen, Garfinkle, & Wolery (2002) compared teacher selection of toys and child choice of toys on the amount of time that three 2-year-old boys with autism appropriately interacted with the toys. Prior to the initiation of the study, the researchers selected a pool of toys for each child based on their preferences and observed the frequency of interaction with the toys during free-play time. These data were collected over a three-month period during daily 45-minute observation periods. Based on these data, six or seven toys were selected for each participant for use in the study. The teacher- and child-choice conditions were alternated daily. However, no condition was used on two consecutive days. The treatment sessions under each intervention condition were comprised of two consecutive 5-minute segments.

In the teacher-choice condition, the teacher randomly selected two toys prior to the treatment session (one for each 5-minute segment). The teacher presented the toy to the child, directed his attention to it, and prompted him to play with it. The teacher then removed herself from the play area. The teacher was instructed to keep the child in the play area and to prompt the child's engagement with the toy. In the child-choice condition, the teacher presented two toys to the child prior to the initiation of each treatment session. After the child indicated a preference for one of the toys, he was taken to the play area. The teacher used the same procedures to initiate the session and prompt the child's engagement with the toy.

The primary dependent variables for the child's performance were the percent of observation intervals in which the child was engaged with the toy, engaged in problem behavior, or not engaged with the toy. In addition, the researchers also tracked a number of teacher behaviors including use of physical prompts, modeling, talking with the child,

Figure 10.5 Illustrative ATD graph from the literature

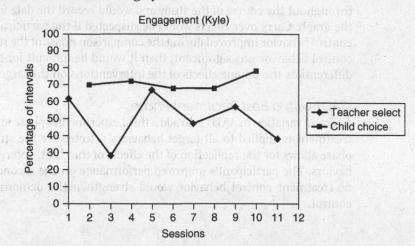

Source: Reinhartsen, D. B., Garfinkle, A. N., & Wolery, M. (2002). Engagement with toys in two-year-old children with Autism: Teacher selection versus child choice. *Research and Practice for Persons with Severe Disabilities,* vol. 27, pp. 175–187. Reprinted with permission.

silent observation, and other behaviors. Data were collected using a 5-second momentary time sampling procedure within alternating 30-second blocks. During the first block the observers tracked the child's behaviors; in the second block they focused on the teacher's behaviors.

Figure 10.5 presents illustrative graphs for one of the children participating in the study. The researchers' overall conclusions were that child-choice condition resulted in higher rates of engagement with toys. The researchers also indicate that neither of the intervention conditions resulted in substantial increases in the rate of problem behavior by participants.

Adapted Alternating Treatment Design (AATD)

Miracle, Collins, Schuster, and Grisham-Brown (2001) used an AATD to compare the effects of peer- and teacher-delivered individualized instruction in teaching basic sight words to four secondary students with moderate and severe disabilities. Prior to the initiation of the study, the researchers identified 15 sight words for each student that might be used in developing a list for shopping at a grocery store. The words were organized into a peer-delivered set, a teacher-delivered set, and a control set, each consisting of five words. The peer tutors and the teacher used an instructional package including a three-second constant time-delay procedure, differential reinforcement, and systematic error correction procedures to teach the words to the students in their self-contained classroom. Each word was presented to the students twice during each session. The peer-delivered and teacher-delivered conditions were alternated each day.

Figure 10.6   Illustrative AATD graph from the literature

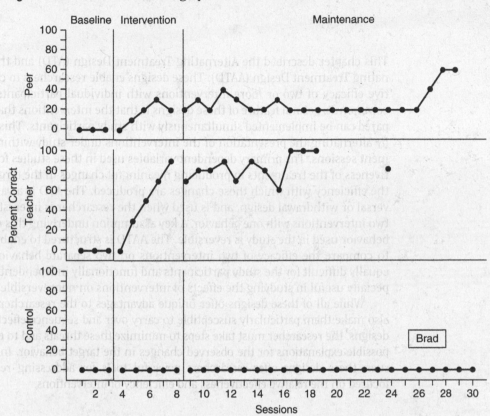

Source: Miracle, S. A., Collins, B. C., Schuster, J. W., & Grisham-Brown, J. (2001). Peer-versus teacher-delivered instruction: Effects on acquisition and maintanence. *Education and Training in Mental Retardation and Developmental Disabilities,* vol. 36, Figure 1, p. 379. Reprinted with permission.

The primary dependent measures included the number of words in each set that the students read correctly and the number of instructional sessions that students required to meet a performance criterion of 100% correct word reading on three consecutive sessions. Trial-by-trail student performance data were collected during each of the peer- and teacher-delivered instructional sessions. Student performance data for the control set were collected during daily probe sessions conducted by the teacher.

Figure 10.6 presents an illustrative graph for one of the students participating in the study. Based on their overall visual analysis of the data, the researchers concluded that peer- and teacher-delivered instruction were effective strategies for three of the four study participants. One of the students did not meet the performance criterion under the peer-delivered condition. The researchers' analysis of the number of sessions to criterion showed little difference between the overall efficiency of the two interventions for the three students who had met the performance criterion.

SUMMARY

This chapter described the Alternating Treatment Design (ATD) and the Adapted Alternating Treatment Design (AATD). These designs enable researchers to compare the relative efficacy of two or more interventions with individual participants or groups. The common structural feature of these designs is that the interventions that are being compared can be implemented simultaneously with study participants. This is accomplished by alternating the presentation of the interventions under study within or across treatment sessions. The primary dependent variables used in these studies focus on the effectiveness of the treatments in producing meaningful changes in the target behaviors and the efficiency with which those changes are produced. The ATD is a variation of the reversal or withdrawal design, and is used when the researcher is interested in comparing two interventions with one behavior. A key assumption underlying this design is that the behavior used in the study is reversible. The AATD is structured to enable the researcher to compare the efficacy of two interventions on two separate behaviors that are both equally difficult for the study participants and functionally independent. The AATD is especially useful in studying the effects of interventions on nonreversible behaviors.

While all of these designs offer unique advantages to the researcher, their structures also make them particularly susceptible to carry over and sequence effects. In using these designs, the researcher must take steps to minimize these threats and to eliminate them as possible explanations for the observed changes in the target behavior. In spite of these issues, these designs offer researchers powerful tools for addressing research questions focused on the relative effectiveness and efficiency of interventions.

REFERENCES

Alberto, P., & Troutman, A. (2009). *Applied behavior analysis for teachers* (8th ed.). Columbus, OH: Merrill.

Barlow, D. H., & Hayes, S. C. (1979). Alternating treatments design: One strategy for comparing the effects of two treatments in a single participant. *Journal of Applied Behavior Analysis, 12,* 199–210.

Barlow, D. H., & Hersen, M. (1984). *Single case experimental designs.* Boston, MA: Allyn & Bacon.

Cooper, J. O., Heron, T. E., & Heward, W. L. (2007). *Applied behavior analysis* (2nd ed.). Columbus, OH: Merrill.

Gast, D. L., & Wolery, M. (1988). Parallel treatment design: A nested single participant design for comparing instructional procedures. *Education and Treatment of Children, 11,* 270–285.

Holcombe, A., Wolery, M., & Gast, D. L. (1994). Comparative single-participant research: Descriptions of designs and discussion of problems. *Topics in Early Childhood Education, 14,* 119–145.

Kazdin, A. E., & Hartmann, D. P. (1978). The simultaneous-treatment design. *Behavior Therapy, 9,* 912–922.

McDonnell, J., & McFarland, S. (1988). A comparison of forward and concurrent chaining strategies in teaching Laundromat skills to students with severe handicaps. *Research in Developmental Disabilities, 9,* 177–194.

Miracle, S. A., Collins, B. C., Schuster, J. W., & Grisham-Brown, J. (2001). Peer- versus teacher-delivered instruction: Effects on acquisition and maintenance. *Education and Training in Mental Retardation and Developmental Disabilities, 36,* 373–385.

Reinhartsen, D. B., Garfinkle, A. N., & Wolery, M. (2002). Engagement with toys in two-year-old children with autism: Teacher selection versus child choice. *Research and Practice for Persons with Severe Disabilities, 27,* 175–187.

Romer, L. T., Billingsley, F. F., & White, O. R. (1988). The behavioral equivalence problem in within-participant treatment comparisons. *Research in Developmental Disabilities, 9,* 305–315.

Sindelar, P. T., Rosenberg, M. S., & Wilson, R. J. (1985). An adapted alternating treatments design for instructional research. *Education and Treatment of Children, 8,* 67–76.

Tawney, J. W., & Gast, D. L. (1984). *Single participant research in special education.* New York, NY: Merrill.

Ulman, J. D., & Sulzer-Azaroff, B. (1975). Multi-element baseline designs in educational research. In E. Ramp & G. Semb (Eds.), *Behavior analysis: Areas of research and application* (pp. 337–391). Upper Saddle River, NJ: Prentice Hall.

DISSEMINATING YOUR
RESEARCH RESULTS

It is widely accepted that the research process is not complete until the results of the researcher's study are shared with other scholars, policy makers, and the public at large (American Psychological Association, 2009). The dissemination of research results has a number of potential benefits, including enhancing the field's knowledge base; improving professional development; improving the effectiveness of educational and community service programs; and shaping policy development at the state and national levels. Dissemination can take many forms ranging from informal discussions with colleagues and students to the publication of books. In fact, most researchers take advantage of as many options as possible to share what they have learned. However, the two most important outlets for the new researcher's work are presenting at national professional conferences and publishing in professional journals. While the thought of presenting at a conference or trying to write a research article can be intimidating, the skills necessary to be successful in these arenas can be learned and mastered through practice. The purpose of this chapter is twofold. First, we provide a general description of the conference presentation and journal publication process. Next, we provide some general recommendations that may assist new researchers to "get their foot in the door" to successfully disseminate their work.

CONFERENCE PRESENTATIONS

Most national professional, consumer, and advocacy organizations host annual conferences. These conferences provide a forum to inform members of recent advances in the field, to exchange ideas, and to network with others who have similar interests. Presenting a paper at one or more conferences not only allows a researcher to share the results of their study with different constituent groups, but also provides opportunities to get feedback on both their research methods and the implications of their results for research, practice, and policy.

The papers presented at professional conferences are typically selected by organizations in two ways. First, the organization may invite outstanding scholars to present to the membership on their research. Second, and the most common avenue for researchers, is to submit a proposal to the organization to make a presentation at the conference. The researcher's proposal is reviewed by the organization for content and quality. And if approved, the researcher will be given a time slot in the conference program.

The Proposal Review Process

Although there is some variation, the proposal review process for most professional organizations includes three steps: (1) a call for papers/presentations, (2) the proposal review, and (3) notification.

Call for Papers/Presentations

A call for papers/presentations is a request by an organization for proposals to present research findings on a topic that is of interest to its membership. The call for papers/presentations will be distributed to members several months in advance of the conference date. The call will typically be published in the primary journals and newsletters of the organization, as well as on its web site. The call will often include the following information:

- The theme of the conference. The theme usually focuses on current issues facing the field or the organization's membership.
- The "strands" or "focus areas" that will be emphasized at the conference. These may include particular topical areas (e.g., alternative assessments, instructional strategies in general education classes) or reflect the structural units within the organization (e.g., learning disabilities, developmental disabilities, education, employment services).
- The presentation formats that are available in the program.
- The application process.
- The deadline for submission.

In recent years, many organizations have expanded the range of presentation formats at their conferences. For example, poster sessions are an increasingly popular format at professional conferences. In these sessions, researchers present the details of their study on an easel or a bulletin board. The researcher stands beside the poster while the conference participants review the information that the researcher has displayed. Two key advantages of poster sessions are that they encourage interaction between the researcher and the participants, and that they allow the researcher to make connections with other scholars who have similar interests. Posters are often grouped thematically and sessions can range between one to two hours in length.

Generally the most common presentation format is the individual paper presentation. In these sessions, the researcher is given a specific amount of time to present the purpose, design, and implications of their study. Another popular format is the symposia, which is a collection of individual paper presentations that are focused on a single topic.

For example, a group of researchers might submit a symposia proposal that includes studies that are focused on alternative methods for assessing problem behavior or the cost-effectiveness of employment programs for adults with developmental disabilities. One of the researchers serves as the symposia "moderator" and introduces the session and each of the individual paper presenters. Symposia frequently have one or more "discussants" who will respond to the issues addressed by each of the papers. Discussants are often established scholars who have done research in the area and who can provide some perspective on the importance of each of the studies for the field and for future research.

A final presentation format is the panel. These sessions are structured to promote discussion and interaction between the panel participants. Although panels can be designed to present the results of research studies, more often they are structured to address broader topics or issues that currently confront the field or organization. The panel members are selected because of their knowledge or expertise in the area. Generally, a panel moderator introduces the panel presenters and the topic. Then panel members are separately asked to offer their comments on the topic. Following the presentations, panel members are encouraged to discuss their viewpoints and audience members are invited to ask questions.

Proposal Review

Presentation proposals are most often reviewed by a committee appointed by the organization. The number of committee members varies based on the size of the organization and the conference. Frequently, a proposal will be reviewed by a sub set of committee members who have knowledge and expertise in a particular area. Each organization has its own standards for evaluating presentation proposals and these are often described in the call for papers/presentations. However, common criteria include:

- The extent to which the proposal aligns with one of the strands or topics emphasized in the call for papers/presentations.
- The importance of the topic to the organization membership.
- The methodological rigor of the study.
- Applications for future research and/or practice.

Notification

The researcher will be notified of the review committee's decision in writing. The first and most positive decision that a committee can make is to accept the proposal. Review committees generally do not provide researchers with recommendations or suggestions to improve the content and organization of the presentation. The researcher is left to develop the paper or presentation based on the information included in the proposal. A second common decision is to accept the proposal but with a change in format. For example, the committee may decide to accept the proposal but ask the researcher to change the presentation format from an individual paper presentation to a poster. This decision does not necessarily reflect the quality of the proposal and may be based on something as simple as the number of proposals received and accepted by the committee.

Finally, the committee may reject the proposal. Although it would be helpful, it is unlikely that the researcher will receive any feedback about why the proposal was rejected.

Although this decision can be disappointing, it should not be assumed that it is based on the quality of the work. A decision to reject a proposal may be based on a number of factors ranging from the fact that it did not align with the focus of the conference to a limited number of presentation slots in the program. There is usually no way to appeal a rejection decision but the good news is that the work put into developing a proposal may not be lost. It is quite possible that, with some revision, a proposal rejected by one organization will be accepted by another.

Recommendations and Pointers

The initial decision to submit a presentation proposal must be based on the rigor of the research study and the importance of the findings. Before submitting a proposal, researchers are encouraged to share it with their colleagues and to get feedback on its potential success. The most important issue is the quality of the research design and the extent to which threats to internal and external validity are controlled in the study. Eye-popping effects by an intervention are not necessary; in fact, much can be learned from studies that do not produce effects or find no differences between interventions. The key is to understand what your results say and why they are important to future research and/or practice. Having said that, the recommendations for increasing your success in having a presentation proposal accepted are relatively straightforward:

- Choose a conference that focuses on the dissemination of research results and has themes that align with the purposes of your study.
- Determine the audiences (e.g., researchers, practitioners, administrators, policy makers) that are most likely to be interested in your results and pick a conference that caters to these groups.
- Pick an appropriate presentation format. Be realistic about the strengths and weaknesses of your study and choose a format that best accommodates them.
- When developing the proposal, strictly adhere to the guidelines. Write the proposal with specific audiences in mind and highlight how the study can benefit these individuals (Figure 11.1).

Recommendations for Poster Sessions

When developing a poster presentation, researchers should strictly adhere to the guidelines provided by the organization. The challenge will be to present, in the limited space provided, the information necessary for conference participants to understand your study. Although posters can be very elaborate (and expensive!), the best course is usually to be as simple and direct as possible. Many researchers use presentation software such as Power-Point to develop slides that are then placed on the easel or bulletin board (Figure 11.2). The advantages to this approach are that it allows for a professional presentation of the information but utilizes materials that are much easier to transport and handle. Obviously, you want to make the poster attractive and give participants a reason to stop. However, too

TITLE OF THE PAPER OR POSTER PRESENTATION

The Relative Effectiveness of Embedded Instruction in General Education Classes and One-to-One and Small Group Instruction in Special Education Classes

PRESENTERS:

Presenter/Chairperson

Name (Last, First) McDonnell, John   Degree PhD
Title Professor
Affiliation Department of Special Education, University of Utah
Address (complete)1705 E. Campus Center Dr., Rm 221 MBH
Salt Lake City, Utah 84112-9253
Phone # (801) 585-0557   fax (801) 585-6476
Email McDonnell@ed.utah.edu

Presenter #2

Name (Last, First) Jameson, Matt   Degree MEd
Address (complete) Department of Special Education, 1705 E. Campus Center
Dr. Rm 221 MBH, Salt Lake City, Utah 84112-9253
Email Matt.Jameson@ed.utah.edu

Presenter #3

Name (Last, First)   Degree
Address (complete)

Email

Presenter #4

Name (Last, First)   Degree
Address (complete)

Email

MOST APPROPRIATE THEME: (identify)

☐ **1. Self-determination and quality of life** (*Best practices, assessment, choice-making, decision-making, problem-solving, citizenship, personal and family quality of life . . .*)

☐ **2. Rights and ethics** (*Ethical values, laws and rights of citizens, community attitudes, respect, ethical dilemmas, issues, bioethics . . .*)

X **3. School inclusion** (*Early intervention, transition, special/regular school, interpersonal relationships. . .*)

☐ **4. Social inclusion** (*Community and work inclusion, interpersonal relationships, sexuality, housing, social participation, retirement . . .*)

☐ **5. Barriers to community living** (*Diagnosis, classification, epidemiology, problem behavior, aloneness, parenting, criminal justice . . .*)

☐ **6. Policies and service delivery** (*School, health and social policies, service delivery and management, quality of services, ISP/IEP, resource allocation . . .*)

☐ **7. Sports and leisure** (*Adapted physical education, facilities, leisure, travelling, vacations . . .*)

175

Figure 11.1 Illustrative presentation proposal for the American Association on Intellectual and Developmental Disabilities (*Continued*)

☐ **8. Health** *(Prevention, promotion, accessibility, healthcare, aging, mental health, genetics . . .)*
☐ **9. Technologies** *(Development, accessibility, utilization, assistive technology, Web access, mobility, home automation . . .)*
☐ **10. Sustainable urban development** *(Facilities, urban development, mobility, signage, home and public accessibility, transportation . . .)*
☐ **11. Spirituality** *(Spirituality, religion, grief and mourning, accessibility to place of worship . . .)*
☐ **12. Education and training** *(Continued education, post-graduate education, training curricula . . .)*

Symposia - Paper presentations - Poster presentations
FORMAT OF PRESENTATION: (Please check your preferred format of presentation.)
☐ **Symposium**   **X Paper presentation**   ☐ **Poster presentation**

Symposia. Symposia last 90 minutes and regroup a minimum of three presentations concern by the same theme and supported by a moderator.

Paper presentations. Paper presentations last 30 minutes each and will be clustered with two other presentations according to themes for a total of 90 minutes per session.

Poster presentations. Poster presentation sessions will be reserved in order to permit all conference participants to attend the poster sessions. One author must be present during the poster session to present to interested participants.

Title: (Maximum of 150 characters)

The Relative Effectiveness of Embedded Instruction in General Education Classes and One-to-One and Small Group Instruction in Special Education Classes

Summary: (Maximum of 200 words)

Embedded instruction has been demonstrated to be an effective strategy for supporting the participation of students with intellectual disabilities in the general education curriculum and general education classes. This session will summarize the results of two single subject studies comparing the relative effectiveness of embedded instruction in general education classes with traditional one-to-one and small-group instructional formats in special education classes. In the first study, the results indicate that both one-to-one embedded instruction and one-to-one massed practice instruction were effective in promoting the acquisition of the target skills. The data showed that one-to-one massed-trial instruction was more effective for two of the students, one-to-one embedded instruction was more effective for one student, and the two strategies were equally effective for the last student. In the second study, the results suggest that embedded and small-group instruction were equally effective in promoting the acquisition and generalization of the target skill with four students. The implications of these findings for the use of embedded instruction as a strategy for supporting the inclusion of students with intellectual disabilities in general education classes are discussed.

If presentation is accepted, I/we (all participating presenters) agree to register, pay the registration fee and attend:

Signature of First presenter/Chairperson John McDonnell

Please send proposal by email to: ***Inclusion2006@uqam.ca*** (please use WORD format or send by Fax at (514) 363-5855). DEADLINE FOR SUBMITTING PROPOSALS: **November 14th, 2005**. An acknowledgment of receipt will be emailed to primary presenter.

Source: Conference Presentation Proposal, American Association on Intellectual and Developmental Disabilities. Reprinted with permission.

176

Figure 11.2 Illustration of a poster presentation

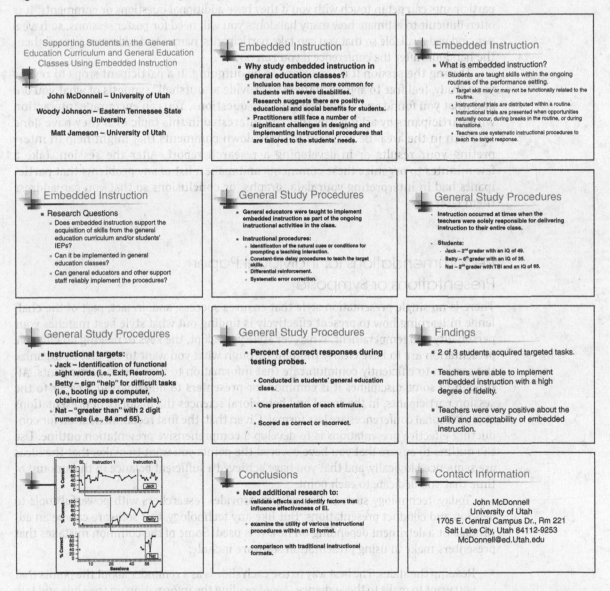

many photographs and graphics can be a distraction. The best advice is to include essential information on the purpose, methods, results, and implications of your study. Make sure that graphs and other data summaries are self-explanatory and are large enough for people to read. It is recommended that you develop an "executive summary" of your study as a handout that participants can take with them. The summary can be a one- to three-page narrative document summarizing the key elements of the study or a handout based on your PowerPoint slides. Make sure that you include your contact information so that participants can get in touch with you if they have additional questions or comments. It is often difficult to estimate how many handouts you will need for poster sessions, so have a pen and pad available so that you can take participants' names and addresses to mail them the handouts after the conference if you run out.

During the session it is important to be outgoing. If a participant stops to review your study, feel free to approach them to provide a "nutshell" synopsis of what you did and what you found and ask if they have any questions. You can encourage interaction with participants by asking why they are interested in this topic or if they have done research in the area. Be prepared to write down comments that might help in interpreting your results or in developing a research report. After the session, take a few minutes to organize these comments and make a list of any problems that participants had in interpreting your data, graphs, or conclusions so that you can address them later.

Recommendations for Individual Paper Presentations or Symposia

There is no single presentation style that ensures success, and, in fact, part of the challenge in learning how to present effectively is finding out what style best matches your personality and temperament. Whatever style you adopt, the keys to making an effective presentation are to have clearly thought through what you want to say and to organize the session to efficiently communicate that information to the session participants. Although in some disciplines it is common for presenters to literally read a paper to the session participants, in the social and behavioral sciences the majority of presentations at professional conferences are less formal. Given that, the first recommendation for conducting effective presentations is to develop a comprehensive presentation outline. Use the outline to ensure that you have covered the points you want to make, that the ideas are sequenced logically, and that you have achieved a sufficient balance in the amount of time that you dedicate to each point.

Today, technology such as PowerPoint provides researchers with powerful tools to develop and conduct presentations. But like any technology, this software can be an advantage or a detriment depending on how it is used. Some of the common mistakes that presenters make in using presentation software include:

- Reading the slides. The best way to use each slide is as a reminder about the points that you want to make to the audience. Avoid reading the information on the slide and talk directly to the audience.
- Putting too much text on a slide. Try to use short phrases that highlight the points you want to make on each slide. You want the audience listening to you, not trying to read your slides.
- Overusing the "bells" and "whistles." Most presentation software comes with a lot of advanced graphics that allow you to "animate" text, graphs and tables, and artwork.

In the hands of a skilled presenter these features can be very effective; however, they also can distract from what the presenter is trying to communicate. Most regular conference participants have seen an interesting and generally well organized presentation fall apart because the presenter was trying to fix a problem with the graphics. A good rule of thumb is to only use a feature when it really enhances the point that you are trying to make.

- Assuming everyone can see the slides. Even with high quality equipment it is sometimes difficult for session participants to see slide images in a large conference room. A handout of your slides will minimize this problem for the participants and will allow them to listen to you rather than trying to take notes.

In organizing the presentation on a single subject research study you should follow the general outline of a research report. A common mistake made by new presenters is not spending enough time describing their study procedures and methods and instead rushing to their results. This inevitably leads to a burst of questions from session participants. It is recommended that you thoroughly describe the subjects, settings, dependent and independent variables, and design and study procedures. This will assist the session participants to understand the context of the study and to better interpret the results. A second recommendation is to make sure that you link your discussion of the results directly to the graphed data while carefully discussing any factors (i.e., change in level, overlap, stability, trend) that weaken the demonstration of experimental control. In your summary of the study, be forthcoming with any potential limitations that might impact internal or external validity. It is also advisable to make a list of potential questions that session participants might ask and be prepared to provide clear and concise answers. Finally, practice the presentation several times to make sure that the ideas flow smoothly and that you stay within your allocated time limit.

Recommendations for Panel Presentations

The effectiveness of a panel presentation hinges on the ability of the panel moderator to promote interaction and dialog between the panel members and between the panel members and the audience. There is no simple formula to achieve these outcomes; however, a few simple suggestions may prove useful:

- Pick panel members who know the area.
- Provide panel members with a clear understanding of the topic or issue that you want them to address. This can be done by providing them with copies of the proposal, by providing examples of innovative papers that capture the essence of the problems or issues to be addressed, and by highlighting for them how their research and their perspective could potentially move the discussion forward.
- Be prepared to ask the panel members questions. Often it is up to the moderator to get the discussion going and the best way to do that is to develop a set of questions that can "prime the pump" and get panel members talking with each other and with the audience.

WRITING RESEARCH ARTICLES

Making presentations at conferences is an effective way to disseminate the results of a study. However, most researchers, especially new researchers, also want to publish their study in a professional journal. While the publication process in the social and behavioral sciences is not without its problems (Borer, 1997; Skolnik, 2000; Smaby & Crews, 1998; Smaby, Crews, & Downing, 1999), it does promote self-regulation by the field in determining whether a study meets accepted scientific and ethical standards. Publication also provides a forum for researchers to share their work with individuals that have similar theoretical perspectives and research interests. Finally, and perhaps more importantly, publication allows the researcher to contribute to the development of an archive of studies that cumulatively builds the knowledge base in a particular area and helps shape the research agenda across time.

A number of authors have offered suggestions and recommendations to researchers on the writing and publishing process (Henson, 2003; Klingner, Scanlon, & Pressley, 2005; Maxwell & Cole, 1998; Ryan, 1998; Spooner, Spooner, Karvonen, & Algozine, 2002; Thompson, 1995). The general consensus is that learning the skills necessary to write journal articles can be mastered with practice and support. However, becoming proficient often takes researchers years of work and effort. Our experience suggests that attending to several key issues can increase the success of new researchers in learning this complex set of skills. The following sections outline the general steps in the publication process and provide recommendations that may assist researchers to become more successful in publishing their research studies.

The Publication Process

The publication process for most journals in behavioral and social sciences consists of six steps: (1) select a journal for possible publication; (2) prepare the manuscript; (3) submit the manuscript; (4) manuscript review; (5) revise the manuscript, and (6) manuscript acceptance and production.

Select a Journal

The first step in the publication process is to select a journal for possible publication. A good place to start is by reading the "Guidelines to Authors" or the "Editorial Policy" published in each potential journal (Figure 11.3). These guidelines will outline the overall mission of the journal and identify the types of articles it publishes. If you are not familiar with the journals it is also recommended that you examine several recent volumes to determine if the articles they publish are consistent with your study. Other criteria that the researcher may want to consider include:

- Circulation rates. The point of publishing your study is to distribute your findings to as large an audience as possible. The circulation rates for journals in a particular area can vary significantly, from several hundred subscribers up to tens of thousands.

Figure 11.3 Illustrative author guidelines/editorial policy

Editorial Policy

Intellectual and Developmental Disabilities (IDD) is a journal of policy, practices, and perspectives in the field of intellectual disabilities. As a journal with an applied focus, *IDD* publishes essays, qualitative and quantitative research articles, conceptual papers, comprehensive reviews, case studies, policy analyses, and innovative practice descriptions and evaluations. The style, methodology, or focus of an article is less important than its quality and contribution to our knowledge. *IDD* publishes journal-length articles, which are subject to peer-review, and commentaries, which appear in a feature called *Perspectives*.

Information for Contributors

Review Process and Editorial Decision
Articles submitted to *IDD* are subject to review by at least two and usually three anonymous reviewers selected by the Editor or Associate Editor. The review process is usually completed within 3 months of receipt of the manuscript. *IDD* strives toward fairness and courtesy in the review process.

Criteria for Acceptance
Articles are judged on relevance to policy or practice, potential reader interest, originality, and clarity of writing. Research articles are reviewed based on standards appropriate to the methodology used in the study. Other articles are reviewed according to scholarly or literary standards. Authors should address the implications of their articles for policy and practice, if not apparent.

Style
Intellectual and Developmental Disabilities adheres to the *2001 Publication Manual of the American Psychological Association* (APA, 5th edition). Manuscripts should be double-spaced on 8½" x 11" paper, with at least 1-inch margins on all sides. An abstract of no more than 120 words should be included. References should be typed double-spaced on a separate page. Articles should not exceed 20 pages in length, including references. Authors are encouraged to submit shorter manuscripts. Highly specialized or technical articles should be 5 pages in length. Because articles are reviewed anonymously, the author's name and other identifying information should appear only on the cover page.

Submissions
Intellectual and Developmental Disabilities uses a web-based manuscript submission and peer-review system called AllenTrack. Manuscripts should be submitted electronically to http://idd.allentrack.net. All manuscripts are peer-reviewed, so potential identifying information should be removed prior to submission. A letter of submission stating that the manuscript is not under review by any other journal should also be submitted. Corresponding authors who require assistance in submitting their manuscripts through AllenTrack should contact the editorial office via phone, 315-443-3851; fax, 315-443-4338; or e-mail, iddaaidd@syr.edu. Authors who choose not to submit their manuscript through AllenTrack may send it as an e-mail attachment to iddaaidd@syr.edu or on diskette to Steven J. Taylor, PhD, Center on Human Policy, Syracuse University, 805 S. Crouse Ave., Syracuse, NY 13244-2280. AllenTrack is able to convert most word 1=1 processing files (e.g., Word, WordPerfect, text, PostScript, and Rich Text Format).

Information for Contributors: Perspectives

Internet-Based Submission of Manuscripts
Intellectual and Developmental Disabilities uses a web-based manuscript submission and peer-review system called AllenTrack. AllenTrack is an on-line software system available that helps manuscripts flow seamlessly into the typesetting process. AllenTrack assists with basic editorial office tracking functions and review correspondence that typically would typically require considerable clerical effort. The system makes the publishing process more efficient, accommodating, and accessible to authors and reviewers all over the world.

Editorial Decision
Commentaries are published in *Perspectives*. *IDD* welcomes thoughtful, well-reasoned, interesting, clearly written contributions. Submissions are reviewed by the Editor and Perspectives Editors, who will make editorial decisions usually within a month after receipt of the manuscript. Detailed comments are not provided for manuscripts not accepted for publication in *Perspectives*.

Style
Commentaries should not exceed 5 pages. An abstract is not necessary.

Submission
Perspectives submissions should be submitted electronically to http://idd.allentrack.net. A cover letter should clearly state that the manuscript is being submitted to *Perspectives* and advise the editor if the submission is under review or has been published by any other journal.

General Information for Contributors

Language
IDD adheres to AAIDD policy regarding the use of "people-first language." Authors should use language that emphasizes the humanity of people with intellectual disabilities. Generic descriptive terms such as people, participants, students, children, and adults are preferred over subjects or informants. Language should be free of gender bias. *He* should not be used generically to refer to persons of both genders.

Copyright Assignment
In view of the Copyright Revision Act of 1976, if a manuscript is accepted for publication, the author(s) must sign a Copyright Assignment and Agreement conveying all copyright ownership, including electronic rights, to AAIDD. Permission to reproduce copyrighted materials for classroom use is granted.

Revisions and Corrections
The Editor reserves the right to reject manuscripts that do not meet the standards contained in this editorial policy and to make editorial changes in accepted articles that do not alter the meaning of the text.

Accepted Manuscripts
Once a manuscript is accepted for publication, the remainder of the production process is coordinated by the Managing Editor. Authors may receive galleys or a copyedited manuscript. Any changes should be sent to the Managing Editor, Stephanie Dean, e-mail: aaidd.journals@yahoo.com, or fax: 614-386-0309.

Data-Sharing
After research results are published, authors do not withhold the data on which their conclusions are based from other competent professionals who seek to verify the substantive claims through reanalysis and who intend to use such data only for that purpose, provided that the confidentiality of the participants can be protected and unless legal rights concerning proprietary data preclude their release.

Source: Editorial Policy. *Intellectual and Developmental Disabilities.* No figure or page number. It appears in every journal issue. Reprinted with permission.

- Acceptance rates. This figure represents the percentage of manuscripts received by the journal that are actually published. Acceptance rates can also vary significantly, from a low of 10% of the manuscripts to a high of over 60%. Lower acceptance rates are generally accepted to mean that the journal has higher editorial standards. This information can often be obtained by calling the journal or by reviewing the annual report of the editor to the journal subscribers.
- The editor and review board. The researcher may want to examine whether the editor and/or members of the editorial board have done work in the researcher's particular work area. Individuals with knowledge about your area of research are more likely to provide an insightful and comprehensive review of your manuscript.
- Publication lag. This represents the time between the date a manuscript is accepted and the time it is published. Most researchers want to get their results out as quickly as possible. However, the rates at which journals are able to get studies in press vary significantly. Some professional organizations regularly publish this information for their journals. For example, the American Psychological Association publishes these data for each journal it sponsors in the annual Summary Report of Journal Operations that appears each year in the *American Psychologist.* In addition, many journals publish with each article the dates that the manuscript was received, when it was initially accepted, and when it was finally accepted. These dates can give you a general sense of how long the journal's review process will take and how long it takes the journal to get accepted papers into press.

Preparing the Manuscript

The *Publication Manual of the American Psychological Association* (APA, 2009) is accepted by many disciplines in the social and behavioral sciences as the definitive guide for the preparation of a manuscript for publication. The manual provides specific directions to researchers on all elements of preparing a manuscript, from writing style to the organization of tables and figures. While the editing policies of many journals in the social and behavioral sciences are based on the APA manual, there are some exceptions. Researchers should read the author guidelines or editorial policy for the selected journal to confirm the editorial guidelines that it has adopted.

Submit the Manuscript

The author guidelines or editorial policy will indicate to whom the manuscript should be sent, the number of copies of the manuscript that should be submitted, and whether all copies of the manuscript should include a title page. In most cases, journals use a blind review process (Henson, 2003). In other words, the reviewers do not know who wrote the manuscript when they complete their reviews. As a result, the journal may ask the researcher to submit a certain number of copies of the manuscript without the cover page.

   Researchers are typically asked to submit a cover letter with the manuscript indicating that the manuscript represents the work of the researcher and co-authors, has not been published in another journal, and is not under review for publication in another journal. It is recommended that you list several ways that you can be contacted regarding the manuscript (e.g., postal address, telephone, e-mail). Most journals will send you a card, letter, or e-mail that confirms they have received your manuscript and will provide an estimate of how long it will take to review it.

Manuscript Review

Having received a manuscript, the editor will review it to make sure that it is consistent with the journal's editorial policy and focus. The editor has the option of returning the manuscript to the researcher if the editor believes that it is not appropriate for the journal. However, this is unlikely to occur if the researcher has done her homework in selecting the journal as a possible outlet for her study. The editor may assign the manuscript to an associate editor to serve as the action editor and to manage the review process. The action editor will send the manuscript to several review board members. Sometimes, the action editor will invite a nationally recognized researcher or scholar to serve as guest reviewer for a manuscript. This typically happens when there is not a sufficient number of review board members with expertise in the area addressed by the study employs or when it uses a unique design or data analysis procedure. As indicated previously, most journals use a blind review process to ensure that reviews are fair and unbiased.

Most journals ask reviewers to follow a prescribed process in conducting their review and to use standardized criteria in making their editorial recommendation. Review criteria often focus on the importance of the study to the field, the rigor of the study design and methods, the interpretation of the data, and the quality of the writing. Reviewers are asked to address these evaluation criteria in writing their reviews and to make a recommendation regarding publication of the manuscript to the editor. Typically, these recommendations can include: accept, accept with revision, revise and resubmit, or reject. A recommendation to "accept" means the reviewer believes that the manuscript can be published in the journal with only minor changes. A recommendation to "accept with revision" means that the reviewer believes that the study makes a contribution to the research base and meets expected basic scientific standards, but changes to the manuscript are necessary to improve its clarity or accuracy. A recommendation to "revise and resubmit" often means that the reviewer has multiple concerns about the contribution of the study to the field, the methods, the data analysis, and/or the interpretation of the results. When making this recommendation, most reviewers will be explicit about what their concerns are and how they should be addressed in a revision. A recommendation to "reject" a manuscript means that a reviewer has significant concerns about a manuscript and does not believe that the researcher can address them adequately in a revision.

Having received the reviewers' evaluations and recommendations, the action editor will make a publication decision and write a letter to the researcher explaining the decision. Generally, the reviewers' evaluations will be enclosed with the editor's letter. It is important to remember that the reviewers' recommendations are only advisory. Most editors will seriously consider the recommendations of the reviewers, but the ultimate decision about whether to publish a manuscript is the editor's alone. Consequently, it is possible that the editor's decision may deviate from the recommendations of the reviewers.

Revising the Manuscript

It is important to remember that very few manuscripts are ever accepted without revisions. In most cases, researchers will be asked to revise or rewrite some sections of the manuscript before it is published. The editor's decision letter typically lays out the specific revisions that must be made to the manuscript. The editor will frequently refer to specific comments or suggestions made by the reviewers and ask that the researcher address them. It is wise to respond to each of the recommendations made by the editor; however, there are times when responding to the editor is simply not possible or when you may disagree with the requested changes. A decision to not respond to an editor's recommendation is appropriate if you can make a good argument for why the change is not necessary or would be detrimental to the manuscript. It is important, however, to remember that the editor has the discretion to send a revised manuscript out for a second review. This almost always happens when the editor's decision is to "revise and resubmit" and it is likely to happen when the decision is "accept with revisions," especially when a number of changes have been requested. The second review will generally follow the procedures described previously. It is likely that the manuscript will be sent to the original set of reviewers.

When the manuscript has been revised, the researcher should send the requested number of copies to the editor with a cover letter. The letter should describe in detail the changes that have been made to the manuscript and the page numbers on which those changes may be found. Finally, if you have decided not to respond to one or more of the editor's recommendations, you should provide a detailed rationale for your decision.

Manuscript Acceptance and Production

A number of important steps occur after the manuscript is finally accepted and it goes into production. Generally, the manuscript will be sent to a technical editor who will review it for syntax, grammatical, and style errors. The technical editor will send the edited manuscript to the researcher for approval of the proposed changes. In addition to minor editing changes the manuscript may include "author queries" that ask the researcher to respond to issues such as confusing text, differences between citations and the references, or inconsistencies between the text and tables. Once the researcher has responded to the proposed changes and returns the edited manuscript, it goes to production and the publisher will develop a "galley proof" of the manuscript as it will appear in the journal. The researcher will be sent the proof and asked to review it for minor typos or small errors.

At some point during the production phase, the researcher (and any co-authors) will be asked to sign a copyright transfer and a certification of authorship. Prior to publication, the researcher and any co-authors are asked to transfer their copyrights to the manuscript to the organization that published the journal. This entitles the organization to control the future duplication, distribution, and sale of the manuscript. It is also common for the researcher (and any co-authors) to sign a certificate of authorship that confirms the order of authorship on the article and verifies that they accept responsibility for the accuracy of the content. Finally, if the researcher has used other copyrighted material in her manuscript, she will be asked to provide evidence that she has obtained permission from the copyright holder to reprint the material.

Recommendations and Pointers

While publishing your study is a critical element of the research process, it is also a very time-consuming activity that can be frustrating and at times disheartening. Although this can not be avoided, the following suggestions may increase your success and make the process more positive:

- Get feedback from peers and colleagues before you submit your manuscript. While it is true that a well written manuscript that describes a poorly designed and implemented study is likely to be rejected, the same is true for a poorly written manuscript that describes a high quality study.
- Your interactions with the editor during the review process should be kept to a minimum. Most researchers are anxious to get their papers into press as quickly as possible, but it is important to understand that the review process takes time. Repeated contacts with the editor during the review process to find out the status of your manuscript is unlikely to have any significant impact on the time it takes to complete the process. Most editors do their best to make sure that reviews are completed as quickly as possible. However, glitches do occur and it is appropriate to contact the editor if you do not receive a confirmation that he has received the manuscript or if you have not heard from the editor following the average publication lag for the journal.
- If the editorial decision on your manuscript is to "revise and resubmit," the researcher must assess the potential for publication against the time and effort required to make the requested changes. In these situations it is important to read the editor's letter carefully; often he will provide some indication of the chances that manuscript has of being accepted if the researcher makes the requested changes. Other factors that might influence the decision include whether the researcher agrees with the editor's decision; whether the requested changes are even possible; or whether the changes can be made within a reasonable time frame. In some cases, it may be wise for the researcher to identify another journal that might be more open to the study or that is more compatible with her vision for the manuscript.
- Don't personalize an editorial decision to reject a manuscript. It is important to realize that many researchers have manuscripts rejected. It is also common for researchers to submit manuscripts to two or more journals before they find a match. Researchers should carefully read the reviews they have received and make an honest appraisal of whether it is worth submitting to another journal or whether their energy would be better spent on the next study. If the researcher chooses to submit to another journal, the researcher should carefully read the reviews that she has received and revise the manuscript to address the primary concerns.

CONCLUSION

Disseminating the results of a study is an important final step in the research process. There are multiple avenues available to researchers to disseminate their findings but the most common approaches are making presentations at professional conferences and publishing in journals. Most new researchers should take advantage of both strategies to disseminate their work. It is often useful to present a study at a professional conference before developing a manuscript for publication. The feedback that the researcher receives about the study during a presentation can be very helpful in developing the manuscript for publication.

Presenting at professional conferences and writing journal articles require a complex set of skills. It is important for new researchers to understand that it will take time to develop these skills. Feedback is an important part of this process even when it is not positive. The challenge is to learn to use that feedback to support continued improvement and professional development.

REFERENCES

American Psychological Association (2009). *Publication manual of the American Psychology Association* (6th ed.). Washington, DC: Author.

Borer, D. A. (1997). The ugly process of journal submission: A call for reform. *Political Science and Politics, 30*(3), 558–560.

Henson, K. T. (2003). Writing for professional publication: Some myths and some truths. *Phi Delta Kappan, 84*(10), 788–791.

Klingner, J. K., Scanlon, D., & Pressley, M. (2005). How to publish in scholarly journals. *Educational Researcher, 34*(8), 21–27.

Maxwell, S. E., & Cole, D. A. (1998). Tips for writing (and reading) methodological articles. In A. E. Kazdin (Ed.), *Methodological issues and strategies in clinical research* (2nd ed., pp. 753–766). Washington, DC: American Psychological Association.

Ryan, M. (1998). Pitfalls to avoid in conducting and describing scholarly research. *Journalism and Mass Communication Educator, 52*(4), 72–79.

Skolnik (2000). Does counting publications provide any useful information about academic performance? *Teacher Education Quarterly 27*(2):15–25.

Smaby, M. H., & Crews, J. (1998). Publishing in scholarly journals: Part I – Is it attitude or technique? It's an attitude. *Counselor Education and Supervision, 37*, 218–223.

Smaby, M. H., Crews, J., & Downing, T. (1999). Publishing in scholarly journals: Part II – Is it attitude or technique? It's a technique. *Counselor Education and Supervision, 38*, 227–236.

Spooner, M., Spooner, F., Karvonen, M., & Algozzine, B. (2002). Contributing to the profession in meaningful ways. *Action in Teacher Education, 24*(3), 10–19.

Thomspon, B. (1995). Publishing your research results: Some suggestions and counsel. *Journal of Counseling and Development, 73*, 342–345.

J Behav Educ (2007) 16:155–189
DOI 10.1007/s10864-006-9011-0

ORIGINAL PAPER

A Field-Tested Task Analysis for Creating Single-Subject Graphs Using Microsoft® Office Excel

Ya-yu Lo · Moira Konrad

Published online: 29 December 2006
© Springer Science+Business Media, Inc. 2006

Abstract Creating single-subject (SS) graphs is challenging for many researchers and practitioners because it is a complex task with many steps. Although several authors have introduced guidelines for creating SS graphs, many users continue to experience frustration. The purpose of this article is to minimize these frustrations by providing a field-tested task analysis for creating SS graphs using Microsoft® Office Excel. Results from the field test are presented and the task analysis, which includes steps for creating a variety of SS graphs, is provided. The article includes various illustrations, a list of prerequisite skills, tips, and troubleshooting items.

Keywords Single-subject graphs · Single-subject design · Graphic presentation · Task analysis · Software

Single-subject (SS) research has played an important role in educational research for several decades. Researchers and practitioners have used SS designs to develop and validate interventions by establishing functional relationships between dependent and independent variables (Horner et al., 2005). A critical component of analyzing SS research data involves the use of graphic displays to interpret treatment effects. As discussed by Cooper, Heron, and Heward (1987), graphs serve multiple functions that essentially provide a major tool for organizing, interpreting, and communicating SS research findings. Graphs are especially useful because they allow for ongoing and continuous evaluation of the data, which is

Y. Lo (✉)
Department of Special Education and Child Development,
College of Education, University of North Carolina at Charlotte,
9201 University City Blvd., Charlotte, NC 28223
e-mail: ylo1@email.uncc.edu

M. Konrad
Special Education Program, School of Physical Activity and Educational Services,
The Ohio State University, 375A Arps Hall,
1945 North High Street, Columbus, OH 43210
e-mail: konrad.14@osu.edu

🙅 Springer

156   J Behav Educ (2007) 16:155–189

imperative for responsive decision-making purposes (Alberto & Troutman, 2006). Therefore, it is important that researchers and practitioners produce clear and precise graphs.

Creating professional quality computer-generated SS design graphs often presents a challenge even for veteran researchers and practitioners. It is no surprise that creating a well-presented graph can be difficult because this task involves a wide array of complex steps. Several authors have provided guidance and tips for constructing reversal and multiple baseline design graphs with slightly different approaches (Carr & Burkholder, 1998; Hillman & Miller, 2004; Moran & Hirschbine, 2002). Despite the availability of these guidelines, we continued to experience frustration at various points along the way as we learned to create SS graphs. This becomes even more challenging for our college and graduate students who have limited prior knowledge or experience in creating computer-generated SS graphs. Some of the more pervasive frustrations we have identified include the following: (a) being unable to align data points with tick marks (i.e., points falling between tick marks rather than on the tick marks); (b) having difficulty getting multiple baseline tiers to align perfectly or stack on one another with each tier being the same size; (c) being challenged to raise the 0 off the x-axis while keeping appropriate scales; (d) having no guidelines for creating multiple data paths (e.g., two dependent variables on the same graph); (e) creating reversal design graphs without having to change the line color and symbol for each individual phase; (f) being unable to move objects such as text boxes outside the graph; and (g) disconnecting a line segment without removing all line segments for the entire data path. Additionally, the earlier guidelines require one to have advanced prerequisite knowledge about toolbars, icons, and various functions within Microsoft® Office Excel, and therefore may not provide sufficient instruction for beginners who are learning to create SS graphs. Our goal, in writing this article, was to reduce the frustration associated with creating SS graphs.

As behavior analysts, we understand how to take a very complicated task and break it into "smaller, teachable units" to create a "task analysis" (Cooper et al., 1987, p. 342). The main purposes of this article were twofold. The first purpose was to provide a task analysis (see Appendix A) for graphing single and double data paths to equip readers with the skills they need to create most SS graphs (including reversal, multiple baseline, changing criterion, alternating treatments, and multi-treatment designs) with as little frustration as possible. The second purpose was to present data from a field test of the task analysis and inform readers about how these data were used to refine the task analysis.

This article differs from the earlier articles in several ways. First, we carefully addressed all the frustrations we and our students experienced when trying to create SS graphs. Second, we included tools to ensure readers' readiness to apply the task analysis including (a) a prerequisite skill checklist and (b) a list of important terms with definitions. Third, we broke the tasks down into very small steps and numbered each step with a box for checking it off when following through the steps. Fourth, we outlined steps for both single and double data paths. Fifth, we included a number of graphics throughout the article to illustrate the steps. These graphics offer visual demonstrations to guide users through the process and are especially useful for users who are less familiar with the Microsoft® Office Excel. Sixth, we included tips for readers to troubleshoot the most common problems. The troubleshooting table outlines 10 common problems users may encounter when creating SS graphs using the task analysis. These were the problems we observed occurring most frequently among the participants in our field test (described in the Method section). We anticipated possible reasons for these problems and provided solutions to troubleshoot as well as to prevent the problems in the future. Finally, a sample multiple baseline design graph with double data paths (see Fig. 1) is presented for demonstration purposes. We provided descriptions of important features of the graph and their corresponding steps that the readers can find in the task analysis.

🖄 Springer

J Behav Educ (2007) 16:155–189   157

Method

Participants and settings

We tested the utility of the task analysis with 21 undergraduate students, 57 post-baccalaureate (post-bac) students, 7 Ph.D. students, and one faculty member in a special education program. All students were selected because they were enrolled in one of four classes that required them to create SS graphs. The faculty member was the instructor for one of the classes (i.e., Single Subject Research) and volunteered to participate. Data collection for the field test was conducted in a computer lab containing 24 individual stations. The computer at each station was a Dell computer equipped with Microsoft® Office Excel 2003.

Instrumentation

Each participant completed a 13-item user satisfaction questionnaire. The first two items asked the participants to rate their levels of experience in (a) using Excel and (b) using Excel for graphing. The remaining 11 items asked the participants to evaluate the utility of the task analysis. Participants rated each item using a four-point Likert scale (ranging from 1 as "strongly disagree" to 4 as "strongly agree"). Cronbach's alpha is .97 and Guttman's split-half is .92, both revealing high reliability for the 11 items regarding the utility of the task analysis.

Field-test procedures

At the beginning of the field test, we distributed to each participant (a) the task analysis, (b) a data set for graphing a three-tiered single data path multiple-baseline design, and (c) a model graph. The participants were instructed to use the task analysis to create a graph like the model graph. A multiple-baseline design graph was selected for testing because it was the most common, yet complicated design for graphing that the participants would have encountered for their course requirements. We speculated that if participants could accurately produce a multiple-baseline design graph using the task analysis, they would also have been able to produce other design graphs. Each participant was provided with one hour to create the graph without any assistance. We allowed the participants only one hour for two reasons. First, each of the course instructors allocated one hour of their class time for graphing instruction as a part of their course. Second, we anticipated that some participants who were uncomfortable or unfamiliar with Excel might require several hours to complete the steps, making it unfeasible for the purpose of the field test.

At the end of the one-hour period, each participant saved their graph to a disk so we could analyze their products. Participants then completed the user satisfaction questionnaire.

Data collection and analysis

The participants' user satisfaction results and graphing products were evaluated.

User satisfaction

For each group of the participants (i.e., undergraduate, post-bac, and Ph.D./faculty), an average of the ratings (with a possible range of 1 to 4) was calculated for each of the 11

158   J Behav Educ (2007) 16:155–189

Table 1 Percentage of participants completing each graphing step correctly

	Undergraduate ($n = 21$), %	Post-bac ($n = 57$), %	Ph.D./Faculty ($n = 8$), %
1. Created one tier graph with data points falling on tick marks	100	98	100
2. Created appropriate x-axis and y-axis scales	100	98	100
3. Created two more tiers stacked on each other	95	90	100
4. Disconnected data points at the condition line	95	65	100
5. Created condition lines (or phase lines)	95	69	100
6. Raised 0 off the x-axis with appropriate y-axis scale	65	75	100
7. Labeled conditions/phases	55	60	71
8. Labeled x-axis and y-axis	40	39	43
9. Provided tier labels	55	50	57
10. Provided tick mark labels with the bottom tier only	40	39	43
Mean percentage of participants completing steps	74	68	81

items on the utility of the task analysis. A mean satisfaction rating was then obtained for respective groups.

Graphing performance

The participants' graphs were rated on 10 criteria corresponding to the major steps listed in the task analysis (see Table 1). Each item was rated as either correct or incorrect for each participant. The proportion of participants (represented in percentages) who produced the correct step was then calculated for each respective group (undergraduate, post-bac, and Ph.D./faculty). The first author scored all graphs, and the second author randomly selected and scored 25% of the graphs independently for interobserver reliability. Reliability was calculated using an item-by-item analysis by dividing the number of agreements by the number of agreements plus disagreements and multiplying by 100. The interobserver reliability ranged from 80 to 100% with a mean of 94%. Chi-square test was used to detect statistically significant differences between each group on their graphing performance.

Results

User satisfaction

On the user satisfaction questionnaire, the participants reported that they had little experience in using Excel with an average of 2.1, 1.9, and 1.9 points, on a scale of 4, for undergraduates, post-bac, and Ph.D./faculty, respectively. These participants also reported that they had little experience in using Excel for graphing (undergraduates = 1.9; post-bac = 1.6; Ph.D./faculty = 1.2).

Overall rating of satisfaction on the graphing steps for undergraduates, post-bac, and Ph.D./faculty was 2.9, 2.9, and 3.4, respectively. No statistically significant difference was found between groups, $F(2,82) = 1.83, p = .17$.

Graphing performance

Table 1 shows the percentage of participants who completed each step correctly within each group. Data on the participants' graphing performance indicated that on average 74% (range

J Behav Educ (2007) 16:155–189   159

40–100%) of undergraduate students, 68% (range 39–98%) of post-bac students, and 81% (range 43–100%) of Ph.D./faculty completed individual steps correctly. There was no difference between groups on all items, except for item 4 (i.e., disconnected data points at the condition line) for which undergraduate students and Ph.D./faculty performed better than the post-bac students, $\mathcal{X}^2$ (2, $n = 84$) = 11.28, $p = .004$. Additionally, the overall performance of each group was represented by the total number of graphing steps the participants produced correctly. The results showed that on average undergraduates completed 7.40 (of 10) steps correctly, post-bac 6.54 steps, and Ph.D./faculty 8.14 steps. No statistically significant difference was found between groups for the overall performance, $F(2, 81) = 1.43$, $p = .24$.

Discussion

The purpose of presenting the field test data was to inform readers about the utility of the task analysis and how refinements were made to produce the final task analysis as presented in Appendix A.

Results on the user satisfaction showed that Ph.D./faculty considered themselves as the least (or equally) experienced (score = 1.9) among the three groups of participants. Yet they provided the highest ratings for all items on the user satisfaction questionnaire (score = 3.4). This may be related to the fact that the participating Ph.D. students (and faculty) were the most knowledgeable about SS designs and were most interested in learning how to create SS graphs due to course requirements and their professional development (e.g., producing a SS research proposal with graphs). On the contrary, undergraduate and most post-bac students had basic knowledge about data collection and A-B designs, but had not learned about concepts of SS designs prior to the field test. This may explain their lower ratings when compared to those made by Ph.D./faculty. Furthermore, it is important to note that the only responses with a rating lower than "2" on the user satisfaction questionnaire items were made by the students with little or no prior experience with Excel. These results show that even though students were inexperienced with Excel, they found the task analysis somewhat helpful.

Regarding the participants' graphing performance, results indicated that overall the participant groups produced an average of at least 6 steps correctly on their graphs (undergraduate 7.40, post-bac 6.54, and Ph.D./faculty 8.14) using the task analysis. Considering the complexity of the graphing components and the participants' reported lack of prior knowledge on Excel graphing, the results were very promising, indicating the usefulness of the task analysis. In terms of the number of participants correctly completing the graphing steps, the results showed an average of 74% of undergraduates, 68% of post-bac, and 81% of Ph.D./faculty completed individual steps correctly. Two factors should be considered when evaluating these data. First, because we provided the participants with only one hour to create the SS graph (due to time constraints and to reduce anxiety), many participants were unable to complete all the steps listed on the task analysis. This is clearly reflected by the graphing products in that a high percentage of participants accurately completed graph components one through five, which were listed as earlier steps in the task analysis (see Table 1). As the participants moved through the task analysis, many of them ran out of time and therefore were unable to complete the latter steps (i.e., corresponding components 6 through 10). In fact, many participants indicated that they would have completed the steps if they were given an additional 30–45 min time period. Second, the majority of the post-bac students were non-traditional students who decided to return to school for a second degree after a long period of work experience either in related or unrelated fields. Many of these students

160   J Behav Educ (2007) 16:155–189

indicated that they had never used Excel before, and reported never having used a computer for academic or professional purposes. This may explain why the percentage of post-bac students who completed each graphing component was lower than the percentage of either undergraduate students or Ph.D./faculty.

Despite the wide range of user satisfaction ratings and graphing performance, the participants agreed that the task analysis was helpful and their graphing products supported their responses. We should emphasize that these results were obtained using an earlier version of the task analysis and were used to improve the task analysis provided in Appendix A. Based on the field test results, we made several changes to the original task analysis by re-wording and adding illustrations and symbols for better clarity. After making several revisions, the final task analysis was given to 15 additional students and faculty members, who then used it to create various types of SS graphs. All of these students and faculty members reported that the task analysis was easy to use and allowed them to create high-quality SS graphs. Two of these students had participated in the original field test and indicated that the improvements were very helpful and most appropriate

The field-tested task analysis presented in this article for producing SS graphs provides great contributions to the field of SS research and practice. First, the task analysis provides detailed step-by-step instructions for graphing most SS graphs with visual demonstrations. Just as researchers and practitioners use task analyses to teach students with deficient skills, we offer a task analysis (with visual prompts) to guide users through SS graphing steps. Second, with the inclusion of a prerequisite skill checklist, glossaries, instruction for graphing both single and double data paths, as well as troubleshooting tables, the task analysis provides useful guidelines to support those offered by previous articles (Carr & Burkholder, 1998; Hillman & Miller, 2004; Moran & Hirschbine, 2002). Finally, by obtaining and reporting formal utility data of the task analysis from 86 participants (and additional 15 users on the final task analysis), we showed that the task analysis has high utility for users with various levels of knowledge and experiences.

Limitations and future research

There are a few limitations pertaining to the field test. First, in collecting social validity data on the task analysis, we did not seek to obtain experimental control. Therefore, based on our data, we cannot state that our procedures for graphing SS data were better than another approach or that our approach was "effective." However, our main purpose in collecting these data was to gain feedback in order to improve the clarity of the steps. Future research should investigate the effectiveness or usefulness of the task analysis using an experimental design.

Second, given that we made several changes to the task analysis over the course of developing it, we cannot be certain that the participants' feedback represents the final version of the task analysis. However, the changes were minor, mostly addressing wording and adding illustrations and symbols. Therefore, we feel confident that the questionnaire results are useful and only would have indicated higher levels of satisfaction had we re-administered the final version of the task analysis. Additionally, we sought feedback from 15 individuals on the final version of the task analysis. Although this feedback was more open-ended and less formal, it supported the field test results.

Third, we did not test our task analysis on Mac systems or on versions of Excel that are older than 2003. Therefore, some users may find that they will need to make adjustments to the task analysis to fit their systems.

J Behav Educ (2007) 16:155–189   161

Finally, we must acknowledge that our approach only represents one way to graph SS research using Microsoft® Excel. It has been an approach that has served us well, and our user satisfaction data indicate that it also works well for others. However, individual users should recognize that these steps, in this order, may not work best for everyone. For example, people who are just learning to use Excel for graphing may view our task analysis as a starting point for learning this process. For people who already have experience using Excel to graph their data, our task analysis may serve as a set of additional tools and tips. For those who already have extensive experience graphing, using this task analysis may be more cumbersome than useful. We encourage experienced users to try this task analysis if they have experienced any of the problems we described in our introduction and troubleshooting tips.

Appendix A

A Task Analysis for Creating Single-subject Graphs

Prerequisite Skill Checklist

The SS task analysis is intended for people who have some basic prerequisite skills. An

individual is prepared to use the task analysis if he or she can do the following:

- ☐ Open Microsoft® Office Excel

- ☐ Use the standard and drawing toolbar features

- ☐ Define basic terminology and concepts (e.g., SS designs, baseline, intervention, phase

    line, data path, and terms in the following glossary section)

Glossary

Worksheet. A worksheet, or a spreadsheet, in Microsoft® Office Excel contains

horizontal rows (represented by numbers 1, 2, 3, etc.) and vertical columns (represented by

letters A, B, C, etc.). Each row and column constructs a cell (e.g., A1, B1) with a gray borderline,

which is invisible in printing.

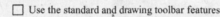

Standard toolbar. The standard toolbar, typically located at the top of the Excel

worksheet by default, contains several basic tools for creating SS graphs. The most frequently

used tools are "Cut," "Copy," "Paste," "Chart Wizard," and "Drawing," which are circled below,

from left to right, respectively.

162   J Behav Educ (2007) 16:155–189

Drawing toolbar. The drawing tools are essential for graphing. The most frequently used tools for creating SS graphs include "Line," "Arrow," "Rectangle," "Text Box," "Line Style," "Dash Style," and "Arrow Style," which are circled below, from left to right, respectively.

Highlight (select) cells. To highlight or select cells (e.g., A1 through D10), place the mouse pointer at the beginning of the cell range you wish to select (in this case, A1), then left click-hold-drag until all the cells you wish to highlight are selected. This creates a gray area of cells.

Right click. For PC users, "right click" refers to making a quick click on the right-hand side button on the top of your mouse. "Right click" serves the same function as "double click." Mac users can use "double click" to perform the same action as "right click" listed in this task analysis.

X-axis. The x-axis is the horizontal axis on a graph. In SS graphs, the x-axis typically represents time (e.g., sessions, days, weeks).

Y-axis. The y-axis is the vertical axis on a graph. In SS graphs, the y-axis typically represents the dependent variable.

Tier. To create multiple baseline design graph, two or more graphs are stacked on top of each other. Each graph is referred to as a tier.

Tips before Starting with the Task Analysis

Checking for toolbars. Before you start with the task analysis, make sure that your standard toolbar and drawing toolbar appear on your Excel worksheet. To make both toolbars appear, select "View" on the top menu of the Excel worksheet. Select "Toolbars," and check to see if both "Standard" and "Drawing" are checked. If not, move your mouse pointer over the

J Behav Educ (2007) 16:155–189

selection and then click on it once. Typically, the standard toolbar is located at the top of the Excel worksheet by default, whereas the drawing toolbar appears at the bottom of the worksheet.

Recording dates/sessions. When structuring your worksheet, you may also use column A to indicate the date/session on which each data point was collected. This is very helpful in tracking back your data. In this case, begin your data in the next column, as indicated in the task analysis. You may also add/insert a new column at any time by clicking on any cell under a column, selecting "Insert" on the top menu, and then selecting "Columns." A new column will appear at the left of the selected/clicked column.

Using "Shift" key. When using "Line" or "Arrow" on the drawing toolbar, hold the "Shift" key as you draw to easily create a straight line.

Using "Ctrl" key. You can smoothly move lines or objects by (a) selecting the line or object, and (b) holding down the "Ctrl" key while using the arrow keys on your keyboard in the direction you wish to move the line or object.

Task Analysis

The task analysis shows how to create three-tier multiple baseline graphs, the most complicated SS graphing task. However, users can easily create reversal, alternating treatment, and multiple treatments designs by treating their graphs as "tier one" and leaving out the steps for creating multiple tiers. In this task analysis, steps for single and double data paths for items A (i.e., structure your Excel worksheet) and B (i.e., create one-tier graph) are listed in separate columns. The left column describes steps for creating a single data path, whereas the right column lists steps for double data paths. Items C through J include steps that are applicable to both single and double data paths. Because each step is essential and missing one step can

164   J Behav Educ (2007) 16:155–189

produce different results, we strongly recommend users check off each step as they follow

through the task analysis.

Single data path	Double data paths
A. Structure your Excel worksheet	*A. Structure your Excel worksheet*
☐1. In cell B1, enter the label of the first tier (e.g., student's name, skill, setting). In cell D1, enter the label of the second tier. In cell F1, enter the label of the third tier. Continue this across row 1 in every other column (B, D, F, H, etc.) until all tiers have been labeled. If the label name (e.g., work completion) is too long to fit in the cell (e.g., B1), you may widen the cell by (a) placing your mouse pointer at the shared borderline of the target cell and the cell next to it at its right (e.g., C1) until a ◆ appears, (b) click-hold-dragging toward your right, and (c) releasing your mouse button when you complete widening. ⬚ DG · fx A B C D E 1 work completion on-task behavior 2 ☐2. Enter data below each tier's label from	☐1. In cell A1, enter the label of the first tier (e.g., student's name, skill, setting). In cell B1, enter the label of the first data path for the first tier (e.g., correct). In cell C1, enter the label of the second data path for the first tier (e.g., incorrect). To widen a cell, see instruction in step 1 in the left-hand column of the task analysis. ☐2. Enter the label of the second tier in cell D1; enter the label of its first and second data paths in cells E1 and F1, respectively. Continue this across row 1, labeling the names and all data paths for all tiers. ☐3. Enter data into columns B, C, E, F, H, I, etc. from top down beginning in row 2 (i.e., B2 ~ , C2~ , E2~, F2~) to reflect data for each data path of each tier. Leave the cell blank if data were not collected for a particular session.

J Behav Educ (2007) 16:155–189

top down beginning in row 2 (i.e., B2~, D2~, F2~). If data were not collected on certain days (e.g., student was absent), leave the cell blank. Entering the word "absent" will inaccurately lead to a "0" score assigned by Excel.

3. Enter the name of the condition in the cell next to the first data point of that condition in column A for the first tier. Continue this in columns C, E, etc. to indicate the beginning of a condition for each tier. See illustration below.

[Note. If you are creating a one-tier graph (e.g., reversal design) for multiple participants, you may also follow steps 1 to 3 so that all the data can be organized into one worksheet.

4. Under the bottom of the worksheet,

4. Enter the name of the condition in the cell next to the first data point of that condition below each tier's label in columns A, D, G, etc. to indicate the beginning of a condition for each tier.

An example of a data entry sheet for a single-tier alternating treatment design is illustrated below.

5. Rename the worksheet tab label as needed by double left clicking on the tab label and typing in the label name (see steps 4-5 in the left-hand column of the task analysis).

place the mouse pointer on "Sheet1" tab label. Double left click the tab. The word "Sheet1" becomes white color in black background. □ 5. Rename the tab by typing in a new label name (e.g., "Data," "Disruption," "Tommy") to help you organize the worksheets. Hit the "Enter" key on your keyboard or click on one of the cells in the worksheet after renaming the tab. [Note: If you have a simple data set (e.g., one dependent variable), this step may not be critical as you can easily locate your data.]	
B. Create one-tier graph	*B. Create one-tier graph*
□ 6. Highlight data for the first tier, beginning with B2 to the last row of data. Make sure that you highlight the data (i.e., numbers) only, not the labels nor the conditions.	□ 6. Highlight the first data path for the first tier, beginning with B2 to the last row of data. □ 7. On the standard toolbar, select "Chart Wizard" (⊞). □ 8. On the "Standard Types" tab • under "Chart type:," select "XY

⚛ Springer

J Behav Educ (2007) 16:155–189

167

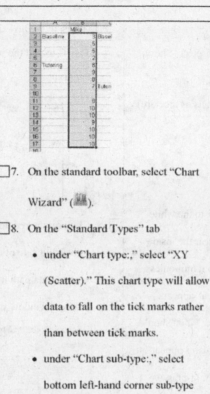

7. On the standard toolbar, select "Chart Wizard" (📖).

8. On the "Standard Types" tab

- under "Chart type:," select "XY (Scatter)." This chart type will allow data to fall on the tick marks rather than between tick marks.

- under "Chart sub-type:," select bottom left-hand corner sub-type (i.e., "Scatter with data points connected by lines").

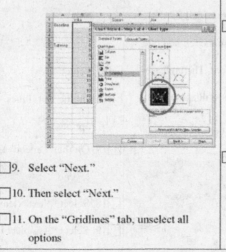

9. Select "Next."

10. Then select "Next."

11. On the "Gridlines" tab, unselect all options

(Scatter)."

- under "Chart sub-type:," select bottom left-hand corner sub-type (i.e., "Scatter with data points connected by lines").

9. Select "Next."

10. On the "Series" tab

- under "Series" (left-hand side), select "Add." "Series2" should be highlighted.

11. In the "Y Values" box, you should see "={1}" at this point.

12. Click on the red arrow at the right-hand side of "Y Values." A small window pops up with a heading "Chart Wizard - step 2 of 4 - Chart Source Data - Values:" The box with "={1}" is highlighted in black.

13. Highlight the second data path of the first tier, beginning with C2 to the last row of data. The data you just highlighted will be surrounded with dashed flashing lines. The

168

J Behav Educ (2007) 16:155–189

12. On the "Legend" tab, unselect "Show legend."

13. Select "Next" (leave others as they are).

14. Select "As object in."

15. Select "Sheet2."

16. Select "Finish."

17. Move the mouse pointer to the white area of the graph (i.e., near the inside edge of the chart). Keep it motionless until the text "Chart Area" appears.

18. Click on the "Chart Area." You should see eight small black squares appear on the chart border. Click-hold-drag the entire chart so that the upper left-hand corner of the chart area rests against the upper left-hand corner of cell B2 (i.e., one column over from the left and one row down from the top). Then release your mouse button. See illustration below.

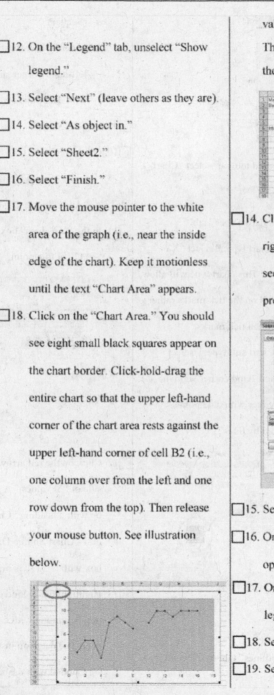

values in the box should change instantly. This is to add the second data path onto the graph.

14. Click on the red downward arrow at the right-hand side of the pop-up window. The second data path now appears in your preview window with a different color.

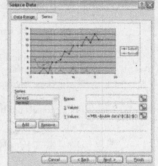

15. Select "Next."

16. On the "Gridlines" tab, unselect all options.

17. On the "Legend" tab, unselect "Show legend."

18. Select "Next" (leave others as they are).

19. Select "As object in."

19. With the presence of the eight small black squares, place the mouse pointer at the black square at the lower right-hand corner of the chart area until the two-way diagonal arrow appears.

20. Click-hold-drag to extend/shrink the chart area through the end of column I and down to the appropriate row (i.e., divide 52 by number of tiers and extend to that row, e.g., through row 17 if there are three tiers). This is to make sure that your graphs will fit onto a letter size (8.5 x 11 in.) paper. If you only have one tier, extending your chart area through row 17 will also be appropriate. Release your mouse button after extending/shrinking.

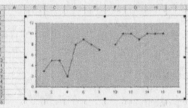

21. Click anywhere outside the graph (i.e., in one of the worksheet cells) and save ( ) your document.

22. Place your mouse pointer on the "Sheet2" tab label of the worksheet. Rename the label (e.g., "graph") by double left clicking on the tab and typing in the new label name to help you organize the worksheets (see steps 4-5). Hit the "Enter" key on the keyboard or click on one of the cells in the worksheet after renaming the tab.

20. Select "Sheet2" or a new sheet (e.g., Sheet3").

21. Select "Finish."

22. Follow steps 17-22 in the left-hand column of the task analysis to extend and drag the Chart Area and rename the tab.

170   J Behav Educ (2007) 16:155–189

C. Modify graphs

[Modify background]

☐ 23. Place your mouse pointer on the gray background. Keep it motionless until the text "Plot Area" appears. Right click on the background (you may also double left click on the background).

☐ 24. Select "Format Plot Area."

☐ 25. On the "Patterns" tab

- under "Border," select "None"

- under "Area," select "None"

☐ 26. Select "OK."

☐ 27. Click on the chart area (outside the "Plot Area") until eight small black squares and the text "Chart Area" appear, then right click.

☐ 28. Select "Format Chart Area."

☐ 29. On the "Patterns" tab

- under "Border," select "None"

- under "Area," select "None"

☐ 30. Select "OK."

☐ 31. Click anywhere outside the graph and save (🖫) your document.

[Modify x-axis]

☐ 32. Move your mouse pointer over the x-axis until the text "Value (X) Axis" appears. Right click on the x-axis and select "Format Axis" (or double click on x-axis).

☐ 33. On the "Patterns" tab

- under "Lines" and then "Weight," select the finest solid line (typically the second

J Behav Educ (2007) 16:155–189

option from the top on the dropdown list)

- under "Major tick mark type," select "Outside" (or "Inside" depending on your

  preference)

- under "Minor tick mark type," select "None"

- under "Tick mark labels," select "Next to axis"

34. On the "Scale" tab

- under "Auto," unselect all options

- in "Maximum," change the number to reflect your total number of sessions (or days,

  weeks, etc.)

- in "Major unit," adjust the number according to your needs [Note: The major unit is
  what the numbers on the x-axis will "count by" (e.g., 2, 5, 10).]

35. On the "Font" tab [Note: If you only have one tier, no change should be made under this

  tab. Skip to step 36. Otherwise, continue with the following bullets.]

- Under "Size," select "10" (or another size as appropriate)

- under "Color," select white color

- under "Background," select "Transparent." This step is done in multiple tier graphs

  because x-axis tick mark labels are not necessary for upper tiers. The selection of

  transparent color allows each tier to remain the same size while "masking" the tick

  mark labels.

36. Select "OK."

37. Click anywhere outside the graph and save (🖫) your document.

[Modify y-axis]

38. Move your mouse pointer over the y axis until the text "Value (Y) Axis" appears. Right

172   J Behav Educ (2007) 16:155–189

click on the y-axis and select "Format Axis" (or double click on y-axis).

☐ 39. On the "Patterns" tab

- under "Lines" and then "Weight," select the finest solid line (typically the second option from the top on the dropdown list)

- under "Major tick mark type," select "Outside" (or "Inside" depending on your preference, but be sure to keep the type the same for both axes)

- under "Minor tick mark type," select "None"

- under "Tick mark labels," select "Next to axis"

☐ 40. On the "Scale" tab

- under "Auto," unselect all options

- in "Maximum," change the number to reflect the maximum level of your dependent variable (e.g., 100 for percentage). This number may need to be set in correspondence with your "Major unit." For example, if the highest score earned by a student was 49 and you set the "Major unit" by fives (i.e., 5, 10, 15, 20), an appropriate "Maximum" number would be "50."

- in "Major unit," adjust the number according to your needs to show what you want the y-axis to "count by" (e.g., 2 for twos, 5 for fives)

- in "Minimum," enter the same number from the "Major unit" box, except this time enter it with a negative sign (e.g., -2)

- in "Value (X) axis Crosses at:," divide the negative number from the "Minimum" box by 2 and enter it in the "Crosses at:" box. For example, if the major unit is 2, enter "-2" for "Minimum" and "-1" for "Crosses at:." This is to raise the y-axis zero value with an appropriate scale. See illustration below for an example.

J Behav Educ (2007) 16:155–189

173

41. On the "Font" tab, under "Size" select "10" (or another size as appropriate). Be sure that the size you select for the y-axis is consistent with the size for the x-axis. Then select "OK."

42. Click anywhere outside the graph and save () your document.

[Modify data path]

43. Place your mouse pointer anywhere on the data path (or one of the data paths if two) until you see the pop-up text "Series# Point#." Right click and select "Format Data Series" (or double click on the data path).

44. On the "Patterns" tab

   • under "Line," then "Color:," select black color

   • under "Marker," then "Style," select solid circle (second option from the bottom; looks like a jagged-edge circle); under both "Foreground" and "Background," select black color

45. Select "OK."

46. For a single data path, skip this step and move on to step 47. With double data paths, repeat steps 43-45 for the second data path, except this time under "Marker," then "Background," select white color instead (keep "Foreground" black).

47. Click anywhere outside the graph and save () your document.

⚛ Springer

174   J Behav Educ (2007) 16:155–189

D. Graph other tiers (For one-tier graphs, skip to Item E or step 64.)

☐ 48. Place your mouse pointer at the outside area of the axes of the first tier until the text "Chart Area" appears. Click on the chart area. Eight small black squares, located on the chart border, should appear.

☐ 49. On the standard toolbar, select "Copy" (▨) (or press "Ctrl"-and-"C" on the keyboard). The chart should be surrounded with a flashing dashed box.

☐ 50. Click on the cell right below the lower left-hand corner of the first graph (e.g., B18).

☐ 51. On the standard toolbar, select "Paste" (▨) (or press "Ctrl"-and-"V" on the keyboard). This is to create the second tier. If necessary, click-hold-drag this graph so that it is directly underneath the first tier. Release the mouse button once you complete dragging the graph. You can use the gray lines on the worksheet to help with this alignment.

☐ 52. Click on the cell right below the lower left-hand corner of the second graph you just created (e.g., B34).

☐ 53. On the standard toolbar, select "Paste" (▨) (or press "Ctrl"-and-"V" on the keyboard). This is to create the third tier. If necessary, click-hold-drag this graph so that it is directly underneath the second tier. Release the mouse button once you complete dragging the graph. You can use the gray lines on the worksheet to help with this alignment.

☐ 54. Repeat steps 52-53 until all the tiers are copied.

☐ 55. Click anywhere outside the graph and save (▨) your document.

☐ 56. Go to the second tier. Place your mouse pointer on the "Plot Area" of the second tier (i.e., the area where the data are plotted). Right click and select "Source Data."

☐ 57. On the "Series" tab, click on the red arrow next to "Y Values." (For double data paths, under "Series" select "Series1" first then click on the red arrow next to the "Y Values.")

J Behav Educ (2007) 16:155–189

175

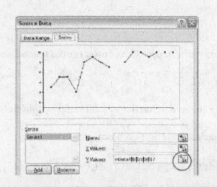

A small window "Source Data - Values:" will pop up, which also takes you back to the

data entry worksheet. You will see a flashing dashed box highlighting the data for tier 1.

Now you will change the highlighted data to the second tier by following steps 58-60.

☐ 58. Highlight the data for the second tier. The data values in the box should change

accordingly.

☐ 59. Click on the red downward arrow at the right-hand side of the pop-up window.

176   J Behav Educ (2007) 16:155–189

☐ 60. Select "OK."

☐ 61. If you have double data paths, repeat steps 56-60 for the second series (i.e., Series2). Otherwise, skip to step 62.

☐ 62. Repeat steps 56-60 for the remaining tier(s) (and series within tiers, if applicable) until all the data values are changed to reflect each tier and series.

☐ 63. Click anywhere outside the graph and save (🖫) your document.

E. Disconnect lines between phases (For alternating treatment design, skip to step 71 to *connect discontinuous data points*.)

☐ 64. In the first tier, move your mouse pointer onto the line segment between the last data point of the first phase (e.g., baseline) and the first data point of the next phase (e.g., tutoring). Click on the line segment once. You should see all data points being highlighted. [Note. (a) The condition/phase labels under columns A, C, E, and etc. in your data entry worksheet will be a great help here to determine where to disconnect the data points. (b) If the data points are really close together, you can temporarily "zoom out" the screen to 200% using the "Zoom" (200% ⬇) tool on the standard toolbar.]

☐ 65. Click on the segment again (DO NOT double left click). This time, only two data points are highlighted. Therefore any change you make will only affect these two data points and the line segment connecting them.

J Behav Educ (2007) 16:155–189   177

☐ 66. Keep your mouse pointer motionless with the two data points highlighted. Right click and select "Format Data Point" (or double left click on the highlighted line segment).

☐ 67. On the "Patterns" tab

  • under "Line," select "None"

☐ 68. Select "OK." Skip to step 70 if you only have one tier with single data path.

☐ 69. Repeat steps 64-68 to disconnect lines between other phases and within the other data path (if double data paths are used). Repeat these steps for all tiers.

☐ 70. Click anywhere outside the graph and save (📄) your document. Then skip to step 75 unless creating an alternating treatment design graph.

[For alternating treatment design] *Connect discontinuous data points*

☐ 71. Click on one of the data paths to highlight all data points for that data series.

☐ 72. On the top menu, select "Tools," then select "Options."

☐ 73. On the "Chart" tab, under "Active chart," select "Interpolated." This action will connect all discontinuous data points within each data path.

☐ 74. Select "OK." [Note: If the student was absent and no data were collected for a particular session, the data points before and after that absent "data point" should be disconnected. Follow steps 64-68 to disconnect these data points.] Then click anywhere outside the graph and save (📄) your document.

F. Create phase lines

☐ 75. Scroll the page to show the first tier (or the tier for which you are drawing the phase lines). Be sure that you click outside the graphs before completing this step. On the drawing toolbar, select the "Line" (⟍) tool by clicking and releasing once.

☐ 76. Move your mouse pointer to the maximum y-axis value between the first two phases. The mouse pointer should look like a plus sign: "+."

☐ 77. Hold down the "Shift" key on the keyboard and simultaneously click-hold-drag downward to draw a phase line, stopping when you just pass through the x-axis by releasing your mouse button. Holding down the "Shift" key will allow you to draw a straight line easily. If you only have one tier or if you are creating a phase line for the bottom tier, stop dragging and release your mouse button when you reach the x-axis.

178   J Behav Educ (2007) 16:155–189

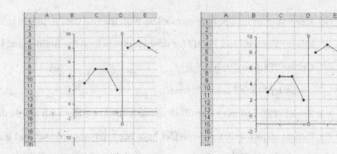

(for top tiers in multiple tiers)   (for one tier or the bottom tier in multiple tiers)

☐78. At this point, the line should be highlighted with an open dot at each end. Click on the "Dash Style" (▦) tool on the drawing toolbar. Move your mouse pointer over the fourth option from the top until the text "Dash" appears, and then click on it. The phase line will become a dashed line.

☐79. Repeating steps 75-78 to create as many new phase lines as needed for your graphs. Follow directions below to lengthen, shorten, or move a phase line.

  • To lengthen or shorten a phase line, select the phase line by clicking on the line until an open dot appears at each end. Move your mouse pointer over one of the open dots until you see a two-way arrow. Click-hold-drag to either lengthen or shorten the line by moving toward the direction you want it to be and then releasing the mouse button.

  • To move a phase line, select the phase line by clicking on the line until an open dot appears at each end. Move your mouse pointer over the phase line until a four-arrow cross appears. Click-hold-drag the phase line to where you want it to be, then release your mouse button. You may also use the arrow keys on your keyboard to move the phase lines to the precise location after clicking on the phase line. Each phase line should rest at the mid-point between the sessions where the data points are disconnected (e.g., falling on session 4.5).

☐80. If you only have one tier, skip to step 82. If you have multiple tiers, continue with step 81.

☐81. Connect the phase lines for tiers 1 and 2 (and tiers 2 and 3, etc.) with a horizontal dashed line. To do so, select the "Line" (◿) tool by clicking and releasing it once. Place your mouse pointer at the bottom end of the phase line for tier 1. With the "+" sign, click-hold-drag toward your right and release it when you reach the top end of the phase line for tier 2. Follow step 78 to change the line to dashed style. You may need to adjust the length of the phase lines so that they are connected to the horizontal connection line to form two right angles.

J Behav Educ (2007) 16:155–189   179

☐82. Click anywhere outside the graph and save ( ) your document.

G. Create label(s) and title(s)

[Create condition/phase label(s)]

☐83. Scroll the page to show the first tier. On the drawing toolbar, select the "Text Box" ( )
tool by clicking and releasing once.

☐84. Move your mouse pointer slightly above the first condition or phase of your first tier. The
mouse pointer should look like an upside-down small case "t." Quick-click once to create a
text box at the top of the first tier.

☐85. Type in the title of the condition/phase (e.g., Baseline). The size of the text box will be
adjusted automatically as you type. You may also adjust the text box by placing your mouse
pointer on any of the open dots located on the border of the text box until you see a two-
way arrow, then clicking and dragging the text box to the direction you want. Release the
mouse button after you complete the adjustment.

☐86. To format the "Text Box," click on the text. You should see the text box surrounded with
open dots and an area with upward diagonal lines.

☐87. Double left click on the border of the text box. A "Format Text Box" pop up should appear.

☐88. On the "Font" tab

• adjust your font, font style, and size as appropriate (By default, texts will be in regular
Arial font in size 10. This is acceptable in most professional journals and therefore no
change needs to be made. It is suggested that you keep the font, font style, and size of
the text consistent within all parts of the graphs.)

☐89. On the "Alignment" tab

• under "Text alignment," for both "Horizontal" and "Vertical," select "Center"

☐90. On the "Colors and Lines" tab, check for the following

Springer

180   J Behav Educ (2007) 16:155–189

- under "Fill," then "Color:," select "No Fill"

- under "Line," then "Color:," select "No Line"

☐91. Select "OK."

☐92. Repeat steps 83-91 until all the phases are labeled above the first tier. [Note. You should

only need one condition/phase label above the first tier if all the tiers for the multiple

baseline graphs share the same condition/phase.]

☐93. To move each text box to the proper place, click on the borderline of a text box until the

four-arrow cross appears and then click-hold-drag the text box and release the mouse button

after you complete your adjustment. The text box should appear at the center of the

condition/phase and fall slightly above the maximum y-axis value of that condition/phase.

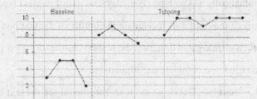

☐94. Click anywhere outside the graph and save ( ) your document.

[Create x-axis and y-axis labels]

☐95. Use the "Text Box" ( ) tool to add an x-axis label right below the last tier by following

steps 83-91. The label should be in capitals. Extend the text box the length of the x-axis.

This allows the label to be centered below the x-axis. If multiple tiers are developed, only

one x-axis label should be created, to be located beneath the last tier.

J Behav Educ (2007) 16:155–189   181

96. Use the "Text Box" (▣) tool to add a y-axis label at the left-hand side of your y-axes by following steps 83-91 except that on "Alignment" tab, under "Orientation," select the bottom middle option so the text is oriented sideways along the y-axes (see illustration below). The label should be in capitals.

If the labels for all the y-axes are the same, create only one text box and align it at the vertical center across the y-axes.

97. Click anywhere outside the graph and save (▣) your document.

[Create tier labels] (This is for multiple tiers only. Skip this step if you have a one-tier graph.)

98. Use the "Text Box" (▣) tool to add the label for each tier (e.g., Mike, on-task, math) by following steps 83-91, except that on "Colors and Lines" tab, under "Line" and then "Color:," you are to select black color. The size of each tier label should be the same. To change the size of the text box, click on the text box until you see open dots surrounded on the border of the text box. Move your mouse pointer over any one of the open dots until you see a two-way arrow. Click-hold-drag in any direction you want to resize the text box. Release it after you finish resizing. Additionally, the tier label should be placed at bottom right-hand corner of the graph or nearby space where data points will not be masked. For consistency, you may want to find the same location within each tier where the space is open for the label. To move a text box, click on the border of the text box until open dots appear on its border. Move your mouse pointer over the boarder until a four-arrow cross

182   J Behav Educ (2007) 16:155–189

appears. Click-hold-drag to the desired location, then release your mouse button. You may also use the arrows on the keyboard to move the text box after you see the open dots surrounding at the boarder of the text box. Finally, click anywhere outside the graph.

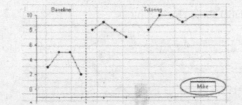

[Create double data path labels] (This is for double data paths only. Skip steps 99-100 if you have single data path graphs.)

☐ 99. On the drawing toolbar, select the "Arrow" ( ) tool by clicking and releasing it once. Then move your mouse pointer to the location where you are to draw an arrow (e.g., close to the selected data path). The mouse pointer should look like a plus sign: "+." Click-hold-drag toward the data path to create an arrow for the data path label, then release your mouse button. The arrow should be pointing to the data path. To reverse the direction of the arrow (if needed), click on the arrow for the two open dots to appear in both ends of the arrow. Place the mouse pointer on the tip of the arrow until the two-way arrow appears. Then click-hold-drag the tip of the arrow in the direction you want it to point. Repeat until all the arrows are created. Click anywhere outside the graph before moving onto step 100.

☐ 100. Use the "Text Box" ( ) tool to create a label for each data path by following steps 83-91. Click anywhere outside the graph and save ( ) your document.

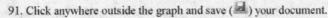

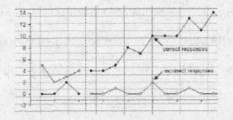

J Behav Educ (2007) 16:155–189   183

H. Make the x-axis value visible for the last tier (If you only have one tier, skip to step 106.)

☐ 101. Move your mouse pointer over the x-axis of the last tier until you see the pop-up text "Value (X) axis." Right click on the x-axis.

☐ 102. Select "Format Axis."

☐ 103. On the "Font" tab

• under "Color," select "Automatic"

• under "Background," select "Automatic"

☐ 104. Click "OK."

☐ 105. Click anywhere outside the graph. You may need to adjust the location of the x-axis label if it came too close to the tick mark labels. Simply select it with the four-arrow cross showing and drag it. Be sure not to drag it below row 52 or it may go off the page.

I. Hide the "0" session and the negative y-axis value

☐ 106. Scroll the page to show the first tier. On the drawing toolbar, select the "Rectangle" (▢) tool by clicking and releasing once.

☐ 107. Move your mouse pointer to the negative y value of the top tier. The mouse pointer should look like a plus sign: "+."

☐ 108. Click-hold-drag toward your lower right-hand corner to form a rectangular box. Release your mouse button after you create a box. The size of the box should be large enough to cover the negative value and the y-axis segment below the x-axis.

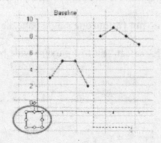

🍷 Springer

184   J Behav Educ (2007) 16:155–189

☐ 109. At this point, the rectangular box should be highlighted (with open dots around the box). If the negative value is not completely covered, either enlarge the box or move it by click-hold-dragging the box with the four-arrow cross.

☐ 110. Keep your mouse pointer on top of the box (with the four-arrow cross), right click and select "Format AutoShape."

☐ 111. On the "Colors and Lines" tab

• under "Fill," then "Color:," select white color

• under ""Line," then "Color:," select "No Line"

☐ 112. Select "OK."

☐ 113. Click anywhere outside the graph. Your negative number should disappear now. If you still see the negative value, do not worry. It is indeed covered up.

☐ 114. Repeat steps 106-113 until all the negative values are covered with the white rectangular box. Alternatively, you can copy (⧉) and paste (⧉) the white rectangular box you just created and then drag the copied rectangles to the appropriate location. For your last tier, the white rectangle will need to be large enough to cover both the negative value and the "0" session. Click anywhere outside the graph and save (⧉) your document.

J. Printing the product

☐ 115. Before printing the product, on the top menu, select "File," then "Print Preview." You can preview your graphs to see if they can fit into one A4 size paper. If they do, select "Print," and print your product. If they do not fit into one single page, select "Setup." Under the "Page" tab, then under "Scaling," select "Fit to 1 page(s) wide by 1 tall." Then select "OK," and then "Print."

J Behav Educ (2007) 16:155–189

185

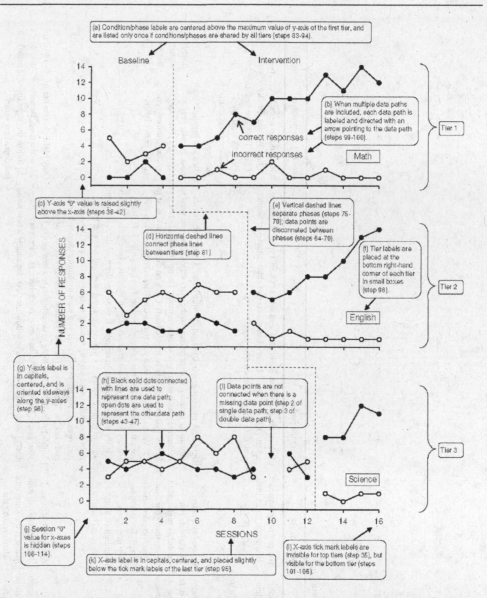

Fig. 1 Sample multiple baseline design graph with double data paths. This sample adheres to the guidelines specified by the *Journal of Applied Behavior Analysis* (JABA, 2000) for preparing single-subject graphs in manuscripts for publication for *JABA*

186   J Behav Educ (2007) 16:155–189

Table 2 Ten troubleshooting tips

Problem	Likely cause	Fixing the problem	Avoiding the problem	Step(s)
1. When I created my graph, the data points did not line up with the major tick marks; they fell between the marks	You probably created a line graph rather than a scatter plot	Click on the chart area. Right click and select "Chart Type." Be sure to select "XY (Scatter)." Then select the correct chart sub-type: "Scatter with data points connected by lines."	When you go to the "Chart Wizard," under "Chart Type," be sure to select "XY (Scatter)" and the correct chart sub-type	6–8
2. I created a graph and there are a couple of strange data points that should not be there. They do not represent any of my data	In your data entry worksheet, you probably highlighted more than your data, which created an extra series. For example, you may have highlighted a phase title (e.g., baseline)	Right click on your graph. Click on "Source Data." Under the "Series" tab, under series, you want to remove the extra series. First you need to determine which series you want to remove. Do this by highlighting Series 1 (it may already be highlighted). Click on the red arrow next to "Y Values." This will take you back to the data entry sheet. You will see a flashing dashed box highlighting the data for Series 1. If these are not the data you want graphed (e.g., if they are phase titles), Series 1 is the series you want to remove. If these are the right data, then you want to remove Series 2. Click on the red downward arrow at the right-hand side of the pop-up window to take you back to the source data options. Highlight the series you want to remove (Series 1 or 2), and click on "Remove." The strange data points should disappear	When you highlight your data, be sure only to highlight data, not session numbers, phase labels, or tier labels	6, 13 (for double paths), and 58
3. When I tried to create an alternating treatments graph (or other graph with multiple data paths), the points did not form two data paths	You probably highlighted both data paths at the same time when creating the scatter plot	For this problem, the best thing to do is to create a new graph. Delete your graph. Go back to the data entry worksheet. Highlight only the first column of data. Be sure to follow the steps for adding a new series	Only highlight one tier of data at a time. Be sure to follow the steps for adding a new series	6–14 (for double paths)
4. My axis line disappeared	You probably clicked on white color or "None" when you formatted the axis line	Right click on the axis and select "Format Axis." On the "Patterns" tab, under "Lines," change the color to "Automatic." This should make the axis line black	When you format your axis lines, be sure to keep the color "Automatic" or black	32–33 and 38–39

Springer

J Behav Educ (2007) 16:155–189

Problem	Probable cause	Solution	Note	Pages
5. After I formatted my y-axis, I noticed that the zero sits way above the x-axis, instead of just slightly above it	You probably did not enter the correct numbers for the y-axis "Scale." It is likely that you mixed up "minimum" with "minor" or "maximum" with "major."	Right click on the y-axis and select "Format Axis." On the "Scale" tab, be sure that none of the boxes is checked. Decide your "Maximum" and "Major unit" first. Your maximum should be the highest score, either the highest score possible or the highest score earned by the participants. Your major unit should be what you want the y-axis to "count by" (e.g., twos or fives). Now you can decide your minimum. This will be based on what you decided to "count by" or your "Major unit." Take this number (e.g., 2 or 5), make it negative, and put it in the "Minimum" box. Now you can decide the "Value (X) axis crosses at:." This will be based on what you just put in the "Minimum" box. Take this number (e.g., −2 or −5), and divide it by 2. This is what goes in the "Value (X) axis crosses at:" box (e.g., −1 or −2.5)	Be sure to follow all the steps when formatting the y-axis. Be careful not to mix up what goes in which box	40
6. I tried to disconnect the data paths between phases, but it disconnected all the data points. There is no line for my data path, just points	You probably selected the entire series, rather than just the segment you wanted to remove	First you will need to undo what you just did. You can simply click on "Undo" on the standard toolbar if this was the last action you took, and then re-start the steps for disconnecting the lines. Otherwise, you will need to right click on the data series and select "Format Data Series." Under "Patterns," then "Lines," select black for the line color and "OK," which will bring you back to your graph. You will need to actually click on the black color once to re-connect the data points, even though the color may have been black.] This time be sure to select only the segment you want to remove. Do this by placing your mouse pointer on the line segment you want to remove and clicking one time on the line segment. (Be sure not to double click or right click at this point.) Then click one more time. Once the line segment you want to remove is highlighted, then you can right click and select "Format Data Point." Under "Patterns," then "Line," select "None" for the line color	Be sure to select only the line segment between the two points you want to disconnect. You can be sure that you have done this when you right click on it. If you are given the option to "Format Data Point," then you have selected just the segment. However, if you are given the option to "Format Data Series," you have selected the entire series	64–70
7. I created an object using a drawing tool, and now I cannot move it outside the chart area	You probably created the object within the chart area, rather than within the worksheet	Delete the object you created. Create the object again; only this time be sure that you create it in the worksheet, not the chart area. Do this by clicking somewhere outside the chart area. You should not see the "Plot Area" or "Chart Area" when you click. Instead you will see a cell in the worksheet highlighted. Now you can draw your object wherever you like and move it anywhere	When you create objects (e.g., lines, text boxes), first click in one of the cells outside the chart area of your graphs. You will know you are outside the chart area if there is a worksheet cell highlighted	75–100 and 106–114

Table 2 Continued

Problem	Likely cause	Fixing the problem	Avoiding the problem	Step(s)
8. I created an object with a drawing tool and it seems to have disappeared	You probably created the object outside the graph and when you clicked inside the graph, you could not see it. Or vice versa: You created an object inside the graph and could not see it when you clicked outside the graph	Most likely, the object you created is still there. To check where it is, click outside the graph to see if you created it inside the graph. Click inside the graph to see if you created it outside the graph	Be sure to create your objects while you are outside the chart area. See troubleshooting item 7 for further explanation	70, 74, 82, 94, 97, and 105
9. I tried to format a text box and when I right clicked to select "Format Text Box," it only gave me a "Font" tab. I need to change the alignment and colors and lines too	You probably right clicked while you were inside the text box rather than on the border of the text box	Try highlighting the text box again by moving your mouse pointer to the border of the box. You should see a four-arrow cross appear. At this point, you will need to keep your hand very steady as you right click. One slight move may place you back inside the text box. If your hand is steady, then right click and select "Format Text Box." This should give you all the tab options you need to format the alignment and colors and lines	When you want to format a text box, be sure to right click on the exact border of the box. A four-arrow cross should appear and the text box should be surrounded with a dark grid area (rather than stripes). Use a steady hand!	86–88
10. When I tried to print my multiple baseline graphs, only one tier printed	You probably left your mouse pointer clicked inside one of the graphs	Try printing again. This time be sure that you click your mouse pointer outside of all the graphs. This will tell the printer that you want to print all graphs. Use "Print Preview" before you print to be sure you have it right	Before printing, click on one of the worksheet cells outside the graphs. Preview the graphs using "Print Preview."	115

Springer

J Behav Educ (2007) 16:155–189   189

Acknowledgments We wish to thank Gloria Campbell-Whatley, David W. Test, and Wendy M. Wood for their kindness to allow us to solicit feedback from them and their students attending Spring 2005 courses of SPED 4270, 5270, and RSCH 7113/8113 at The University of North Carolina at Charlotte. Thanks also are extended to anonymous reviewers as well as a number of students for their constructive feedback on the manuscript.

References

Alberto, P. A., & Troutman, A. C. (2006). *Applied behavior analysis for teachers*, 7th ed. Upper Saddle, NJ: Prentice Hall.

Carr, J. E., & Burkholder, E. O. (1998). Creating single-subject design graphs with Microsoft Excel. *Journal of Applied Behavior Analysis, 31*, 245–251.

Cooper, J. O., Heron, T. E., & Heward, W. L. (1987). *Applied behavior analysis*. Columbus, OH: Merrill.

Hillman, H. L., & Miller, L. K. (2004). Designing multiple baseline graphs using Microsoft Excel. *The Behavior Analyst Today, 5*, 372–387.

Horner, R. H., Carr, E. G., Halle, J., McGee, G., Odom, S., & Wolery, M. (2005). The use of single-subject research to identify evidence-based practice in special education. *Exceptional Children, 71*, 165–179.

Journal of Applied Behavior Analysis. (2000). Manuscript preparation checklist. *Journal of Applied Behavior Analysis, 32*, 514.

Moran, D. J., & Hirschbine, B. (2002). Constructing single-subject reversal design graphs using Microsoft Excel™: A comprehensive tutorial. *The Behavior Analyst Today, 3*, 179–187.

Name Index

SUBJECT INDEX